The Box
That Changed
The World

Fifty years of container shipping –
an illustrated history

The Journal of Commerce

Commonwealth
BUSINESS ◆ MEDIA

Dedication

*The Containerization and Intermodal Institute
dedicates this book to the genius of Malcom P. McLean
and the vision of those who followed him in developing
containerization and more efficient global commerce.*

*CII was established in 1960,
just four years after the sailing of the IDEAL X,
to fill a need for educating people
about a new international intermodal shipping business.*

*The publication of this book will help to create
a credible history of this great innovation
and to educate generations that follow about
the importance of connecting the people of the world
through global trade.*

CONTAINERIZATION & INTERMODAL INSTITUTE

Dedication

Evergreen dedicates this book to Evergreen Group Chairman Dr. Yung-fa Chang whose humble beginnings served as a driving force in his resolve to venture into the waters of the world with investment, innovation and insight to build a multifaceted transportation company that began with a single chartered bulker in 1968.

Dr. Chang's commitment to all citizens of the world includes a promise to build the best shipping company and ensuring an ongoing emphasis on serving the customer so that global trade can grow and flourish.

We salute his place in history and in the history of containerization.

Dedication

*In the journey of these fifty years, Horizon Lines dedicates this book
to all the talented, innovative and determined people who helped create
and foster containerized shipping around the world.*

Dedication

Maersk Line and Maersk Logistics
dedicate this book
to the many people and organizations
that have provided outstanding services
and dedication to the container shipping
industry over the past 50 years.

✳ **MAERSK LINE**   ✳ **MAERSK LOGISTICS**

Dedication

*To the genius of its creator and the vision of the men and women of the
New York Shipping Association and the International Longshoremen's Association
who collaborated in the successful completion of the first voyage and the
subsequent development of the rules, operations, equipment and management
of the single greatest goods movement innovation in history.*

This is where it all started...here in the Port of New York and New Jersey.

**New York Shipping
Association, Inc.**

Dedication

*The Port of Houston Authority salutes the people with the vision, courage
and spirit to ensure our port holds a premier role in history
as the first to house cargo containers.*

*On April 26, 1956, the world's first container ship, the Ideal X, carried
58 containers and her normal liquid cargo from New York to Houston,
forever transforming the shipping industry.*

*Shipping magnate Malcom McLean – owner of that first container ship and
founder of Sea-Land – put his resourcefulness to work to start a revolution.
Equally visionary Port of Houston commissioners and professional staff
fueled that revolution by establishing Houston as Sea-Land's only
U.S. Gulf Coast port-of-call for its container vessels for years to come.*

The Box
That Changed
The World

Fifty years of container shipping–
an illustrated history

ARTHUR DONOVAN AND JOSEPH BONNEY

Contents

Foreword

Containerization is a truly remarkable story – how an idea of using truck-trailer-sized boxes to move goods along a continuum from origin to destination forever changed the concept of shipping as a port-to-port enterprise and helped unleash the forces of globalization. But containerization, as this book describes, is not remarkable so much for the inherent transportation breakthrough it represented. Rather, what is most impressive is how quickly it dislodged the centuries-old practice of loading goods into ships piece by piece. That is why Malcom McLean figures so prominently in this story. It was no secret to anyone involved in shipping in the mid-1950s that in containers lay the potential to achieve the quantum leap forward in cost reduction and efficiency that shipping companies were desperately looking for. By loading containers filled with cargo away from the port, instead of handling cargo on the docks essentially one piece at a time, ships' time in port would be reduced by days, pilferage of cargo would all but disappear, and transit times for cargo would be greatly reduced. This idea had its origins well before McLean's time, and had been tried in various ventures before McLean launched his first container service in 1956. But no one had officially lit the match that sparked the revolution. McLean did. His first service from New York to Houston moved cargo along a route that was not widely used for general cargo by ship. Most cargo moving between the Northeast and the South went by truck or rail. For the longshoremen who would be the most impacted by a switch from traditional cargo handling methods to containers, though certainly uneasy at the radical approach that containers represented, McLean's service was new business, and they were glad to see it. It was McLean's success with this service that sent the message not that containers were a good idea, but much more importantly, that a container service could work. Once that happened, it took just over a decade – a speck in time – before the main services along East-West trade corridors linking North America, Asia and Europe were all converted to containers. Shipping has never looked back. And as subsequent global developments favorable to trade made headlines one by one – the fall of the Berlin Wall, the capitalist shift of China, the conclusion of major free-trade agreements, containerization was there. It stood ready to help convert the raw potential of people free to make money into the wonderful reality of emerging economies, wealth creation, low inflation, and global sourcing and distribution of raw materials and merchandise; in essence, globalization. Ultimately, that is the legacy of McLean and the contribution of the container to the world we live in. It is a story that we at *The Journal of Commerce* and Commonwealth Business Media are honored to be able to tell in this book. We hope you enjoy it.

— Peter M. Tirschwell
Editorial Director, *The Journal of Commerce*
Vice President, Magazine Division,
Commonwealth Business Media Inc.

Marketplace For The Global Village

*"The real driving force behind globalization is...
the declining cost of international transport."*

—*The Journal of Commerce*, April 15, 1997

Stroll through a shopping mall and look at the labels. You'll find shoes and shirts from China and Guatemala, televisions and computers from Japan and Taiwan, housewares from Thailand and the Philippines. Visit a supermarket and the story is the same – the shelves are loaded with cheeses, meats and condiments from around the world. Even the car you drive may have been assembled with parts delivered on a just-in-time basis by a supply line stretching halfway around the world.

This international flow of goods is made possible by containerized shipping, a way of packing and moving cargo that in the last 50 years has dramatically reduced the cost of freight transportation. Containerization uses standard-sized steel boxes to move cargo by ship, truck and train. By improving speed and reliability, and reducing costs of handling, loss and damage, the system allows products and materials to be carried thousands of miles yet still be sold more cheaply than comparable goods made nearby. Customers at Wal-Mart, Ikea or Home Depot can take advantage of the low prices because the retailers and their suppliers are plugged into international supply chains that depend on efficient container transportation. Manufacturers have access to a wider range of suppliers of raw materials and buyers for finished products.

Though containers have become part of the everyday landscape, their role in the global economy is largely invisible. This book tells the story of containerization and how it has developed since the morning of April 26, 1956. On that date a company owned by a former trucker, Malcom McLean loaded 58 reinforced highway trailers, with their wheels and undercarriages removed, onto a deck fitted atop a World War II tanker for a six-day voyage from Newark to Houston. At the time the event attracted relatively little attention. It took another decade for the innovation to spread internationally and even longer for it to function smoothly and efficiently. The change was the biggest to hit shipping since the switch from sail to steam propulsion a century earlier.

McLean was proud of having introduced the container ship, but he never claimed to have invented containerization. Others had used various forms of containers to move shipments by land and sea, but McLean was the first to build an enduring system around the concept. Containerized shipping combines the three traditional modes of transportation: ocean shipping, railroads and trucking. It did not take great imagination to see that if they could use a common cargo container, great efficiencies could be realized. But first, McLean and those who followed had to overcome regulatory barriers, technical challenges and it-can't-be-done attitudes. This book describes the development of containerized transportation, the people who made it happen, and how this innovation has transformed freight transportation and helped give birth to the modern global economy.

*   *   *

Malcom McLean put it succinctly: "Freight is a cost added to the price of goods." As Adam Smith pointed out in his 1776 classic *The Wealth of Nations*, the extent of the markets in which products can compete is limited by the cost of transportation. The price of any product sold in a distant market must at least cover both the cost of production and the cost of transporting the product to market. By reducing transportation time and cost, containerization has expanded companies' potential markets. This in turn has confirmed Smith's famous conclusion that the larger the market, the greater the impetus to increase productivity through specialized production – the "division of labor." What emerges from increased specialization through the division of labor and the expanded markets encouraged by reduced transportation costs is a self-reinforcing "virtuous circle" of progressive innovation and continued market expansion.

These are precisely the phenomena that are driving the growth of the global economy in the 21st century. McLean was not thinking of Adam Smith 50 years ago when he was looking for new ways to reduce the cost of hauling goods long distances. But were Smith alive today, he would understand immediately how containerization led to a new form of global commerce that, while unforeseen, has been enormously beneficial.

*   *   *

The container revolution, which began as a revolution in freight transportation, quickly mushroomed into a revolution in global commerce. Today the cost of transporting goods from factories to markets halfway around the world is typically one percent or less of the retail price. It costs roughly 34 cents to bring a pair of shoes that sells for $45 from a factory in Asia to a store in America, 40 cents for a video game system that costs $130, $12.50 for a television that sells for $2,500, and $90 for an $11,000 motorcycle. It has been said that containers "spelled the death of distance for manufacturing." With the near elimination of transportation costs in a global economy that is open to trade, the volume of goods moving between continents has soared. Without containerized shipping, the Asian economic miracle of the last quarter century would not have developed as it did.

The container revolution has also brought about a cultural revolution. In the mid-20th century, social commentator Marshall McLuhan noted the ways that electronic media — movies, radio, recorded music, and television — were transforming the world's cultures. McLuhan realized that the new media were becoming the dominant providers of the world's images, information and cultural values. He observed that because these media project their messages at the same time, around the world, the medium itself was becoming the message. In the 20th century, cultural norms and information flow around the world as rapidly as news and other cultural information moved around villages in the pre-industrial era. It was, McLuhan said, as if all mankind now lived in a single "global village" created by new forms of communication.

Today the rapidity and low cost with which shipments can now be moved around the world is doing for goods and materials what the electronic media did for visual and aural representations. Thanks to containerization, nearly everything produced for global consumption is available nearly instantaneously, nearly everywhere, at nearly the same price. McLuhan's global village of images, information and ideas has been matched by a global village of goods. Containerization helped make it happen.

PART ONE

Road To Port Newark

CHAPTER ONE

The Seed Is Planted

"A truck is a box, and a ship is a ferry, a bridge."

— Malcom P. McLean

1937 was a tough year in America, and an especially tough year for Malcom P. McLean. The nation's economy was still mired in the Great Depression and McLean, 23 years old, was struggling desperately to find business for the small North Carolina trucking company he had started six years earlier. Born and reared in the south-central North Carolina community of Maxton, McLean was the fourth of seven children. McLean's father was a farmer and mail carrier, a descendant of a long line of Scottish emigrants who had settled in the state's tobacco-growing region.

When Malcom finished high school in 1931, there was no money for college and, he recalled later, "Jobs were as scarce as pearls in oyster stew." Several of his former high-school classmates invited him to come with them to New Orleans, where they planned to sign on as seamen and see the world. He chose not to go, but he had no intention of spending his life working a farm. He took a job in a grocery store, then left to operate a service station at the nearby village of Red Springs. He supplemented his pay by using his battered old car and a borrowed trailer to transport freight locally.

As the Depression tightened its grip on the country, the government began creating federally funded jobs through the Works Progress Administration. McLean heard that the WPA was building a road nearby and needed to have some dirt hauled. He bought a used truck for $125, with a $35 down payment and the balance in weekly installments, and was hired for the job. Six months later, he had saved enough money to buy another truck. McLean planned to use it to haul vegetables to the Northeast, but he quickly learned that the trucking companies already supplying these markets were not about to share the work with a newcomer. He turned instead to the local textile mills, which were expanding as Northern mills moved south in search of

Opposite: Near High Point, North Carolina, in the 1930s.

cheaper labor. He started asking around at nearby mills to see if he could haul anything for them, but again he found that larger competitors had that business locked up. A mill in Fayetteville agreed to give him some business. With this break, and a fortuitous upswing in textile production, McLean was off and running. He later said that when he began competing to haul the mills' scrap material, he quickly learned a lasting lesson – "if the price is too high, the freight doesn't move." McLean priced his services to attract and keep business. By 1935 he had acquired eight tractor-trailers and was carrying all the freight he could handle between North Carolina and New York, Boston and other Northern cities.

Then his luck turned bad. Brutal winter weather contributed to a series of accidents that immobilized his trucks and cost his company badly needed business. Soon McLean was down to his last truck, which he drove himself. Family members stepped in to help. His sister Clara gave up her secretarial job to manage the company office. Younger brother James spent his summers running the service station that Malcom had leased a few years earlier. But the already depressed economy had taken a dip, and with less freight available to haul, McLean Trucking was in trouble. He had taken on $15,000 in debt and it began to appear that the company, along with many of the textile mills that had used his services, might not survive the hard times.

Just before Thanksgiving 1937, a few days after Malcom's 24th birthday, he picked up a load of cotton bales and headed north to Jersey City, New Jersey. He drove all night to deliver the bales to be loaded aboard the *Examelia*, an American Export Lines ship that would take them to Istanbul. Arriving in Jersey City the next morning, he was irritated to learn that the dockworkers would not be able to unload his truck until the end of the day. McLean did not welcome the news. He had planned to empty his truck and quickly return to North Carolina for another load. Instead, he would have to waste the day waiting around the docks, watching the longshoremen load the *Examelia*.

Except for the use of steam-powered winches and cranes, the Jersey City longshore gangs were handling cargo "breakbulk" style, the same way the Phoenicians did thousands of years ago. The process still relied heavily on muscle and manpower. Ships remained in port for days while longshoremen wrestled individual boxes, barrels and bales into and out of tight spaces below decks. Damage was frequent and expensive, as were losses from pilferage. To discourage theft, some importers of shoes shipped

Handling bagged cocoa beans at Boston in 1958. Bags were hoisted from the ship, rolled into a warehouse and stacked. Dockworkers' cargo hooks frequently ripped the bags, causing the spillage visible in the ship's hold.

Muscling quarter-ton bales of cotton into the irregular spaces of a ship's hold was slow and difficult.

their goods in separate lots – with left shoes in one consignment, right shoes in another – and matched them up later.

With hours to kill, McLean had the opportunity to observe and think. Years later, he described what he saw:

> I watched all those people muscling each crate and bundle off the trucks and into the slings that would lift them into the hold of the ship. On board the ship, every sling would have to be unloaded by the stevedores and its contents put in the proper place in the hold. What a waste in time and money! Suddenly the thought occurred to me: Wouldn't it be great if my trailer could simply be lifted up and placed on the ship without its contents being touched? If you want to know, that's when the seed was planted.

That seed eventually would develop into a global transportation and logistics system that would help change the way the world does business. Nineteen years later, McLean would launch the modern era of containerized shipping by loading 58 reinforced truck trailers, their wheels and undercarriages removed, on the deck of a converted tanker. After containerization had become a vital cog in the global economy, McLean frequently told the story of his epiphany on the New Jersey waterfront. The tale was repeated so often that some wondered whether it was apocryphal. McLean, who died May 25, 2001, was respected as a shrewd, intelligent and forward-looking businessman and earned a reputation as a skilled raconteur. Did his idea for modern container shipping come in 1937? It is entirely possible that it happened that way.

*   *   *

On the day that McLean spent cooling his heels on the Hudson River waterfront, he might have seen a system for loading and unloading cargo that looked very like the type of containerization he would later introduce. Such a model was in operation in 1937 in Hoboken, New Jersey, less than a mile from the dock to which McLean had delivered his load of cotton. The Hoboken pier and its looming gantry crane were part of a transportation system belonging to Seatrain Lines.* Seatrain was a specialized freight liner company that began operations in 1929. It carved a profitable niche for itself by handling rail freight cars in nearly the same way that McLean would later handle cargo containers the size of truck trailers. Seatrain can be legitimately described as a precursor and model for containerization.

Given the proximity of the Seatrain and American Export piers on the New Jersey side of the Hudson River, McLean could have seen the Seatrain gantry crane in operation as it moved railcars on and off a ship. One of Seatrain's ships, the *Seatrain Havana*, arrived at the company's dock on November 23, 1937, two days before Thanksgiving, approximately the time McLean was waiting at nearby Jersey City. Even if McLean did not see the Seatrain cargo-handling system in operation, he doubtless would have been aware of it. Seatrain had been in business for eight years and was well-known in the shipping industry. Its system had been fully described in several trade journals.

Seatrain was the brainchild of Graham M. Brush, a World War I naval aviator who founded the carrier and served as its president. Brush spent several years working out the details of this new system while employed by a New York passenger liner company. Brush realized, as did McLean a generation later, that

*Seatrain began operations near the Bethlehem Steel shipyard in Hoboken and years later moved operations a short distance upriver to Edgewater, New Jersey.

Graham M. Brush was the innovator behind the Seatrain system.

the time and cost involved in loading and discharging shipboard cargo could be dramatically reduced if freight was packed in large, standard-sized containers that could be directly transferred to and from an existing mode of overland transportation. When Brush created his system, the most widely dispersed and suitable containers available were standard railway freight cars. He therefore designed and built his Seatrain ships so they could carry railcars by sea.

Under his system, oceangoing ships were refitted to carry loaded railcars on three cargo decks and their main deck. The railcars were lifted on and off the ship by large gantry cranes permanently installed on piers in the ports where the ships called. The railroad freight cars that served as containers in this system were brought aboard with their wheels still attached. Four sets of parallel rails, extending nearly the length of the ship, were welded to each of the decks. Freight cars were lifted from rails on the dock and lowered to the sets of rails in the ship. Each car was then pushed forward or aft and securely fastened to the deck. It was an ingenious system, and in 1929 the first Seatrain ship, a converted tanker renamed the *Seatrain New Orleans*, began carrying loaded railway freight cars between New Orleans and Havana.

Seatrain was not the first company to carry railway freight cars across waterways. Railway companies had long used ferries and barges to move railcars across the Great Lakes and across rivers and bays. Barges loaded with railcars and towed by tugs were a common sight in New York harbor. Most of the port's piers lay across the Hudson River from the region's main railyards.

The most ambitious of these earlier rail-water links was built by Henry Flagler, a co-founder of Standard Oil and one of the earliest and most notable real-estate developers in Florida. Flagler pushed his Florida East Coast Railway down the state's Atlantic Coast as his development activities worked their way south from St. Augustine to Miami. He then decided to continue even farther south and laid out the Overseas Railroad from Miami to Key West. This engineering feat was completed in 1912, making Key West the southernmost deepwater port with direct connections to the U.S. rail network. Flagler then brought rail ferries from the Great Lakes to carry freight cars between Key West and Havana.

Flagler's Overseas Railway was a unique and monumental enterprise, but it was completed near the end of the heroic age of railroad building and proved to be of limited commercial use.

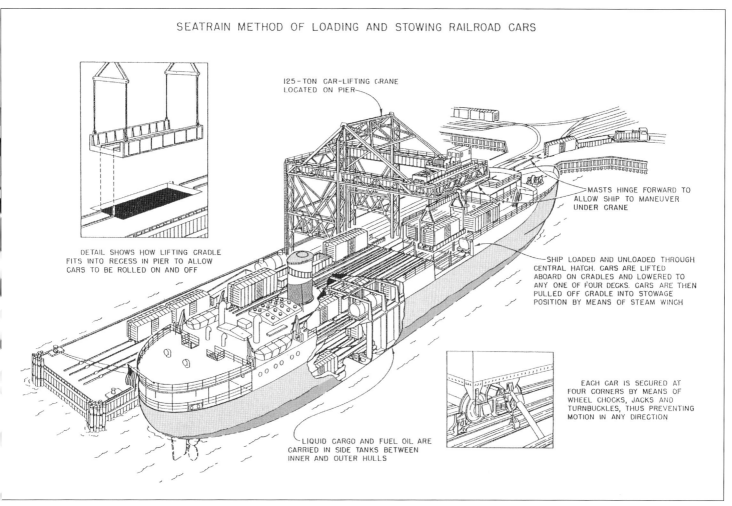

125-TON CAR-LIFTING CRANE LOCATED ON PIER

DETAIL SHOWS HOW LIFTING CRADLE FITS INTO RECESS IN PIER TO ALLOW CARS TO BE ROLLED ON AND OFF

MASTS HINGE FORWARD TO ALLOW SHIP TO MANEUVER UNDER CRANE

SHIP LOADED AND UNLOADED THROUGH CENTRAL HATCH. CARS ARE LIFTED ABOARD ON CRADLES AND LOWERED TO ANY ONE OF FOUR DECKS. CARS ARE THEN PULLED OFF CRADLE INTO STOWAGE POSITION BY MEANS OF STEAM WINCH

EACH CAR IS SECURED AT FOUR CORNERS BY MEANS OF WHEEL CHOCKS, JACKS AND TURNBUCKLES, THUS PREVENTING MOTION IN ANY DIRECTION

LIQUID CARGO AND FUEL OIL ARE CARRIED IN SIDE TANKS BETWEEN INNER AND OUTER HULLS

This cutaway drawing shows how Seatrain stowed railcars on its ships.

Key West was far from the nation's industrial centers and main rail corridors, and the Overseas Railway carried little freight and became best known as a passenger line offering dramatic ocean views.

Brush, having no commitment to Florida, wisely decided to use his water-rail service to connect Havana and New Orleans, the South's largest port, which had river and rail links to America's industrial heartland. Working with Joseph Hodgson, a freight manager with the New York and Cuba Mail Steamship Company, Brush purchased a British-built tanker and had it refitted to carry railcars above and below deck. Cuba was a natural choice, an independent nation located near the United States that had developed its rail system according to U.S. standards. Railcars could be transferred freely between U.S. and Cuban railroads.

Brush launched his new Seatrain service on January 12, 1929, with the first departure of the *Seatrain New Orleans* for Havana. Although 1929 would hardly prove to be an auspicious year for launching such an enterprise, Seatrain survived and flourished.

Above: The Seatrain New York in the 1930s, leaving New York on a voyage to Havana and New Orleans. In the background is the Empire State Building.

Opposite: Seatrain ships had four decks with tracks on which railcars were secured. This photo was taken at Hoboken, New Jersey, in the 1930s. The stack of a Morgan Line freighter is visible in the background, upper left.

*The Port of New York Authority was renamed the Port Authority of New York and New Jersey in 1972.

Seatrain's initial voyage to Cuba proved an immediate success. Brush summarized the system's advantages in a 1932 article in the Port of New York Authority's* magazine, *Port of New York*:

> The new element which Seatrain introduced was its ability to come into port, unload and load in ten hours a cargo which an ordinary ship required six *days* to handle, and to steam out again. In so doing, Seatrain had dispensed with an enormous amount of handling of goods, lighters, trucks, storage, packing, etc. The goods, packed originally at the factory or the mine or the farm in the freight cars, slipped on board Seatrain and across to Havana untouched by hands…Many ships must spend half their time in port, loading and unloading, and half of each dollar in terminal expenses. The Seatrain vessel has been at sea 84 percent of the time, and a ship earns only while in motion carrying cargo.

Seatrain's ability to turn a ship around in 10 hours gave it an enormous advantage over its competitors, and the company's single ship soon had gathered up most of the then-extensive trade between New Orleans and Havana. The *Seatrain New Orleans* enabled U.S. producers of perishables, petroleum products, coke, lumber and other commodities to seize markets that had been supplied by other countries. Without the need for piece-by-piece transfer at dockside, the Seatrain system not only saved time but did a better job of protecting cargo, which arrived in much better condition than was possible when using traditional stowage methods. This feature of Seatrain's success was a direct result of using

railroad freight cars as containers. The *Port of New York* magazine article noted that there were 12 million railcars on U.S. railroads, and that, "They represent just about perfect packages," permitting perishables to be shipped in refrigerated cars and other products to move without transshipment or repacking. In three years, the *Seatrain New Orleans* carried more than 400 million ton-miles – tons of cargo multiplied by mileage moved – without a single claim for loss or damage being presented by any cargo underwriter. Brush had developed a system for handling general cargo that provided nearly all the same advantages offered by the kind of containerization McLean introduced 25 years later.

*   *   *

Seatrain was operating what now is known as an intermodal service, the coordinated movement of freight using two or more modes of transportation. As a departure from the traditional way of handling cargo, the Seatrain operation naturally generated resistance. Some emerged when the *Seatrain New Orleans* docked in Havana at the end of its first voyage. The expectation was that the ship's loaded railroad cars would be hoisted ashore and delivered to destinations elsewhere in Cuba for unloading. Cuban longshoremen assigned to the ship had a different plan. They told the ship's captain that they would bring the railcars ashore, unload the railcars' contents, then reload the cargo before turning the railcars over to the Cuban railways. An agreement was finally worked out to avoid the unnecessary work, but the Havana dockworkers had made a point, one that would be repeated at other ports in the years to come.

Brush's success in capturing most of the traffic on the New Orleans-Havana run also attracted opposition from competitors. In the highly regulated world of freight transportation, mixing two previously separate modes of transportation set off a variety of alarms. Before Seatrain began offering service on the New Orleans/Havana run, the venerable Mallory and Morgan lines dominated the trade using conventional freighters. The two carriers complained that Seatrain's rates were too low. But U.S. transportation law draws a sharp line between domestic and international maritime service. Domestic service is protected from foreign competition and is regulated by the federal government. International service, which in certain ways is subsidized and protected, must compete with foreign carriers for cargo.

Rates charged by ships engaged in domestic coastwise trade

The Seatrain New Jersey passes the Jersey City waterfront in the 1930s.

were regulated by the U.S. Maritime Commission. Railroads were required to file their rates with the Interstate Commerce Commission, which then made them public.* Seatrain filed its rates with the ICC, probably because the cargo it carried arrived at and left the dock by rail. But Seatrain's competitors were ship operators, not railroads. Two of those operators, the Mallory and Morgan lines, carried coastwise cargo but evidently also had been carrying freight to and from Cuba at domestic rates. Upset that an interloper was competing with a new and more efficient system of cargo handling, they complained to the ICC. Mallory and Morgan argued that Seatrain's lower rates should be approved by the commission, as theirs were. But was Seatrain engaged in coastwise water carriage? The answer was clearly no, for Cuba was an independent nation. The ICC therefore rejected the

*The ICC lost most of its regulatory authority through deregulation of the trucking and railroad industries in 1980. In 1995 Congress abolished the ICC, assigning its remaining activity to the new Surface Transportation Board in the Department of Transportation.

This aerial photo of a Seatrain ship shows the dockside gantry crane that lifted railcars on and off the ship.

request by Mallory and Morgan. The commission ruled that Seatrain was engaged not in domestic service but in international maritime commerce, over which the ICC had no jurisdiction. Brush had found a chink in the regulatory armor and had figured out how to exploit it to his considerable benefit.

Hoboken was an extension of Brush's initial trial with the *Seatrain New Orleans*. Brush had operated successfully for three years on the New Orleans/Havana run before extending operations to the Northeast. In 1931 he arranged to have two additional ships built so that Seatrain could add service to and from the New York area. Here too, government involvement, in this case federal subsidies, played a crucial role in Brush's success.

Seatrain needed rail access to the New York waterfront, so Brush bought the Hoboken Shore Railway, originally built to bring coal to the Hudson River docks. He also ordered two new ships to be built by Sun Shipbuilding & Drydock Company in Chester, Pennsylvania. The *Seatrain New York* and *Seatrain Havana* were delivered in September 1932. Although laid out like the original *Seatrain New Orleans*, with four sets of tracks on the main deck and three lower decks, the new ships were larger and faster than the older ship. Each could carry 100 loaded freight cars, the equivalent of a train a mile long. They could steam at 16.5 knots, fast enough to provide fourth-morning delivery to Havana and sixth-morning delivery to New Orleans.

At a time when the government was desperate to revive American shipyards, Brush seized the moment. During World War I, the United States had embarked upon an accelerated shipbuilding program to provide merchant vessels to support American participation in the war. The explosion of shipbuilding produced a huge excess of recently built vessels that depressed freight rates and all but eliminated shipbuilding activity in the 1920s. To revive U.S. shipyards and help American-flag ship operators compete in international service, Congress passed the 1928 Mail Subsidy Act to subsidize the operation and construction of ships built for international commerce. Brush's new Seatrain ships were the first to be built under this act. President Herbert Hoover attended the launching of the two new ships and praised Brush for demonstrating how the "resourcefulness and ingenuity of American designers and operators may facilitate the development of our invaluable ocean-borne commerce."

The *Port of New York* article that described Seatrain's new service to New York also hinted that shippers would be able to send freight cars by sea in domestic service between New York and New Orleans. The article mentioned that arrangements could be made to transfer freight cars from one ship to another in Havana, thereby providing one-week delivery from New York to New Orleans. Once again, the distinction between domestic and international commerce was being purposely blurred. Federal law stipulated that postal subsidies could be used only to support international liner service. Using an offshore port as a switching point for what was in reality domestic service between New York and New Orleans clearly violated the intent of the Mail Subsidy Act. Furthermore, the notion that railcars bound for New Orleans would be moved from one ship to another was largely a ruse, for it is known from first-hand testimony that many railcars went from New York to New Orleans, and from New Orleans to New York, without being landed in Havana. Brush's alertness made regulatory and promotional opportunities work to his benefit. It was one of the secrets of Seatrain's success. It wasn't done by technological innovation alone.

Seatrain's ships also broke new technical ground. In a 1932 article in the widely circulated professional journal *Marine Engineering and Shipping Age*, W.P. Spofford said the *Seatrain New York* and *Seatrain Havana* "had to be designed backwards, starting with the fact that the owners wished to carry 100 standard railway freight cars on four decks, four cars wide." Naval architects were not accustomed to having the dimensions of the cargo determine the lines of the ship.

Under the prophetic title, "Container Ships," an unidentified writer, presumably the journal's editor, suggested that the new Seatrain ships signaled the beginning of a new system of marine transportation in which ships serve "as a link in a complete scheme of transportation, including rail, truck, and ship, providing door-to-door service." The article said Seatrain's service appeared to be "a step in the direction of conforming ship transportation to the best and most economical practices on land. However, within the last few years, the motor truck, with its greater flexibility, has become a powerful factor in the transportation problem, necessitating the development of a standard container which can be used by the truck and by the railroad as a unit of cargo transportation."

The author then described the outcome of a 1930 European competition organized by railway and automotive groups to determine the dimensions of a container for international shipping. The box they arrived at was roughly 12.5 feet long, 7.5 feet wide and 7.3 feet high. But rather than focusing on this particular set of dimensions, the author suggested more generally that "the trend of efficient shipping lies in the direction of conforming to the standard unit of shipment, the container." He then turned his attention to the Seatrain system. "The Seatrain project uses the boxcar as a unit, but, if carried to its ultimate conclusion, a similar type of ship could be designed using the container unit and saving the weight of boxcar underpinning and rails."

Spofford's article examined other ways to increase the efficiency of the Seatrain system, and his discussion ranged far beyond the Seatrain model. Because this was an abstract rather than a treatise, the author rather abruptly ended his brief essay with a few general observations:

> A cargo carrier's first job, obviously, is to carry cargo. According to Mr. Brush, too much money and too much time is being spent in the terminals....Whether the container-ship is the answer to the cargo-shipping problem depends to a large degree upon the international use of containers of a uniform size and type, and upon the development of suitable pier equipment. In any event, the future cargo ship will be designed to reduce material handling to a minimum.

It is clear that containerization as we know it today was being seriously considered well before Malcom McLean was biding his time on the dock in Jersey City. But as Brush and McLean would have reminded anyone who is prone to stay in the world of ideas and abstract thinking, the people who actually make history are the doers, those who build things newer and better than what came before. Brush and McLean fit that category. They were innovators and entrepreneurs, men who earned a place in history by building more efficient systems for moving goods over land and sea.

*   *   *

Malcom McLean's irritation at having to waste a day hanging around the New Jersey docks was understandable. Trucking in 1937 was a difficult business with shaky economics. In the 1920s the trucking industry seemed to appear out of nowhere, but it soon was challenging the older modes of freight transportation. After World War I ended in 1918, ambitious truckers back home began competing with the railroads for express and intercity freight, and captured much of this highly profitable cargo.

Railroads objected to the new competition. They had to buy their rights-of-way, build their tracks, pay taxes on costly capital assets, and employ shop forces to maintain and repair their locomotives and railcars. Truckers, on the other hand, had free access to public highways and cheap equipment. During World War I an enormous American Army in Europe required thousands of trucks for transport of troops and supplies, even ambulances to carry the wounded from the front. The automotive industry met the production challenge, providing the trucks the Army needed. After the armistice, the government put the fleets of surplus trucks on the market at low prices. Finally, the railroads were closely regulated by the Interstate Commerce Commission, while truckers were free to haul freight across state lines on whatever roads they chose and at whatever rates shippers were willing to pay.

Railroaders' complaints might have been ignored if the trucking industry had somehow been able to balance the supply and demand for its services. But the industry was too fragmented and competitive for such a balance to emerge spontaneously, especially in the midst of the Depression. The cost of entry in trucking was comparatively low, and in a period of widespread business failure, there were too many trucks competing for too little freight. Intense competition depressed freight rates and drove all but the strongest firms into bankruptcy. In the

Unloading rubber at New Orleans. Narrow breakbulk wharves provided little space for mechanized cargo handling.

depressed 1930s, long-haul trucking was a sick industry whose return to health was considered an essential part of efforts to revive the economy. The architects of the New Deal soon felt compelled to grapple with its problems.

When members of President Franklin Roosevelt's brain trust turned their attention to the trucking industry, they first tried to promote self-organization and self-regulation, but this strategy failed to achieve its objective. When bankruptcies and instability continued to plague the industry, they took the next logical step, to bring interstate trucking under the regulatory supervision of the Interstate Commerce Commission.

The ICC, created in 1887 to regulate railroads, was the grandfather of all federal regulatory agencies. Trucking was brought under the ICC's regulatory umbrella by the Motor Carrier Act of 1935, which gave the commission the responsibility and power to limit the number of trucking companies competing for business. The ICC also was directed to define the routes over which truckers could operate, and to set and publish the rates truckers could charge when carrying freight on established routes. Lawmakers believed the ICC, drawing on its decades of experience regulating railroads, would be able to protect the public from excessive rates while shielding truckers from cutthroat competition. Such was the legislative intent behind the Motor Carrier Act, which set the terms for ICC regulation of the interstate trucking industry for the next 45 years.

The administrative arrangements created by the Motor Carrier Act would never have been approved had the Depression not already brought the trucking industry to its knees. The government was stepping in to limit the unbridled competition that previously had characterized the U.S. economy. Federal regulation ended the cowboy days of interstate trucking, when anyone could buy a truck, find a load of freight, and haul it across state lines on public highways.

Under the new law, anyone wanting to start an interstate trucking company first had to obtain a certificate of convenience and necessity from the ICC. The commission was empowered to balance the demand for trucking services and the carrying capacity of the certified interstate motor carriers.

There was one loose end to be tied. By the time the Motor Carrier Act had been passed, thousands of trucks were already hauling goods on interstate routes linking farms to markets and factories to towns. The ICC could not do its assigned job if all these businesses were allowed to keep competing for freight. To

Financed partially by GI Bill loans to owner-operators, McLean purchased 600 GMC diesel tractors with sleeper compartments after World War II.

solve the problem, the Motor Carrier Act included a grandfather clause for existing interstate trucking companies. Those carriers would be granted operating certificates, but others would have to apply as new companies.

This simple-sounding accommodation turned out to be a major undertaking. Between 1935 and 1938, truckers filed thousands of applications under the grandfather clause. Companies that claimed to have been operating before the law frequently described their businesses in the broadest possible terms, which added to the ICC's difficulty in evaluating their applications. By 1938, when the commission closed its books on the grandfather clause, it had processed more than 93,000 applications, 42,000 of which were denied, dismissed or withdrawn.

Meanwhile, Malcom McLean was struggling to keep his trucking firm afloat. In the spring of 1938, with the textile industry largely shut down by the depressed economy, he was forced to find additional funds to stay in business. He reluctantly sold two-thirds of his much reduced company to two partners for $500 each.

The situation was touch-and-go. McLean realized that if his company failed, he was unlikely to stay in interstate trucking.

Certificates of convenience and necessity were intended to limit competition, and if McLean did not get a certificate under the grandfather clause, he would likely be shut out for good. Such thoughts must have tormented him during the long hours he spent behind the wheel of his company's only remaining truck in 1937 and early 1938.

*   *   *

Those Depression years turned out to be the worst that McLean Trucking had to endure. When a wealthy farmer agreed to co-sign a $1,000 loan from a local bank, McLean bought back the shares in his company he had sold a few months earlier. In the late 1930s the textile mills began operating again and McLean quickly acquired more trucks to handle his expanding business. He incorporated McLean Trucking in 1940. By then Europe was at war and U.S. industry was reviving rapidly. In that year McLean's company was running 30 rigs and reported gross revenue of more than $230,000.

When the United States entered World War II, Malcom kept the company going while his brother James went off to war. Amid wartime shortages, Malcom made do with the resources he had and those he was able to acquire in an economy in which fuel, tires and other materials were rationed. When peace returned he was ready to expand his trucking company as rapidly as the domestic economy and his regulatory permits would allow. The dark days of McLean Trucking were behind him.

McLean's eagerness to expand and grow, which had been held in check during the years of the Depression and war, could again be turned loose. McLean Trucking began expanding at a furious rate. By 1950 the company was operating 162 trucks, making it one of the top motor carriers in the Southeast. "I saw that my only opportunity was to build and build and build [to] make a big trucking company out of a relatively small one," McLean later said. Still thinking regionally, he noted that expansion "would provide employment...would increase available money in the area...[and] would offer security to hundreds of families."

McLean moved the company's headquarters to Winston-Salem, North Carolina. From this central location he cast his eye across the entire state and region. "All throughout North Carolina and adjoining states new business and industries were springing up, demanding service that we were ill-equipped to supply," he later said. McLean sat down with his closest associates and "mapped out a program intended to fulfill the needs of the entire area." They had already doubled the number of trucks the company was running, but they were not yet keeping up with the demand for trucking services. McLean came up with an imaginative way to expand his truck fleet.

Like other states, North Carolina in the postwar years was crowded with veterans looking for jobs. McLean felt an obligation to help them, and he recognized a way to expand his business at the same time. Paul F. Richardson, a future president of Sea-Land Service who joined McLean Trucking as a management trainee in 1952, recalled an innovative action by McLean that accomplished both objectives.

Richardson said McLean realized that the returning veterans qualified for the Servicemen's Readjustment Act of 1944, better known as the GI Bill of Rights. The GI Bill is most famous as the program that made college education and advanced technical training available to veterans. But the program also provided funding for veterans who wanted to start their own businesses.

McLean Trucking expanded rapidly after World War II.

McLean called a number of these men together and asked if they would like to be owner-drivers in his company. He quickly had a long list of applicants eager to operate their trucks as part of the McLean fleet. In effect, McLean expanded his fleet with the government's money: all those GI loans to the company's owner-drivers. He went to General Motors with this list and in 1950 placed an order for 600 GMC diesel tractors with sleeper accommodations; to be delivered over two years. It was a bold stroke, even for McLean. It was the largest such order GM had ever received.

McLean's drivers pushed themselves and their rigs hard while driving as fast as they dared along endless stretches of still mostly two-lane highway, sustained by coffee, cigarettes and sandwiches. Four-lane highways were rare. Legislation to create the interstate

Malcom McLean was featured in a May 1950 article in American magazine. The man on the left is unidentified.

highway system wouldn't be enacted until 1956. Drivers for rival companies often referred to the middle, or passing, lane of three-lane highways as "The McLean Lane." The third lane was meant for passing slow traffic, but McLean's drivers had a different attitude; they barreled along the middle lane as if they owned it.

In the early 1950s McLean Trucking employed 2,000 people at 37 terminals from Georgia to Maine, and was grossing $12 million a year. It was the largest motor freight carrier in the Southeast and the second-largest in the nation, and McLean's success was beginning to attract national attention.

Fortune magazine wrote about McLean's safety campaigns, programs that used down-home psychology to reduce losses from accidents and damage. McLean understood life behind the wheel of a truck. He identified the foremost hazards of trucking as poker, women and long stretches away from home. He measured safety in terms of freight delivered in perfect condition, and made Christmas bonuses proportional to the profits of each terminal, after cargo damage claims had been paid. Drivers who had no accidents in a three-month period got a gift certificate for three percent of their gross pay, redeemable at the Sears and Roebuck store in Winston-Salem – as McLean expected, most were redeemed by the drivers' wives.

In December 1950, McLean offered a special prize, a furnished house worth $25,000 that would be raffled off among the drivers who had perfect driving records during the next 12 months. Ninety-six out of 171 drivers qualified, and the raffle was won by a driver who had covered 80,000 miles without a dent. With drivers who were achieving this level of reliability, McLean decided to stop carrying insurance on his freight. The money he saved on premiums more than paid for the prizes he awarded to his employees.

By 1952, McLean decided it was a good time to reap some of the rewards of his early work. He sold a quarter of the company stock in a public offering. McLean was thinking about extending his reach in the transportation business and was looking for new sources of credit and capital. Not yet 40 years old, he saw no reason to slow down. He was still a young man looking forward, not back. Always a builder, McLean had his eye on new, tantalizing opportunities.

CHAPTER TWO

Fishybacks And Finance

*"The whole thing sounded so natural. I felt I had to do it.
I kept saying to myself, 'What if somebody else does it and I don't?'"*

— Malcom P. McLean

Although his company was thriving, Malcom McLean saw storm clouds ahead for the trucking industry. He realized that the cost of hauling his trailers over the highways was going to keep rising, and he began looking for other ways to move them long distances. The foremost challenge he faced, and the one for which truckers were held directly responsible, was the undeniable fact that tractor-trailers were hammering America's aged and over-crowded system of state highways into powder.

In a 1952 article titled "Where Do Trucks Go From Here?" *Business Week* noted that truck traffic was more than doubling every 10 years. The number of registered trucks had increased from one million in 1920 to four and a half million in 1940, and to nine million in 1951. More than half of these trucks were owned by individuals who operated only one vehicle. Only one million trucks, those engaged in interstate commerce, had own-ers who were required to file detailed reports with the Interstate Commerce Commission. Taken as a whole, the article observed, the trucking industry had "started out as a chaotic, catch-as-catch-can business in the early 1900s [and] is still essentially a small-business operation." The cost of entry remained relatively low, returns on investment were relatively high, and truckers were not obliged to make any direct payments for the highways they used. Operating under these favorable conditions, "the trucking industry tumbled into maturity."

The real problem, the one of greatest concern to both long-haul freight carriers and state highway officials, was that the number of ton-miles hauled by trucks was far outstripping the increase in miles driven. Trucks were getting larger. Operator expenses were largely proportional to miles driven, while rev-enues were proportional to ton-miles carried. Because larger trucks generated higher revenue, an increasing number of larger trucks were being driven over the nation's roads. From 1930 to

Opposite: McLean Trucking was prospering when Life Magazine published this photo of Malcom McLean and sister Clara and brother James, middle, in 1949.

1950 the number of trucks having axle weights of more than 18,000 pounds doubled, and these were the trucks that were wearing out the highways. In the 1950s highways and secondary roads were still entirely a state responsibility and, as one of the enduring themes of country music emphasized, the state police and truck drivers were natural antagonists on the open road. The railroads sided with the states on this issue. They seldom missed an opportunity to remind the public that while railway companies owned and maintain their tracks, truckers used highways built and maintained at public expense.

As states encountered rising highway construction and maintenance costs, they began to push back. Some imposed highway-use taxes based on weight and mileage, or built toll roads that made it difficult for truckers to avoid paying for weight and mileage. The truck companies complained that such taxes created barriers to commerce and were unfair. Nine states had instituted specific taxes on out-of-state trucks based on weight and distance traveled, and others were planning to follow suit. Truckers faced stringent enforcement of weight restrictions in a growing number of states, notably Virginia, through which McLean trucks had to pass on some of their busiest routes. Federal regulatory pressure also was increasing. The ICC, worried about growing concentration in the trucking industry, was considering changes that would require its permission before any additional mergers or consolidations could be finalized.

In 1952 McLean realized that the freebooting days of long-haul trucking were coming to an end. And if his thoughts drifted to the idea of moving trucks on coastal ships, that at least gave him an option he could consider while trying to avoid the cul-de-sac that long-haul trucking was facing.

McLean thought first of having a railroad company carry his trailers on rail flatcars, a cross-modal arrangement called piggyback. This would have enabled him to avoid the rising road taxes and save on fuel and drivers' labor. But when he proposed this to the Southern Railway, a carrier whose main route ran between Washington and New Orleans, railroad officials told him they weren't interested. The real issue, and the reason that Southern declined McLean's offer, was a long-brewing and intensely felt sense of antagonism between railroads and truckers. Rail and trucking were locked in a struggle for dominance in long-haul overland transportation. Were the railways going to maintain the dominant position they had held for decades? Or would the upstart truckers capture most of the higher-value cargo the rail-

Growth in rail piggyback services was stunted by regulatory restrictions until the mid-1950s.

roads used to carry, leaving the railroads only coal and other low-value bulk commodities? McLean did not see the problem in these terms. He had no designs on the railroads. He just wanted to move his trailers at the lowest possible cost.

*   *   *

Today, intermodalism is standard practice around the world. But in the two decades following World War II, it seemed to contradict all the basic assumptions of the deeply conservative regulatory system that governed interstate transportation. The Interstate Commerce Commission, whose original mandate had been reinforced and expanded by the Transportation Acts of 1920 and 1940 and the Motor Carrier Act of 1935, saw its task as defining and policing the boundaries that separated rail, truck and water transportation. Each of these modes of transportation was to concentrate on providing the services for which it was

Circuses began moving their wagons on railcars in 1872. This photo of a Sells-Floto Circus train was taken in Florida in the early 1900s.

best suited. The ICC acted as a referee in the fierce battle for freight being waged by railroads and truckers. The ICC saw its mission as promoting rail-truck cooperation that would benefit consumers. The commission did not function as a super-manager looking for ways to coordinate the operations of the different transportation modes so that freight moved as quickly and as cheaply as possible. Promoting intermodal transportation was neither a policy goal nor an established practice for the ICC. In freight transportation it was every mode for itself, with the ICC enforcing the rules laid down by the federal government.

Hauling trailers on railroads was not new. In 1872, P.T. Barnum's circus began moving its wagons on rail flatcars. In the 1880s, the Long Island Rail Road carried farmers' horse-drawn carts for transport to markets. As early as 1901, Bowling Green Storage and Van Company used 16-foot-long steel "lift vans" that carried household goods on trucks, trains and ships. There were additional examples in other parts of the world. The first recorded intermodal carriage of freight by truck trailers on railroad flatcars was in 1926 on the Chicago North Shore and Milwaukee Railroad. Several other railroads had dabbled with intermodal service after World War I, but the practice was not widespread.

One reason the railroads did not pursue piggyback service aggressively was a setback they had suffered in a 1931 ICC decision known as the Container Service Case. In that decision, the ICC required rail rates for intermodal shipments to be related to the class-rate structure in railroads' common carrier tariffs. Specifically, the commission said carload rates for the most expensive commodity in a container of mixed commodities would apply to the entire shipment. The decision made piggyback rates more expensive, and discouraged their use for the next two decades. In 1935, the Association of American Railroads went further, adopting a resolution against through joint rail-truck rates and through routes unless they did not impinge on another railroad's territory.

As time passed and trucking became better established, the introduction of new transportation technologies and new ways of moving freight created pressures to which regulators had to respond. The legislators and officials who drafted the policies and headed the bureaus that governed interstate transportation did not foresee that treating each transportation mode as a separate entity would create a sense of competition rather than one of cooperation. In transportation, modalism became the industrial equivalent of nationalism in international politics. A concept originally developed to articulate a sense of distinct identity and purpose evolved into a creed to which competing groups appealed when defending their interests and actions against incursions by others.

By the 1950s, antagonism between truckers and railroaders had grown so pervasive and intense that it effectively blocked rational consideration of new ways of moving freight that coordinated the efforts of two or more transportation modes. McLean's suggestion that a railroad carry his trailers piggyback required cooperation of this sort, but the railroad saw his suggestion as a declaration of war and responded accordingly.

In *Piggyback and Containers*, author David DeBoer has described how the railroads reacted to the challenges and opportunities presented by piggyback service. For years truckers and railroads had cooperated in various ways when moving less-than-carload consignments of freight. But in the post-World War II era, railroads and truckers increasingly found themselves competing for intercity freight, and railroads refused to even discuss cooperation with truckers. The American railroad network had been fully developed, with every railroad company serving a defined area and providing an established menu of services, an arrangement that was certified and policed by the ICC. As a result, DeBoer wrote,

> ...anything that could possibly upset this carefully crafted equilibrium was not to be taken lightly. "If the trucker originated freight in some other railroad's territory," went the argument, "wasn't this as bad as a railroad building track there?" "Well, the trucker has the freight now anyway," went the response, "so why don't we get a piece back for the railroad?" "Well, what about helping the enemy?"

Southern Railway saw McLean's suggestion that it carry his trailers piggyback not as a proposal that could work to the mutual advantage of both parties, but as a ruse to put the camel's nose under the tent. This reaction was typical of the era, as the industry journal *Railway Age* observed in 1952. Piggybacking, it reported, "has been and is opposed on many railroads which ought to be able to generate a large traffic in the movement of trucker's trailers. It might profitably be recalled that not all alliances of mutual advantage are contracted for reasons of affection – there are also what the French call marriages of convenience."

Although the challenge of piggybacking was widely seen as a threat to the railroads' traditional role as the premier carrier of overland freight, the advantages of piggybacking could not be denied. Such an arrangement would reduce the repeated handling of the items being shipped. The New York, New Haven and Hartford Railroad was one of several lines that had provided such service in the 1930s. Besides the regulatory impediments established by the ICC, there were troublesome mechanical problems involved in securing the trailers to flatcars, and especially in loading and unloading trailers on trains. The layout of the classification yards where trains were made up and broken down could not be easily altered to facilitate loading and unloading trucks on flatcars, and new equipment designed for this purpose needed to be built if piggybacking was to become a viable option.

In 1952 Gene Ryan, a transportation consultant in Chicago, attacked this problem head-on and launched the Rail-Trailer Company. Ryan designed equipment that would quickly move trailers on and off flatcars outside railroad classification yards. General Motors backed Ryan, but the railroads resisted building the rail-truck terminals required to make the Ryan system work. Railroad operating departments were unwilling to commit capi-

The New York, New Haven and Hartford Railroad won an ICC decision that encouraged piggyback services. This photo shows a New Haven piggyback train at Cos Cob, Connecticut, in the mid-1950s.

tal resources to the venture, and railroad traffic departments saw piggybacking as a threat to boxcar revenue. This initiative suffered the fate that so often awaits innovations "not invented here," and despite Ryan's best efforts, the railroads continued to view piggybacking as a marginal activity at best.

The railroads' reluctance to promote piggybacking did not eliminate pressure for some kind of intermodal service. The issue was again addressed in a 1953 suit filed by the New York, New Haven and Hartford Railroad. The case arose when the New Haven petitioned the ICC for a declaratory judgment on the legal status of numerous aspects of piggyback service. In its ruling on "Twenty Questions Concerning the Movement of Trailers by Rail," the commission's findings were burdened with the kind of hair-splitting distinctions so often encountered in regulatory litigation, but the main points established by the decision were unmistakable.

Effectively reversing its 1931 ruling, the ICC ruled that "all freight" tariffs were legal and that the goods did not have to be charged at the rate of the highest commodity in the trailer. The ICC found that freight movements by rail were not governed by rules written to govern highway movements. That meant that the railways therefore did not need a trucking certificate to operate their own trucking services. The ICC said railroad-owned trucking companies were allowed to pick up and deliver trailers and that railroads could carry trailers of private trucking companies that worked exclusively for a single shipper and were not common carriers. Railroads and common-carrier trucking companies were allowed to establish joint rates and routes. The Twenty Questions Case quickly led to the establishment of a formalized series of plans for intermodal service, and the railroads' piggyback business expanded rapidly. By 1955, about 30 railroads were carrying piggyback freight. The Twenty Questions Case laid the groundwork for the development of modern intermodal transportation.

*   *   *

In the early 1950s, Seatrain Lines, which pioneered the use of railcars as seagoing containers, began expanding aggressively into the U.S. domestic market. Seatrain had suspended its commercial operations during World War II, while its ships were used to support military operations overseas. After the war the company built two new ships and began moving railcars on routes linking Edgewater, New Jersey, and Savannah, New Orleans and Texas City, Texas. In 1952, the ICC approved a Seatrain request that it be allowed to transfer the *Seatrain Havana*, which had been serving ports on the Gulf of Mexico, to the New York-Savannah run; the ship was promptly renamed the *Seatrain Savannah*. Several railroads immediately protested the ICC's decision, but two railroads in Georgia and New York supported the ICC, as did the Port of New York Authority and more than 80 shippers and their organizations. Although we have no record of Malcom McLean's reaction to this development, it was about this time that he accelerated plans for introducing his own shipboard trailer-container service along the Atlantic and Gulf coasts.

In light of these events, and despite unrelenting opposition to road-rail operations among traditional railroad executives, it is hardly surprising that McLean began looking for a more promising way to move his trailers long distances. If the railroads were going to haul trailers, it looked as if they would be hauling their own trailers or trailers owned by the companies whose goods they were carrying. Established long-haul common carriers such as McLean Trucking, the companies the railroads characterized as the enemy, would be shut out of piggybacking. Evidently McLean would have to come up with another way to move his trailers along

the Atlantic Coast if he was going to avoid running them over the increasingly congested highways. If he continued moving all of his trailers over the road, he faced delays and rising costs, and if he didn't act quickly, he soon would be squeezed by Seatrain's expanding liner service and by the new piggyback rail services. And if that happened, freight rates and profit margins would fall and he would be forced into a ruinous competition for customers.

Though many railroads continued to resist cooperation with trucking companies, the limitations of rail service and the advantages of truck transportation were becoming more apparent, as was the possibility that truckers might have another option – moving trailers by ship. Transportation economist Marvin Barloon summarized these points in a *Harper's* magazine article with the intriguing title, "The Second Transport Revolution." Barloon's article showed how trucking was steadily transforming freight transportation in America:

> In 1929 the intercity truck lines moved only two ton-miles of freight for every fifty carried by the railroads. But in 1955 they carried over nineteen to the railroad's fifty. There are already nearly as many highway trailers and semi-trailers in the country as there are boxcars,

Seatrain extended service to Texas City, Texas, near Houston, in 1940 and resumed service there in 1952.

and in a year's time they carry more freight than the boxcars do....Year by year, the trucks gain. We have long regarded the highways as supplementary to the railroads. But, as the stream of highway freight continues to grow, it moves ever closer toward an ultimate central position as the trunk-line structure of our transportation system.... The railroad revolution of the nineteenth century opened the floodgates to reconstruction of the nation's industry and institutions and to a geographical regrouping of her populations. The transport revolution of the twentieth century shows signs of an equally thorough overhauling of our institutions and geography.

The article then detailed why the railroads were finding it so difficult to compete with truckers for general freight.

To shippers and consumers it becomes progressively more important to move things straight from A to B without stalling around at X, Y, and Z on the way. Intercity trucking provides movement which is fast and direct, and it provides tailored or individualized service....A truck loaded in Cleveland at four o'clock Wednesday afternoon will pull up to the receiver's dock in Rockford, Illinois, Friday morning. The same shipment by rail would take a week.

Barloon pointed out that the railroads could not match truck service because railcars had to be made up into trains in classification yards, and that the trains then had to stop at intermediate points to drop off and pick up railcars. "This is why the average freight train speed between terminals in 1955 remained just under nineteen miles an hour....The average rail freight haul is 429 miles, but because the freight car spends most of its time being switched from train to train, it covers only forty-eight miles in an average day."

Readers who suspected that Barloon had some animus against the railroads were wrong, for that was not the reason for highlighting the advantages of trucking. He noted that railroads were making technological improvements, but said, "almost all of this progress is in the direction of cost reduction rather than of service improvement." He wrote that railroads' only hope of rivaling fast highway service was through carrying highway trailers on railcars. "However, rail executives almost universally regard this development as a means of getting traffic back from the highways rather than of making existing rail service more attractive. They rarely offer it to shippers as a substitute for boxcar carriage via the classification yard system. But business once lost to the highways is hard to get back. If railroad executives do not promote the piggyback system much more aggressively than they have shown any sign of doing, it can do little more than retard the growth of highway freight."

Barloon then made an observation that a half-century later seems especially prescient: "Trucking is the great paradox of the twentieth century. This era is generally identified as that of mass production and mass merchandising. But, in transportation, the mode offering the most individualized service is the one moving ahead most rapidly."

The article provided additional insights about other aspects of freight transportation that were changing in the 1950s. Barloon noted that high port costs had kept coastal shipping traffic "in the doldrums" since the beginning of World War II. "As a standard rule of thumb, goods can be moved eight miles on the deep waters at the same cost as one mile by rail. But, because of high costs in the seaports, five major intercoastal carriers were spending half of their total income in 1953 in merely loading and unloading the cargo." He said the carriage of highway trailers by ship offered a solution. "By this method a ship which would normally require four or five days to load is packed with trailers and out to sea in eight hours or less. On the Atlantic Coast the cost of

Stowing breakbulk cargo was labor-intensive. These longshoremen were at work in the Port of New York and New Jersey in the 1950s.

holding and loading a ship in port may run as high as $270 per hour, and the trailer-carrying vessel brings the loading costs down from half of the total revenue to some two or three percent.

Barloon's article was published in 1957, less than a year after McLean had begun hauling trailers on ships, but McLean had been thinking along those lines for several years. Although he had never set foot on a ship, McLean began in the early 1950s to look closely at what one author called his "sea-going piggyback idea."

*   *   *

McLean understood the cost advantage of using ships to carry trailers long distances. Once he had determined that the railroads were not interested in moving his trailers on long hauls, he began paying close attention to coastwise shipping, an industry that had been moribund for three decades primarily because of its port costs. McLean first considered ships that could carry truck trailers that were driven on and off. While examining this option, McLean had a full-scale mock-up constructed of the interior space available in the kind of trailer ship he had in mind, so that he could see if the idea would work. One way or another, McLean was going to get at least some of his trailers off the highway. He told the ICC in 1954 that "highway transportation costs have shot up 50 percent since 1940," and he was determined to find a cheaper way to move interstate freight.

There were several obstacles to moving trucks on ships. One of the biggest was that although ships can carry freight at inexpensive rates, they require expensive capital investments. A 1920 U.S. law, the Jones Act, requires ships engaged in coastal and intercoastal service to be constructed in U.S. shipyards and manned by American seafarers. But the crash shipbuilding program of World War II had left the federal government with many surplus ships that could be made available for commercial use. If a few of them could be acquired cheaply, perhaps "fishyback" could replace piggyback, and the hazards and costs of long-haul trucking could be avoided.

The Higgins Box

A ndrew Jackson Higgins, whose World War II landing craft helped Allied forces storm beaches from Normandy to Okinawa, was a font of ideas. One of them was containerized shipping.

The New Orleans boatbuilding yards of Higgins Industries Inc. turned out 20,000 landing craft, PT boats and other vessels during the war. In 1945, seeking to keep his company thriving during peacetime, Higgins outlined a plan for containerized shipping that resembled what Malcom McLean introduced more than a decade later.

Higgins proposed using 10- and 20-foot-long containers that would be carried on truck chassis, railcars, ships and barges throughout the United States. The containers would have been steel-framed, with doors at each end, wooden sides and floors, and steel skids underneath. The boxes would have moved on conventional vessels, including shallow-draft ships that Higgins would build to serve inland points.

An industrialist with little transportation experience, Higgins appeared to have been primarily interested in providing the containers. The system would have been run by a neutral management group responsible for overseeing selected ship, barge and truck operators.

World War II boatbuilder Andrew J. Higgins had dreams of a waterborne container service.

Higgins described his plan in a 50-page booklet aimed at potential investors. In an indication of how thoroughly transportation was regulated in that era, about half of the booklet was devoted to a discussion of how rates would be set to comply with U.S. inland transportation regulations.

Though the Higgins container system would have been revolutionary, it never was implemented. After the war, Higgins Industries was crippled by union jurisdictional disputes, cash-flow problems and a 1947 hurricane that wrecked the company's underinsured plant. Higgins died in 1952, just four years before McLean launched his container-shipping venture.

Early in 1954 McLean began to show his cards. He sent requests to the ICC asking for permission to begin moving his trailers by sea, to build ships to carry them, and to expand his company into a $50 million land-sea transportation service operating between Southern and Eastern ports. A year earlier McLean Trucking had reported that it was running 1,425 trucks and trailers on the road, was operating 37 terminals, and had grossed $19.2 million. McLean noted that the service he planned to start would be similar to "the 'sea trains' used by the railroads to carry freight cars by water." He reported that 90 percent of his business was north-south freight and said that although moving trailers on ships from Wilmington, North Carolina, to New York would take 30 hours, as opposed to 18 hours by road, his costs would drop by 50 percent, which would enable him to take business away from the railroads. He planned to begin this new service in 1955.

McLean's decision to begin "fishyback" service has traditionally been characterized as an idiosyncratic venture undertaken by a shrewd if somewhat maverick trucker, an innovation that emerged on the fringe of a settled transportation industry. There is some truth in such a description, but the appearance of genius and eccentricity begins to fade when one looks more closely at the options available at the time and the purposeful nature of McLean's campaign. While a successful trucker, McLean saw himself in a more general sense as providing transportation services, and, being an entrepreneur, he was ready to innovate if that would enable him to do his job at less cost. In the 1950s he was indeed an unusual figure in freight transportation, yet the choices he made were firmly based on experience and careful calculations of costs.

During the early months of 1954 McLean disclosed additional information about his new venture. He started with his salesmen. At a staff dinner in February at the Waldorf-Astoria Hotel, he told his Northeast sales representatives he was going to start a "sea-land" service that would use ships to carry trailers between Northern and Southern ports. McLean planned to begin the service by acquiring the S.C. Loveland Company, a coastal steamship and tug-and-barge operation based in Providence, Rhode Island. McLean Trucking asked the ICC for permission to use Loveland's operating authority to operate roll-on, roll-off ships carrying highway trailers between Wilmington, North Carolina, and New York, and between New York and Providence.

The same month Malcom disclosed his plans to his salesmen, his brother James, the executive vice president of McLean Trucking, was sent to Miami Beach to explain the company's plans to the general executive board of the Teamsters union. The union leaders were assured that while McLean's new plan might cause some temporary dislocations for drivers, its overall effect would be to create new business for truckers. No drivers would lose their jobs, but if an initiative of this sort were not launched, "the outlook for continued expansion of the truck industry was poor." Dave Beck, the union's president, gave his blessing to the project, saying it would help the trucking industry beat off railroad competition. Malcom McLean also reached out to Patrick McGinnis, a former securities broker who in April 1954 became president of the New York, New Haven and Hartford Railroad, which had pressed the ICC to loosen its restrictions on piggyback shipments. McGinnis

EASTERN SALES MEETING
McLEAN TRUCKING COMPANY
TO EXPLAIN NEW "SEA-LAND" SERVICE
THE WALDORF-ASTORIA   NEW YORK CITY
FEBRUARY 20, 1954

DRUCKER-HILBERT CO.
N.Y.

Malcom McLean explained his "sea-land" plan to his Northeast sales staff on February 20, 1954. McLean is seated in center. His brother James is to his right, fifth from left. Others include Paul F. Richardson, top right, and Richard Shellenback, later a Sea-Land sales executive, middle row, far right.

announced that if joint rates could be developed, the New Haven was definitely interested in coordinating McLean's new trailership service with its own piggyback operations.

Speaking to the Teamsters leadership in February 1954, James McLean briefly described how McLean Trucking was planning to move truck trailers by sea. Bethlehem Steel's shipbuilding division had drawn up preliminary plans for four ships, each of which would cost $5.5 million and could carry 240 trailers. These ships would carry "loaded trailers between Atlantic Coast ports in the North and South." Each ship would be equipped with ramps over which trailers would be rolled on and off the ship, making it possible to load or unload the vessel in four hours. On March 17, 1954, *The Journal of Commerce* published a photograph showing a model of a terminal to be built at Port Newark for McLean Trucking to use in handling four new roll-on, roll-off, or "ro-ro" ships.

Another feature of this new service was highlighted by a McLean representative who participated in a 1954 Washington symposium organized by the recently founded International Cargo Handling Coordination Association. The symposium heard first from H.J. Hvide, president of the American & Overseas

New York Central Railroad operated Flexi-Van, an intermodal rail service, in the 1950s and 1960s. Aluminum containers were carried on special railcars with built-in turntables. A truck driver unlocked the container from the railcar, rotated the container 90 degrees, hooked it to his tractor and chassis, and hauled it away.

Chartering Corporation, a company that planned to use two converted World War II LSTs (Landing Ships, Tanks), amphibious ships that load and unload vehicles over bow ramps. These ships were to carry loaded truck-trailers in a service operating on the Hudson River between Albany and New York City. The general counsel of McLean Trucking then described the service his company planned to begin, noting that "one of the results…is the development of at least a partial answer to the insistent cargo-handling problem of the water carrier."

Clearly McLean, having thought through all the problems involved in inaugurating his new service, figured he had a winner. By moving loaded trailers he could avoid repeated cargo handling and the related cost of hiring longshoremen to handle and stow boxes and bags of cargo piece-by-piece. Moving freight in trailers would eliminate this cost, reduce turnaround time, and greatly reduce losses to breakage and pilferage. If McLean could offer service like this, he reasoned, he would have all the business he could handle.

In light of later events, McLean's plan to build roll-on, roll-off ships is surprising. McLean's trailer ship proposal, described in the April 1954 issue of *Marine Engineering*, was entirely unlike the much more modest system, using modified World War II ships, that he ended up putting into service in April 1956. The new ships described in his 1954 proposal would be ro-ros, rather than ships carrying cargo that was lifted on and off; they would be new construction; they would be 650 feet long and operate at up to 20 knots; and they would carry trailers still attached to their wheels and undercarriages and stowed on two trailer decks below the main deck. His main objective was still to use water transport to move trailers more cheaply than they could be driven over highways.

The *Marine Engineering* article said McLean's initiative was designed to help revive coastwise shipping.

> By helping to restore water service which formerly existed on the East coast, the [ro-ro] service will fill an important need for dry-freight water transportation between points along the Eastern seaboard. Considerable coastwise service never was resumed after conventional dry-cargo ships were taken from this trade for use overseas during World War II. Vessels operating in coastwise service were reduced in number from 490 in 1938 to only 196 in 1948. Some of the reasons this service has not been restored include lack of suitable vessels, high cost of cargo handling (including pilferage), delay in ports, inefficient port facilities, and lack of co-ordination with land carriers moving between ports and interior points.

McLean knew the system he was proposing was similar in both its concept and in many of its details to the Seatrain operation that moved fully loaded railcars by sea between New Jersey and ports in Cuba, the Gulf of Mexico, and along the Atlantic Coast. His proposed system also resembled the piggyback services used to move loaded truck-trailers on railroad flatcars. But the article added, "The McLean co-ordinated system is designed to be of particular value to the motor-carrier industry, as well as to the shippers who use it."

The *Marine Engineering* article also suggested that, besides commercial applications, McLean was thinking of another possible market. The Army had expressed interest in the development of trailer ships. The article said McLean planned to use private capital to build new ships that will make "a material contribution to the nation's security requirements." The announcement that laid out the terms addressed in this proposal was published on January 31, 1954, when "the Military Sea Transportation Service requested funds to begin construction of a 'roll-on roll-off' ship of a type long sought by the Army." It was less than a month later that McLean called his sales staff together in New York and told them that he would soon be offering container service along the Atlantic Coast.

*   *   *

Military shipping and commercial in the United States have long had an on-again, off-again relationship. During both world wars, the U.S. embarked on a rapid buildup of its privately owned merchant marine to support military activity, then struggled to deal with the peacetime glut of shipping capacity.

As it had in World War II, the military made extensive use of commercial ships during the Korean War, when 180 mothballed merchant ships in the National Defense Reserve Fleet were activated. These ships, together with the MSTS's own ships, carried about 60 percent of the cargo that was sent to Korea during the three-year conflict. The rest was carried under government contract by commercial ships.

During the Korean War, the maritime industry and its friends in government began pushing for closer integration of civilian and military operations. In 1951 the Defense and Commerce departments negotiated an agreement on how the Military Sea Transportation Service would proceed when acquiring additional shipping services. First priority was to be given to ships operating in U.S.-flag liner service, second to chartering U.S.-flag vessels, third priority was to reactivate ships in the National Defense Reserve Fleet, and last priority was to use available space on foreign-flag ships or obtain vessels operating under foreign flags.

In July 1954, two members of the pro-business Eisenhower Administration, Defense Secretary Charles E. Wilson and Commerce Secretary Sinclair Weeks, agreed on a plan that went much further in requiring the Army to make use of America's civilian maritime resources. The Wilson-Weeks Agreement limited the Military Sea Transportation Service to a nucleus fleet of 56 passenger transports, 34 cargo ships, and 61 tankers, except in times of emergency. If other shipping resources were needed, they were to be obtained according to the priority list agreed to in 1951, with privately owned U.S.-flag merchant ships given first priority. The military was not happy about these restrictions, which limited its control over the design, construction and operation of the vessels it needed to fulfill its logistical and operational obligations. The military would also have to pay for the higher operational costs involved when using American commercial ships and crews. The U.S.-flag liner industry enthusiastically welcomed the Wilson-Weeks agreement, for it promised to expand considerably the demand for commercial services.

McLean had access to an ample supply of mothballed World War II freighters and tankers. These Victory ships were laid up on the Hudson River above New York City.

In an effort to stimulate the shipbuilding industry, the government also sought to liberalize restrictions on subsidies so they could be used to build ships for domestic as well as international service. Special "trade-in and build" legislation also was passed. This law gave the secretary of commerce the authority to buy prewar and war-built ships on terms favorable to the carriers. The government would then hold the funds received in tax-free accounts that could be used to pay for the building of equivalent tonnage in American shipyards. Other incentives also were created. New federal ship-mortgage guarantees greatly reduced the risks and financing costs of ordering ships for use in domestic markets.

McLean was doubtless pleased with this new emphasis in federal policy, but his first concern was with following through on the development of his new sea-land service. Once he had obtained new federally funded trailer ships, he would be in position to bid for contracts to carry military cargo. This was the good news, but it was soon offset by the bad, for it quickly became clear that his request for federal mortgage guarantees for the construction of new Army-style ro-ro ships was going nowhere. But one way or another, he remained determined to get his new "sea-land" service up and running.

By the beginning of 1955, after years of planning to build roll-on, roll-off trailer ships, McLean was changing course. He was still sold on the idea of moving trailers by sea, but he was not convinced that the way he proposed to do so in the first half of 1954 was the way to go. A number of unresolved problems led him to reconsider his original plans. Were Wilmington and Providence the best ports to serve? What kind of port facilities

North To Alaska

At least three pioneering container services operated in the 1950s in the U.S. Pacific Northwest, western Canada and Alaska. All predated the start of Malcom McLean's first shipments of containers by sea.

Alaska Steamship Company began carrying containers between Seattle and Alaskan ports in 1953, using World War II Liberty ships that were fitted with squared-off holds. The ships carried 60- and 144-cubic-foot collapsible containers under deck, and 24-foot containers and 40-foot truck trailers on deck. The shorter boxes were stowed two or three tiers high. Eventually, two of the ships were fitted with steel frames above deck to help secure the containers.

The Alaska Steamship service operated as many as 15 vessels before falling victim to competition from Sea-Land, which entered the Alaska market in 1964, and to the slow speeds of its aging ships. Alaska Steamship ceased operations and sold its last ship in 1972.

Another containerization pioneer, the White Pass & Yukon Railway, carried small containers via Canadian Pacific coastal steamers between Vancouver, British Columbia, and Skagway, Alaska, where cargo was transferred to boxcars for shipment on a narrow-gauge

Alaska Steamship carried small boxes stacked atop Liberty ships between Seattle and Alaska. The company built a model to demonstrate the system to customers.

railroad to Whitehorse, Yukon. On November 26, 1955, the railroad began operating its own ship, the *Clifford J. Rogers*, which carried containers 25 feet long, eight feet wide and eight feet high. The *Rogers* was replaced with a larger ship in 1965. White Pass & Yukon ceased operation in the early 1980s.

Still another carrier, Ocean Van Lines, carried containers on barges between Seattle and Alaska from 1949 to the late 1950s, using 30-foot aluminum boxes manufactured by Brown Trailer Company. Malcom McLean heard about the containers and ordered 33-foot containers from Brown when he launched Pan-Atlantic's container service in 1956.

would be required, and how could they be acquired? Was there an alternative to taking on the huge cost of building new ships? Could truck-trailers built for highway use survive the additional strains of ocean voyages? And would the railroads persuade the ICC to deny McLean permission to start his new "sea-land" service? The difficulties McLean faced suddenly loomed large; course adjustments were called for.

*   *   *

While reviewing the companies that were already in the coastwise shipping business, McLean came across one that had many of the assets he needed to start his trailer ship service. It was the Waterman Steamship Corporation, headquartered in Mobile, Alabama. Waterman was a family-controlled company that had been founded in 1919. An unsubsidized American-flag shipping company, it operated 30 cargo ships on intercoastal routes between the East and West coasts of the United States, on coastwise routes between U.S. ports in the Gulf of Mexico and along the East Coast, and between the U.S. mainland and Puerto Rico. Waterman ships also operated on international routes, calling at ports in Asia and Europe. The Port of New York Authority was at that point putting the finishing touches on newly built wharves and warehouses in Newark, New Jersey, a facility that was to be leased to Waterman. And best of all, from McLean's point of view, Waterman was for sale.

In June 1954, while his application to acquire S.C. Loveland was pending, McLean offered to buy Waterman. His offer was rejected but the following January he succeeded in buying one of Waterman's subsidiaries, Pan-Atlantic Steamship Corporation. This purchase would provide him the operating certificate he needed to move his trailers by ship between Gulf and East Coast ports, as well as seven ships and the Gulf Florida Terminal Company of Tampa. McLean finally had the ships and operating rights he needed to put his trailer ship concept into effect. He told the press he intended to move forward without delay: "Acquisition of the Pan-Atlantic Steamship Corporation will permit us to proceed immediately with plans for construction of the trailerships. When these new ships have been built, coordinated Pan-Atlantic sea-land service can be inaugurated immediately between Atlantic ports and Gulf ports."

McLean said the trailer ship service would supplement Pan-

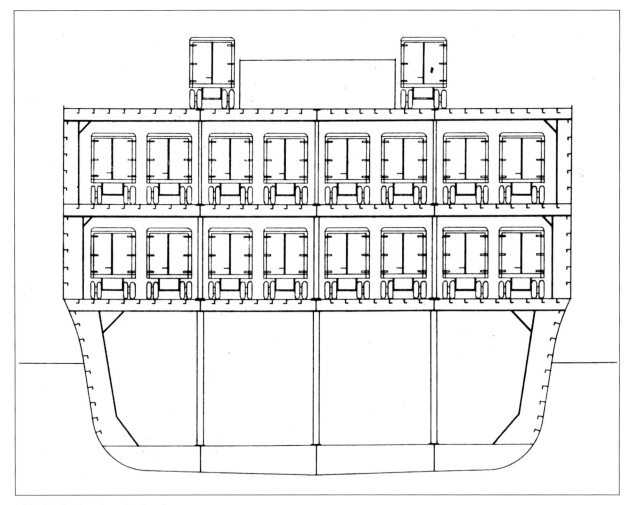

This sketch of Malcom McLean's planned roll-on, roll-off trailer ship was prepared by Bethlehem Steel's shipbuilding division and distributed by McLean Trucking in early 1954.

Atlantic's existing services. He said the ships would carry 286 loaded trailers, each 35 feet long, that would be rolled on and off the ship. McLean said the acquisition did not alter McLean Trucking's plans to acquire S.C. Loveland and to use that company's operating rights to begin "sea-land service" along the Atlantic Coast.

The ICC would not allow McLean to own two competing companies – McLean Trucking and Pan-Atlantic – that provided transportation services in the same market. To get around that prohibition, McLean quietly arranged to divest himself of control over his trucking company before buying Pan-Atlantic. Malcom, together with his brother James and his sister Clara, still owned 75 percent of McLean Trucking. On January 21, 1954, Malcom resigned as president of McLean Trucking and arranged to have the company's closely held stock re-registered to a new company, McLean Securities Corporation, with the voting rights placed in trust. No longer having control of the company, Malcom then sold his shares and used the $6 million payment he received to buy Pan-Atlantic from Waterman on the same day.

When the transaction became public, a furor ensued. Within a month, seven major railroads, including the New Haven, moved to block McLean's plan to establish a sea-trailer service. They filed a complaint with the ICC saying that McLean still controlled an interstate trucking company. The complaint was dismissed eight months later, when McLean used an open ICC hearing to explain what he had done to avoid the prohibited conflict. McLean had his prize, and soon he would have all of Waterman, too.

*   *   *

Banker Walter B. Wriston grasped the possibilities of McLean's idea for moving containers on ships.

In the early 1950s, when McLean's success as a trucker was beginning to attract national attention, he had the good fortune to be noticed by an energetic young banker, Walter B. Wriston of New York's National City Bank. It was not long before the two men began working together in ways that served them both. McLean, trying to lower the cost of moving his trailers between coastal cities, was seeking financial backing to acquire the ships he needed. Wriston was eager to find growing businesses in which his bank could invest.

Despite their complementary motivations, McLean and Wriston made an unlikely couple. The urbane Wriston was the son of an iconoclastic president of Brown University and a graduate of the Fletcher School of Law and Diplomacy at Tufts University. McLean was a product of rural North Carolina, a man with keen intelligence but with a formal education that did not extend past Maxton High School. What they had in common was soaring ambition and a willingness to gamble on unproven ideas, a trait that made each of them a maverick in his own industry. McLean was pleased to find a deep-pocketed banker who could keep up with his lightning-quick calculations of costs and revenues; Wriston was delighted to find an industry-builder who validated his ideas on how bank reserves should be invested. In later years, Wriston would make a lasting mark in banking, rising to chairman and CEO of Citibank, where he led the industry into automatic-teller machines, credit-card lending and international bank branches.

When Wriston joined National City in 1946 after Army service and a year at the State Department, one of his first clients had been a businessman named Aristotle Onassis. The Greek entrepreneur had few resources, but saw that there was money to be made in post-war shipping. Wriston recommended that his bank provide backing for Onassis because the investments he planned to make would generate healthy cash flows. Here was a banker McLean could work with.

Assigned to National City's transportation unit, Wriston and his colleagues noticed that they had only a few trucking accounts. When they searched out the nation's top 10 trucking companies, they found that McLean Trucking kept popping up as one of the country's most profitable motor carriers. When National City saw in the mid-1950s that McLean Trucking had a net worth of $25 million, Wriston decided it was time to take a trip down to Winston-Salem. As Wriston's biographer tells the story, "He discovered in the idea-a-minute Malcom McLean something of a soul mate," a man with an endless curiosity about how the world really works.

Wriston was especially pleased that McLean thought of himself as working in the transportation industry, rather than in the trucking business. This was a highly unusual self-perception at the time, but McLean, unlike his contemporaries, seemed to consider the regulatory roadblocks that separated the transportation modes as merely temporary obstacles. "McLean," Wriston said, "saw the ship as just another piece of highway to transport goods on." Wriston also reported that, "McLean had approached a top railroad executive with a proposal to transport containers on flatbed railcars in piggyback fashion. The railroad man rejected that suggestion out of hand, saying that he didn't want to do anything that would help truckers, his archcompetitors. If not 'piggybacks,' then why not 'fishybacks'? McLean asked himself." And so, after one of Wriston's analysts reported that the numbers on McLean Trucking checked out, the New York banker prepared to work with his newfound friend and client in North Carolina.

Three months after buying Pan-Atlantic, McLean offered to purchase the rest of Waterman. This time, the offer was accepted. Putting the deal together involved considerable arm-twisting in New York and Mobile, and the saga of its closing sheds considerable light on how McLean and Wriston did business.

At the end of World War II, Waterman was one of the world's largest shipping companies, with more than 120 ships operating under its company flag, but by 1955 it had shrunk considerably, along with the rest of the American merchant marine. Waterman, however, had a substantial number of non-maritime investments. The company McLean acquired included several valuable prop-

The Wacosta, one of Waterman's breakbulk freighters, later was converted into a container ship by Sea-Land.

erties in the Mobile area: the Grand Hotel and Golf Course at Point Clear, the 16-story Waterman Building in downtown Mobile, the Gulf Shipbuilding Company and the Ryan Stevedoring Company. When Wriston and McLean took a closer look at Waterman, they discovered that it had been so conservatively managed that it had no debt and held cash reserves of $25 million, while the company's entire market value at that time was only $20 million.

McLean, acting through the C. Lee Company, a new entity wholly owned by McLean Securities Corporation, offered to buy Waterman for $48 per share, which came to just under $42 million. His offer was accepted pending the resignation of the current board of directors. Waterman had another offer in hand as well, one made by a consortium of several New York shipping interests, but for slightly less money than McLean offered.

McLean and Wriston put their bid together in a series of late-night meetings in New York's Essex House Hotel. National City Bank would lend the entire $42 million needed to buy Waterman. McLean would secure the loan with $7 million in preferred stock, but without putting any personal funds at risk. It was one of the earliest "leveraged buyouts," and the loan nearly equaled the bank's legal lending limit. Not surprisingly, Wriston had some trouble selling the concept to the bank's senior officers. The plan was to declare a $25 million cash dividend as soon as the transfer was completed and immediately reduce the loan by that amount. Things got a bit tense when it was revealed that another National City Bank lending unit was backing the other bidder, but McLean persuaded the bank to approve the deal.

Not all members of the Waterman's board of directors were happy with the deal. When it was pointed out that the board assembled in Mobile to approve the sale did not have a quorum, it appeared that the closing would have to be postponed, and the transaction might not go through. At that point one of the New

Helen Delich Bentley covered the container revolution as a Baltimore Sun reporter and later served on the Federal Maritime Commission and as a Maryland congresswoman.

York lawyers rushed out to the street and corralled a likely looking passer-by. He was immediately elected a director, told how to vote, and then politely ushered out the door, somewhat befuddled but with a $50 bill in his hand. And with that, the deal was done.

*   *   *

Soon after the aquisition, McLean recouped much of the purchase price of Waterman by selling off the Mobile company's shipyard, stevedoring company and hotel and golf course. The company pension plan was also terminated, with its assets distributed to the participants. But McLean had every intention of hanging on to Waterman's ships. He also decided to keep the company's headquarters in Mobile and soon moved to that city himself.

McLean took over as the chairman of Waterman's board of directors and installed his brother James as the company's president. It was soon announced that the company had sent two surplus World War II tankers, the *Ideal X* and the *Almena*, to a Bethlehem Steel shipyard in Baltimore. James McLean told the press that the work being done was "experimental" and was "related to a plan to put an extensive trailership service in operation to serve Atlantic and Gulf ports." The same newspaper story also reported that Pan-Atlantic had asked the U.S. Maritime Commission to approve a request "to turn in seven vessels and replace them with trailerships." Word of McLean's grand plan was beginning to spread.

Immediately after the sale, Waterman had announced it intended to surrender its operating rights to carry cargo between Pacific and Atlantic ports via the Gulf. McLean's intention was to have the surrendered operating rights transferred to Pan-Atlantic. Less than a month later, aggrieved railroads that operated along the Atlantic Seaboard asked the ICC to investigate whether McLean had violated antitrust laws with the attempted maneuver.

Legal sanction for McLean's new coastwise service came in September 1955. The ICC granted Pan-Atlantic Steamship preliminary approval to use "ships as 'sea tractors' to haul freight-laden highway trailers." The examiner who made this announcement explained that "the trailers would serve as mere containers for the freight actually transported." This careful distinction between the box and what it was carrying was important, for the liner company was being "authorized to haul 'commodities generally' between Gulf and North and South Atlantic ports." The Atlantic Coast Line Railroad brought the issue to the ICC because, it asserted, "Pan-Atlantic was primarily a breakbulk water carrier without authority to haul trailers on especially built 'trailer ships,'" but the ICC examiner concluded otherwise.

The examiner supported his finding with a revealing argument. He pointed out that "Seatrain Lines, Inc. transported freight generally loaded in railroad freight cars," and that "Pan-Atlantic's operating certificate likewise appeared to be 'all-embracing.'" He further noted that "the term 'commodities generally' did not include restrictions 'regarding containers of any kind in or on which, or the manner in which, the freight may be carried'." And on the basis of this distinction, *The New York Times* reported, "the hopes of Malcom P. McLean climbed another rung."

McLean celebrated this breakthrough by immediately announcing that his company would soon be offering trailer ship service to ports such as Boston; New York; Philadelphia; Baltimore; Georgetown and Charleston, South Carolina; Jacksonville, Miami, Tampa, Port St. Joe and Panama City, Florida; New Orleans; and Houston and Galveston, Texas. Reporting on the Pan-Atlantic acquisition, the *Baltimore Sun's* Helen Delich wrote that in an interview the week before the transaction, McLean said "that he had some novel ideas concerning the handling of cargoes on regular dry-cargo vessels in addition to initiating the trailer ship on a wide-scale basis."

The container revolution was set to begin.

CHAPTER THREE

The Revolution Begins

*"It is probably most accurate to think of McLean as the Robert Fulton of containerization.
Just as Fulton did not invent the steamboat, but instead was the first to make a going
concern of the steamship business, similarly McLean did not invent containerization,
but was able to raise an industry around this technology."*

—Mark Rosenstein

April 26, 1956, was a chilly, dreary day in Newark, New Jersey, with intermittent drizzle and a high temperature of 48 degrees. Across the Hudson River in New York City, the wet weather forced the postponement of that night's baseball game between the Brooklyn Dodgers and the New York Giants at the Polo Grounds. That morning on a dock outside Shed 154 at Port Newark, Malcom McLean and about 100 Pan-Atlantic Steamship employees and guests gazed upon a strange-looking ship, a 524-foot-long tanker with a metal platform installed above the pumps and piping that cluttered the vessel's main deck. The ship had been launched near the end of World War II as the *Potrero Hills*. McLean renamed it the *Ideal X* because it was ideal for his experiment.

The *Ideal X* represented a change in McLean's plans for the company's venture into the coastwise trailer ship business. McLean had detoured from his original idea for roll-on, roll-off ships with ramps for trailers to be driven directly on and off the ship. The trailers being stowed on the top deck of the *Ideal X* had been separated from their wheels and undercarriages and were lifted aboard with a dockside crane. The trailers – the word "container" was still not widely used – were not the standard ones hauled along highways. These boxes had been specially reinforced to withstand the rolling of the ship, and as McLean was careful to note, each was filled with paying cargo. As McLean and his guests watched, longshoremen lifted 58 of the containers, at the rate of about one every seven minutes, and secured them on the ship's raised deck. Even with a half-hour delay caused by trouble with the crane, the loading was completed in less than eight hours. The ship sailed that evening for Houston, where it arrived six days later at City Dock 10.

New Trailership Service Starts

Pan Atlantic Steamship Corp. yesterday inaugurated the first trailership service out of New York when its converted tanker, Ideal X, left Port Newark, N. J., with 58 fully-loaded truck trailer bodies as well as tank cargo.

Much of the freight would have been shipped entirely by overland route were it not for the new service which will be operated on a once-a-week schedule sailing every Thursday, James K. McLean, president of Pan-Atlantic, said.

"We are convinced," he said, "that we have found a way to combine the economy of water transportation with the speed and flexibility of overland shipment."

The service provides sixth-day arrival in Houston the following Wednesday.

*The Journal of Commerce,
April 27, 1956*

*Opposite: History was made when
McLean's first container was stowed
on the Ideal X.*

On hand for the maiden voyage were Donald V. Lowe, chairman of the Port of New York Authority; Austin J. Tobin, the port authority's executive director; Newark Mayor Leo P. Carlin and Malcom P. McLean.

Newark Mayor Leo P. Carlin and Donald V. Lowe, chairman of the Port of New York Authority, spoke at a ceremony and luncheon marking the start of the new service. In his official remarks, Carlin told McLean: "With the first sailing of a container ship, you will have converted a challenging, revolutionary transportation concept into a practical reality." The front page of that afternoon's *Newark Evening News* carried a three-column photograph and a brief story ("Sea-Land Shipping; 'Piggy Back' Tanker Service Starts"). Elsewhere, the event attracted little attention. The next day's *New York Times* printed a one-column story on page 39. *The Journal of Commerce* published a three-paragraph story under the headline "New Trailership Service Starts."

Today the first voyage of the *Ideal X* is viewed as the start of modern container shipping. The effect of this development would be profound and extensive. It would alter the appearance and operations of ports and the work that surrounded them. It would cause venerable shipping lines, agencies and stevedoring companies to disappear, while creating profitable opportunities for new competitors. Most important, containerization would create a new world of opportunities for buyers and sellers of goods and, by doing so, help transform the global economy.

In early 1956, no one could foresee all of this. Even within the shipping industry, few recognized the impact that containerization would have. Less than two weeks after the *Ideal X* left on its first voyage with containers on deck, New York port officials announced plans to develop a new cargo-passenger pier near the foot of Houston Street on the West Side of congested lower Manhattan. The chain of events set in motion that day at Port Newark would make this project obsolete almost as soon as it opened, but in the spring of 1956, conventional wisdom supported decisions to invest in traditional cargo-handling technology.

And why not? New York City piers still hummed with activity. Under pressure from shippers and newspapers, port officials had recently cracked down on the entrenched "loading racket," in

which criminal-linked companies charged exorbitant rates to transfer cargo between truck and pier. Cargo activity was so brisk that trucks clogged narrow dockside streets, waiting for hours to pick up and deliver cargo. Tugs pushing barges shuttled railcars back and forth between New Jersey railheads and ship piers where cargo was loaded breakbulk style, by the pallet, box, bag or bale. Amid this activity were the comings and goings of large trans-Atlantic passenger liners, such as the *United States, America* and *Queen Elizabeth*. On a good day, 25,000 longshoremen worked in and around dozens of piers in the nation's busiest port.

By contrast, the terminal from which the *Ideal X* sailed in April 1956 was a backwater. Port Newark had been created during World War I to handle government cargo. Over the years, it continued to handle intermittent shipments of lumber, scrap iron and various bulk commodities. But it had advantages. Unlike New York's "finger piers," which jutted out into the water, ships at Port Newark were moored parallel to the wharf, and the ample space between warehouse and water permitted trucks to be driven all the way to pierside. Truckers also had quick access

Tank Vessels Begin Trailer Runs in April

Special to Journal of Commerce

MOBILE, Ala., Feb. 19.—A new service between Houston and New York using tankers to carry full trailer loads of dry cargo will be started by Pan-Atlantic Steamship Corp. in April, it was announced at the weekend by James K. McLean, president.

Beginning of the service is the first phase in a truck-water program being undertaken by Pan-Atlantic, a subsidiary of McLean Industries, Inc., according to Mr. McLean.

The announcement followed six months of sea trials for the two vessels to be engaged in the service initially, Mr. McLean said.

Both ships are T-2 type tankers, converted for Pan-Atlantic by the addition of a cargo deck. Each has a carrying capacity of 2,320,-000 pounds of dry cargo, in specially built trailer bodies. The ships will also carry crude oil on northbound trips.

Converted at Bethlehem Steel Corp.'s Baltimore yard, the ships have a deadweight tonnage of 16,500. Each vessel is equipped to carry 58 fully loaded, 33-foot trailer bodies, each with load capacity of 40,000 pounds.

Special equipment is now being installed at the Pan-Atlantic terminals in Houston and Port Newark for the loading and unloading of the trailer bodies.

The Journal of Commerce, February 20, 1956. This announcement followed successful sea trials.

to the New Jersey Turnpike, which had opened only five years earlier. Port Newark was out of the mainstream, but Malcom McLean didn't care. It had what he needed.

* * *

In the months leading up to the first sailing of the *Ideal X*, McLean had indicated that he still planned to carry out his original plan to use roll-on, roll-off ships instead of a system in which cargo was lifted on and off. In November 1955, McLean said Pan-Atlantic planned to trade in seven war-built freighters and build seven ro-ro ships of the kind the military liked. "The new vessels will be of the 'rollon-rolloff' type advocated by the Department of Defense," McLean announced. "Our company is proud that it can provide these special-type ships which will fulfill a vital need in the defense of America in a national emergency and also make an important contribution to our peacetime commerce." Maritime Administrator Clarence G. Morse said only minor details were yet to be worked out for construction of the ships, and that 87.5 percent of the vessels' estimated construction cost of $9 million each would be covered by government-backed mortgages.

In a magazine article in January 1956, Morse reported with evident satisfaction that plans had recently been announced to support the building of ships "designed with the shipper in mind":

> Trailer ships, now more popularly called "roll-on-roll-off," are a very important element in the Maritime Administration's projections for service to American shippers. With interest mounting in this type of vessel, largely limited to coastwise service, we may have found an answer to the rejuvenation of the domestic trades. Various companies have expressed interest in obtaining Federal mortgage insurance to aid them in financing construction of some 35 of these ships.

Morse went on to say that "Pan-Atlantic's Trailer Ship Service" will probably be "the first implementation of the new trailer ship service in American coastwise steamship operation." He said the plan was for Pan-Atlantic to return seven old ships in exchange for government mortgage insurance on seven new vessels. Morse also said that the Office of Defense Transportation was asked to authorize an accelerated tax write-off for these ships. Construction was to begin within three months after all financial arrangements had been completed, and the ships

were to serve ports along the Atlantic and Gulf coasts. The article pointed out that the ships would be substantially like the 20-knot ro-ro vessels that were being constructed for the Military Sea Transportation Service to carry more than 200 loaded truck trailers to help supply military transportation needs. These trailers would be loaded and discharged via ramps that required no special shoreside facilities.

The following month, however, McLean revealed that he had opted to convert tankers to carry containers that were lifted on and off ship instead of trailers that were rolled on and off. In February 1956, newspapers reported that although Pan-Atlantic still hoped to build the ro-ro trailer ships, it would launch its new service with two tankers on which top decks had been installed at Bethlehem Steel's Key Highway shipyard in Baltimore. The conversion had been done the previous year, but Pan-Atlantic had given the converted ships a six-month trial to work out "questions of balance and the handling of trailers" on the tankers' new decks.

This was the "experimental" work to which James McLean had cryptically referred after the Waterman acquisition. The Coast Guard was concerned that highway trailers could not withstand the stress of shipment by sea and would be a hazard to the ship and its crew. To satisfy the Coast Guard and the American Bureau of Shipping, which certifies the safety of ships, McLean had had his Pan-Atlantic tankers carry around two old but substantially reinforced Fruehauf highway trailers loaded with coke briquettes. The tankers carried oil between the Gulf Coast and the Northeast. At the end of each voyage, the

McLean's tankers hauled test shipments of coke briquettes in trailers that had been reinforced with triangular steel frames.

McLean's first containers were designed with steel pedestals that fit into holes on the tankers' decks.

*After that initial order, McLean's containers, including boxes carried on the maiden voyage of the *Ideal X,* were built by the Strick division of Fruehauf Trailer Corporation. The company's president, Roy Fruehauf, recognized containerization's potential and offered to finance McLean's purchase of containers and chassis.

Coast Guard checked the condition of the containers. The test continued until the ship captain's log showed that the ship and its trailers had withstood sufficiently rough weather to convince the authorities that the loaded trailers could be carried safely on deck.

Besides difficulties surrounding government approvals and financing, McLean had other reasons to look beyond roll-on, roll-off ships as the vehicle for his seagoing trailers. Trailers' wheels and undercarriages occupied space that otherwise might be used to carry paying cargo. He began inquiring about having strong, custom-made containers built for his novel shipping service.

*   *   *

Late one spring afternoon in 1955, Keith W. Tantlinger received a message at the Toledo, Ohio, headquarters of Brown Trailer Company. The message said George Kempton, executive vice president of Waterman and Pan-Atlantic, was interested in buying some containers but wanted to talk with an engineer, not a salesman. Tantlinger, Brown's vice president of engineering, returned the call. Brown Trailer had built 200 reinforced aluminum containers, each measuring 30 feet long, eight feet wide and eight and a half feet high, for Ocean Van Lines, a company that transported military cargo from the Pacific Northwest to Alaska. These containers were stacked two-high on oceangoing barges and, after reaching Alaska, were locked onto trailer chassis and hauled to their destinations. Kempton said he and McLean wanted to learn more.

Tantlinger received the message on Friday, April 1. The following Monday he was in Mobile to tell McLean and his team at Pan-Atlantic about the seagoing boxes. McLean was impressed and agreed to pay approximately $2,800 apiece for an order of 33-foot-long containers. He would get the first two containers in two weeks, and he agreed to order 200 more if the first ones tested successfully.* McLean was satisfied with the trailers, but he had one other request. He wanted Tantlinger to move to Mobile to help with his new venture. Tantlinger left Brown to become vice president of engineering at Waterman and Pan-Atlantic.

Now that McLean had his containers, his next problem was how to move them quickly and safely on and off the tankers that would take them to sea. Because the boxes would not be attached to truck chassis, Tantlinger and his fellow engineers had to come up with a suitable lifting system. They located a pair of used revolving cranes at Sun Shipbuilding in Chester, Pennsylvania. The cranes had the capacity and reach that was needed and the price was less than half the cost of new cranes. More important, the Sun cranes were available immediately. One was installed at Newark and the other at Houston after the wharves were reinforced to support the cranes' weight.

While the cranes were being readied, Tantlinger was busy solving another problem. Lifting an object as large as a trailer body normally would require four longshoremen on the dock to use ladders to secure hooks to the container's corners, and four more to disengage the hooks on deck. To speed the process, Tantlinger designed and patented an automatic spreader. This was a steel apparatus that allowed a crane operator to press a button that automatically grabbed the container for lifting. The dimensions of the spreader were approximately the same as those of the container's top. When the crane lowered the spreader onto a container, an electrical device was used to lock the spreader to the box at its top corners. When the container had been placed on the ship, the locking device was disengaged electrically.

It was a simple and fast way to move 25-ton containers

Keith W. Tantlinger was described by Malcom McLean as "the one who did the most to get the containers on ships."

The McLean Test

The containers carried by the *Ideal X* and its sister converted tankers were made of semi-monocoque or stressed-skin aluminum, meaning that the box's outside structure supported most of its load.

Keith Tantlinger, the Brown Trailer executive who had sold the units, assured Malcom McLean that the structurally riveted roof, though only 1/32 inch thick, was so strong that a man could jump on it. McLean ordered two of them for testing.

Two weeks later, the boxes were delivered to the Baltimore shipyard where the *Ideal X* and another tanker were being fitted with a deck to carry contain-

ers. Tantlinger and McLean planned to meet for breakfast at the Lord Baltimore Hotel with several other Pan-Atlantic Steamship officials, and then go to the shipyard.

Tantlinger arrived early and waited "for what seemed like three or four hours" before discovering that the rest of the group had gone directly to the shipyard.

He hailed a taxi and rushed to the shipyard, where he was astonished to see McLean and his companions on the roofs of the boxes, jumping up and down to test the manufacturer's claim about the containers' strength.

New containers were fitted onto the steel decks installed on Pan-Atlantic tankers at Bethlehem Steel's Key Highway shipyard in Baltimore.

between ship and shore. As Tantlinger noted when recalling the first voyage of the *Ideal X*, "In April 1956, none of the guests had ever seen a shipping container the size of a semi-trailer, let alone a mysterious device dangling from a crane that mysteriously engaged and disengaged them." The pieces of the new system had fallen into place by the time McLean invited shipping executives, port officials and newspaper reporters to the launching of his new transportation service. Meanwhile, McLean had already planned his next moves.

* * *

His timing was impeccable. There was an ample supply of used ships available for conversion into container ships. With more war-built cargo ships than peacetime commerce required, the government found itself with a surplus of ships that were being placed in mothball fleets or sold off at low prices. These boom-and-bust cycles in maritime investment were highly disruptive to the overall health of the U.S. shipping industry, for they broke the linkage between the costs of building and operating merchant ships and the economic returns realized when they were used in commercial service. But they provided a pool of ships that would be used to launch containerized shipping.

At the end of World War II, the U.S.-flag merchant fleet contained more than 4,400 ships. Of this number, about 2,500 were the celebrated Liberty ships, which were mass-produced during the war but were of low value commercially, since they could only chug along at 11 knots. At the end of the war, the economies of the European nations and Japan, which had had sizable merchant fleets before the war, were in ruins. The United States had to immediately address the problem of getting its allies and former adversaries back on their feet. The Marshall Plan was one response to this need. Rebuilding national shipping fleets was another. The 1946 Merchant Marine Sales Act made surplus U.S. merchant ships available to both U.S. and non-U.S. buyers. By 1949, American companies had purchased more than 1,000 surplus merchant ships from the government and buyers from other nations had purchased more than 1,100. The remaining surplus ships, many still in good condition, were placed in the newly formed National Defense Reserve Fleet. These were the ships that during the 1950s and 1960s were sold to McLean, laying the foundation for the container revolution. The government did its best to obtain reasonable payment for these vessels, which had been built at public expense. But because they were steadily losing value while mothballed, the government was willing to sell them cheaply.

The *Ideal X* was a government-surplus tanker that had been built at Marinship Corporation in Sausalito, California, in 1945. A second converted tanker, the *Almena*, soon joined it. McLean bought a third tanker, the *Marine Leader*, for $1.275 million shortly before the inauguration of container service by the *Ideal X*. The *Marine Leader* was renamed the *Maxton*, in honor of McLean's hometown. All three ships were modified to carry the containers built by Brown and, later, those made by Fruehauf as well.

The boxes that these converted tankers carried were 33 feet long, eight feet wide and eight feet, six inches high. This length was chosen because it was the maximum that could be evenly divided into the distance between the tanker's aft and mid-deck houses and still comply with Eastern states' 35-foot limits on trailer lengths. The elevated deck supporting the containers was equipped with cone-shaped pedestals that were fitted into holes on the deck to hold the boxes in place.

A week before starting his new container service, McLean reached a three-way agreement with the International Brotherhood of Teamsters and the International Longshoremen's

Pedestals on the bottoms of Pan-Atlantic's initial "sea-land service" containers had to be fitted into holes on special trailers. This photo was taken at Houston in 1956.

Association that defined the work jurisdiction of the two unions to prevent work stoppages. The Teamsters would drive the trucks to and from the dock, and the longshoremen would transfer the boxes to and from the ship. Newspaper accounts noted that the agreement included a proposed Pan-Atlantic roll-on, roll-off service that would use seven specially designed vessels capable of carrying 286 loaded trailers. McLean was still publicly committed to the idea of using a roll-on, roll-off system. But he had already begun converting the general cargo ships that came with his purchase of Pan-Atlantic into container ships that, like the Seatrain ships, would carry metal boxes above and below deck. Although the boxes were transported without their chassis, McLean and his designers persisted in calling the new boxes "trailers," and the *Ideal X*, *Almena* and *Maxton* were known as "trailer ships," suggesting a continuity with trucking.

*　*　*

McLean knew from his earliest days in the trucking business that even the best equipment is no good without customers. He sent his salesmen out to round up business for Pan-

Loading of the Ideal X and its sister ships was speeded by a spreader that automatically grabbed and released containers by their top corners. The photo at right, taken in Houston, shows one of Pan-Atlantic's cranes and the deck installed over a tanker's deck pipes.

Atlantic's new service. Many of the service's early customers had moved freight with McLean Trucking, and McLean was thoroughly familiar with the north-south market that Pan-Atlantic was pursuing. The new service's first domestic accounts included Nabisco, which sent crackers and cookies south from its bakeries in the Northeast; Heublein (alcoholic beverages), Gillette (shaving products) and Melville (shoes). McLean had carefully calculated the costs of the new venture. "I don't think that anyone in this period had a better sense of north-south costs than Malcom," said Paul F. Richardson, who was still at McLean Trucking but would later join his former boss at the new container-shipping venture. Richardson said McLean "knew every angle of costing…. He'd take a pencil and, on the back of an envelope, calculate the costs for a trucking run more precisely than anyone else could do it."

McLean paid close attention to the work of his sales force. He hired a group of young recent graduates, many of them former athletes, and turned them loose to convert frequently skeptical customers to the notion of moving their overland freight by ship. One of those early hires was R. Kenneth Johns, a Mobile native and recent Auburn University graduate who joined the

The Ideal X was christened the Potrero Hills when it was built at Marinship Corporation in Sausalito, California, in 1945. Sold by Pan-Atlantic and renamed the Elemir in 1959, the vessel resumed service as a tanker before it was damaged in a Pacific storm and scrapped in Japan in 1965.

company in 1957. Johns, who would later become president of Sea-Land Service, said McLean inspired devout loyalty among his salesmen. "Before one single trailer had been shipped, Malcom had convinced all of the young guys he'd hired for his sales force that this thing was going to work…And if we hadn't believed in what he was doing, we'd have been skinned when we made our pitches to potential customers." McLean held regular Monday afternoon meetings with his staff. "We made pitches to him," Johns said. "He would sharpen them. We hear today about 'direct reporting' as a management 'best practice'. With Malcom, you just told him what you had to say in plain English. And he'd tell you back. You couldn't get any more 'direct' than that."

Pan-Atlantic's young sales representatives encountered resistance from many customers who were apprehensive about putting their over-the-road freight on a ship. They wanted to see how the Pan-Atlantic project worked before committing themselves. "Once the snowball started to move, they got caught up in it," Johns said. "When reports came back that trailers shipped by sea actually arrived safe, unbattered, etc., the next sale was easier. There was at least a 20 percent savings for using us…The real secret of containerization, for me, was as much in the selling as in the technology. The latter was a breakthrough, but you had to make people aware of it."

*   *   *

Within months after launching its coastwise container service, Pan-Atlantic was operating four converted tankers – the *Ideal X*, *Almena*, *Maxton* and *Coalinga Hills*. Each was fitted with a top deck that carried 58 containers. The ships eventually carried as many as 62 boxes. By the end of 1956, the Port of New York Authority reported that Pan-Atlantic had moved more than 67,000 tons of containerized freight through Port Newark. Malcom's brother James said the company had found a better way to move cargo: "We are convinced that we have found the way to combine the economy of water transportation with the speed and flexibility of overland shipment. By minimizing special packaging requirements and intermediate handling as well as delivery and interchange, we have met the objections which many shippers previously made to shipping by water."

The primary flow of containerized cargo on the ships was southbound. The tankers continued to carry oil from Houston to the Northeast on a few early voyages, but their dual use did not last long. As Pan-Atlantic's container business took off, the converted ships soon were used exclusively for containers. McLean used the converted tankers to launch his container service because they were available at a bargain price, could be put into use quickly and if the venture did not pan out, they could be used for their original purpose, carrying oil.

Soon the tankers were replaced by a different group of ships. These also were converted World War II-era vessels but were former C-2 freighters instead of T-2 tankers like the *Ideal X*. The T-2 and C-2 designations were used by the Federal Maritime Board, and later the Maritime Administration* to identify U.S.-flag ship types. The letters identified the ship type – "T" for tankers, "C" for general-cargo ship – and the numbers represented sizes, with larger numbers (C-3, C-4 and so on) denoting larger ships. McLean acquired six C-2s that were converted to carry containers and put into use in 1957-58. Renamed the *Gateway City*, *Azalea City*, *Bienville*, *Fairland*, *Raphael Semmes* and *Beauregard*, these ships took containerization to a new level.

Each of the six converted C-2s was redesigned to carry 226 containers stacked in cells, or steel frames, below deck and on

Paul Richardson joined McLean Trucking in 1952 as a management trainee and later rose to president of Sea-Land Service.

* The Federal Maritime Board was divided in 1961 into the Federal Maritime Commission, an independent regulatory agency, and the Maritime Administration, whose mission is to promote the U.S. maritime industry.

Pan-Atlantic Container Ships Set for Coastal Run in Fall

The first U. S. flag vessel designed exclusively to handle container shipments with self-contained loading cranes will be placed in operation this Fall by Pan-Atlantic Steamship Corp., the company has announced.

Next month, the Gateway City, first of ten C-2 cargo ships being converted by the company is scheduled for completion followed shortly thereafter by the Azelea City.

The company will then be ready to begin regular weekly sailings between Newark, Miami, Houston and Tampa. Two more similar ships are expected to be ready by October at which time New Orleans will be added to the route and sailings will be increased to two per week between Newark, Miami and Houston.

Pan-Atlantic, a subsidiary of McLean Industries, Inc., now maintains a container operation between Newark and Gulf ports with four T-2 tankers upon whose decks containers are carried in both directions as well as oil cargoes on Northbound voyages. These vessels will be withdrawn as the converted ships take over.

The company, which pioneered its "Sea-Land" service between New York and Houston last year, will expand the schedule further and extend the operation to other coastal cities as additional converted ships are completed. Company officials explain that cranes, developed by Pan-Atlantic engineers and carried on the vessels themselves, eliminate the need for shore installations. They make it possible to serve any port having adequate water and dockside

(Continued on Fifteenth Page)

The Journal of Commerce reported on McLean's planned expansion on July 11, 1957.

hatch covers above deck. Keith Tantlinger said this was uncharted territory for engineers: "In 1956 there were no five- or six-high stackable containers, no cellular container ships, and there was no one who knew or could even predict the behavior of stacked containers in a cell, or how closely the cell guides should support the individual stacks."

Tantlinger and his fellow engineers built a cell-guide prototype at the Alabama State Docks in Mobile. There, with a stiff-leg crane, they used trial and error to determine the ideal clearance for containers. Too much clearance, and the container stack would shift while at sea. Too little clearance, and the flexing of the ship would cause the containers to jam in the cell guides. Over and over, the engineers lifted and lowered a container into the steel frame. "We nearly wore that container out hoisting it loaded, partly loaded and empty, canted to match all simulated listing angles and hanging vertically...while we varied both list and drag angles," Tantlinger said. The engineers finally decided the ideal clearance would be 1¼ inches more than the container's length and three-fourths of an inch more than its width.

The next problem was cranes. Land-based revolving cranes were adequate for lifting containers on and off a converted tanker's open deck but they were poorly suited to the job of stowing containers in the tight confines of below-deck cell guides. Tantlinger and his fellow engineers decided that the best solution would be a crane that straddled each row of containers and could be precisely positioned to lift and lower containers in and out of the cells. McLean also wanted the cranes installed on the ships so that they could call at any port where trucks could be driven alongside a ship.

McLean was eager to get the converted freighters into operation as quickly as possible. He set a tight schedule. By the time the design for the cell guides had been worked out, only 90 days was left for procurement, installation and testing of the cranes. Tantlinger engaged the Mobile engineering firm of Ewin, Campbell and Gottlieb to help with a project that all involved later said should have taken a year or two to complete.

The engineers had no time to design a new crane from

scratch. They had to find existing cranes and quickly adapt them for use on the ship. They found what they needed at the Skagit Steel and Iron Works in Sedro-Woolley, Washington. Skagit had made logging cranes and had some that could be adapted for installation aboard Pan-Atlantic's ships.

Because the decks of the C-2s had their wheelhouses amidships, each ship would need two cranes — one forward, one aft — that could be rolled along the deck for positioning over each row of containers. The cranes' hinged arms were folded downward when not in use. When the ship had been made fast alongside a dock, the cranes' arms were raised into place so that they extended over the dock.

Handling containers in below-deck cells also required modification of the spreader to fit inside the ship's cell guides. After the two shipboard cranes were installed on the first converted C-2,

the *Gateway City*, the process was repeated in rapid succession on the other ships.

Even after the cranes and cell guides were installed on the *Gateway City*, no one was sure how well they would work at sea. Tantlinger said one "well-recognized naval architect" predicted that the flexing of a ship's hull would crush the containers "like walnuts" in their confined cell guides.

Tantlinger said that despite their planning, he and his fellow engineers were nervous. "No one preceded us and all we could do was use our best collective judgment and hope," Tantlinger recalled. "If the ship listed consistently during the loading of a single cell, theoretically all the containers would be hard against the cell guides on one side. We certainly hoped our container stack would not be swaying as a unit with each roll of the ship. There was no way to determine or even predict the result. The risk was ridiculous, but we had to try."

Before the *Gateway City* made its first voyage from Newark to Miami, Houston and Tampa on October 4, 1957, Tantlinger went to an F.W. Woolworth five-and-dime store in Newark and purchased the store's entire stock of children's modeling clay.

The Gateway City approaches Miami on its maiden voyage from Newark on October 7, 1957. As containerized cargo increased, the city's port later was moved from the mainland to Dodge and Lummus islands.

Opposite: To determine optimum clearance for cell guides on a container ship, engineers built a prototype at the Alabama State Docks in Mobile. A crane lifted and lowered containers in the guides while hydraulic jacks tilted the frame to simulate a ship's movement during loading. At left is Nelson K. Rogers, a Pan-Atlantic engineer.

Each of the converted C-2s carried two cranes – one forward of the wheelhouse, the other aft. They extended over the ship's sides and were folded down when not in use. The cranes were positioned over a row of container cells. The crane operator rode on the spreader, which grabbed the boxes with an automatic twistlock, lifted them from the dock and lowered them directly into the cell.

The clay was packaged in inch-square bars, wrapped in cellophane. Tantlinger returned to Port Newark to watch the containers being stowed on the *Gateway City*. Before each hatch on the ship was closed, he cut the soft clay blocks with his pocketknife and wedged them, cellophane and all, between the container corner posts and the cell guides. When the ship docked in Miami a few days later, Tantlinger retrieved the clay blocks and measured them to see how much they had been compressed by movement during the voyage down the East Coast. The container stacks had moved no more than 5/16 of an inch.

* * *

With the switch to the converted C-2s, Pan-Atlantic upgraded its container fleet to boxes 35 feet long, the maximum length permitted by Eastern states and the length McLean had wanted all along. The new trailers were built and financed by Fruehauf Trailer Company, which in the years ahead would manufacture thousands of containers for McLean. The 33-foot containers that the company used to launch its coastwise container service were phased out as the converted C-2s entered service. So were the *Ideal X* and its sister ships that McLean had used to launch Pan-Atlantic's "sea-land" service. By February 1958, all of the converted tankers had been sold. The *Ideal X* was scrapped in Japan in 1965.

The *Gateway City* began service from Port Newark to Miami, Houston and Tampa on October 4, 1957. There was an immediate and dramatic improvement in cargo-handling productivity. A C-2 breakbulk freighter would normally hire five work units, or gangs, of 21 longshoremen each to shift cargo from the vessel's five holds. With cargo being moved at a rate of about 40 tons per hour when discharging and loading cargo this way, a conventional freighter would stay in port six to eight days. The *Gateway City* required only two gangs of longshoremen, and was able to move cargo at the rate of 264 tons an hour. A ship could be

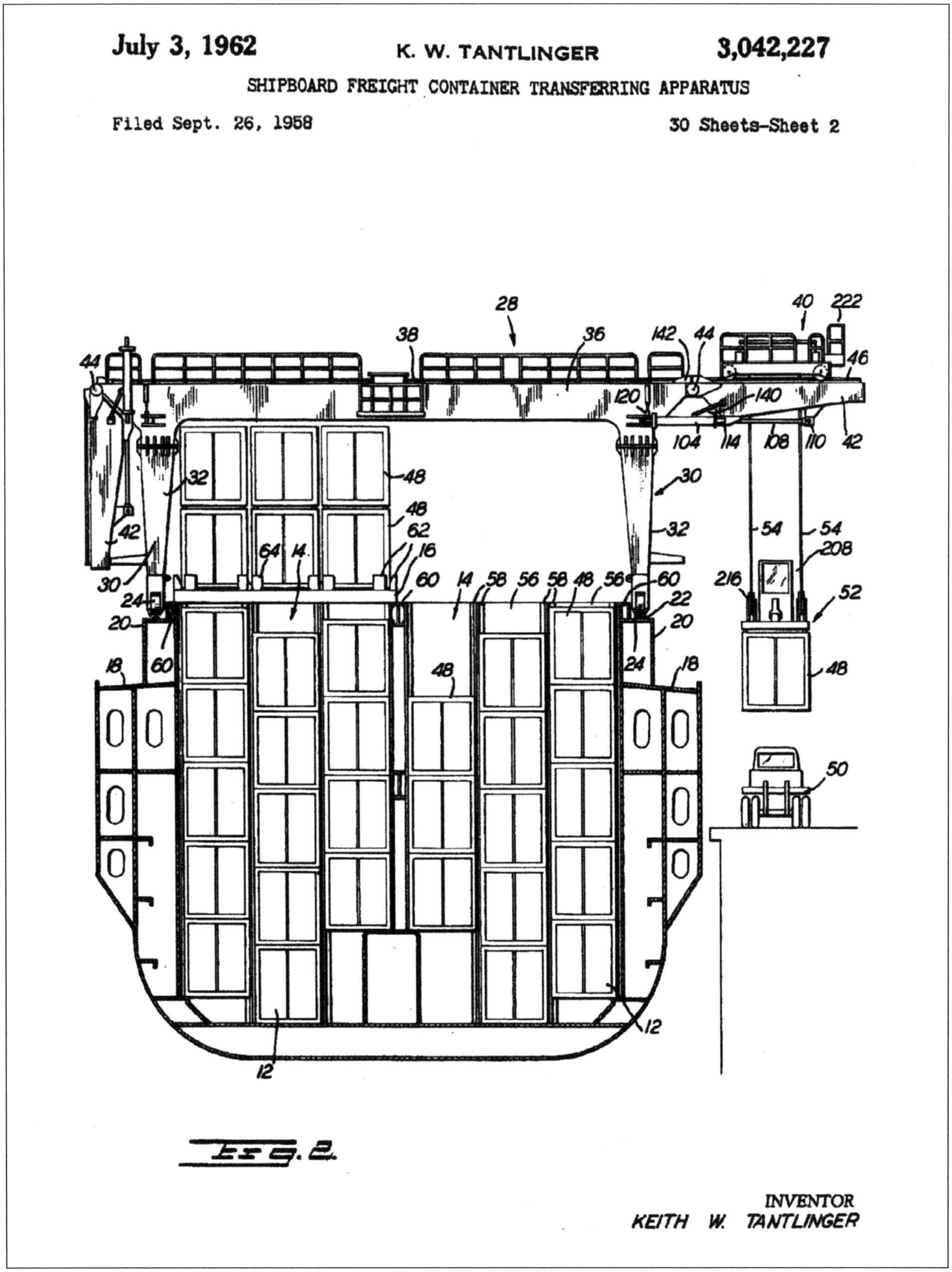

FIG. 2.

INVENTOR
KEITH W. TANTLINGER

This patent sketch of the container cranes installed on Pan-Atlantic's
converted C-2 freighters shows a cross section of the ship and containers.

Pan-Atlantic's boxes bore the company logo and "Sea-Land Service," which in 1960 became the company's name. This photo was taken in Miami in 1958.

turned around in as little as 14 hours.

There still were doubters. Critics of McLean's new system pointed out that containerized shipping did not permit the ship's full cubic capacity to be used. On a breakbulk ship, longshoremen would tightly stow bags and boxes of cargo in every available space. McLean acknowledged that container cell guides left unused spaces in cargo holds, but he said it was a fair trade-off: "We sacrifice tonnage for quick turnaround in port. That's the theory of the trailer ship. A ship earns money only when she's at sea. Costs are fixed at sea. Where costs rise is in port. The quicker you can get back to sea, the more money you can make."

In August 1958, Pan-Atlantic moved beyond its coastwise niche when the *Fairland* inaugurated service to San Juan, Puerto Rico. The new service had a rough beginning. Five months before the first Pan-Atlantic sailing to San Juan, the *Bienville* had sailed to San Juan, carrying the first shipload of containers bound for Puerto Rico. The *Bienville* was operating under the

The Story Of
The Twistlock

Guests watching the first containers lifted aboard the *Ideal X* were fascinated by the dock crane's spreader, an automatic container-securing device controlled by the crane operator.

The spreader was an invention of Keith W. Tantlinger, vice president of engineering at Pan-Atlantic and Waterman. It overlapped the top of the container and picked it up with curved bars that hooked into the sides of the box's top corners.

The device worked fine on the *Ideal X* and its sister converted tankers but would not work on a cellular container ship. The spreader's locking mechanism protruded beyond the top of the container and would not fit the tight confines of a cell guide.

Tantlinger devised a solution: the twistlock. The device was based on the principle of a bolt-action rifle. It could be lowered into slotted eyelets in the top corners of the container and automatically engaged and disengaged from above, without extending beyond the edge of the container. The device made it possible to develop the cell guides that would permit containers to be stowed below deck.

Today the twistlock is ubiquitous at container terminals. McLean agreed to release the patent rights to Tantlinger's twistlock and corner-post design in 1965, and the International Organization for Standardization used it as the basis for what now is the worldwide standard.

James LaRose, a principal at the Mobile, Alabama, engineering firm of Gottlieb, Barnett and Bridges, has described the device's invention as "the indispensable event of the container revolution. The twistlock was to containerization what the rubber tire is to the automotive industry. It is hard to imagine life without it."

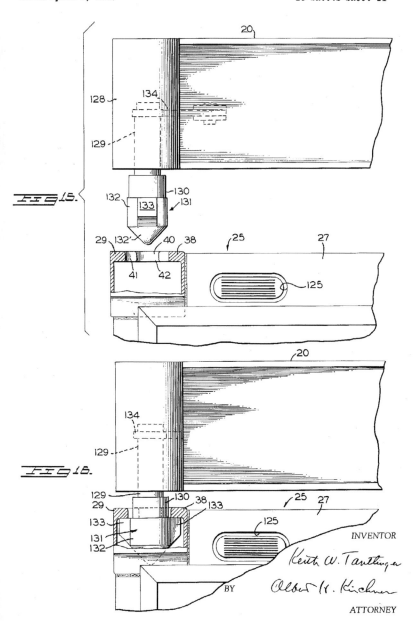

March 27, 1962   K. W. TANTLINGER   3,027,025

APPARATUS FOR HANDLING FREIGHT IN TRANSIT

Filed April 8, 1958   18 Sheets—Sheet 11

A sketch of the first twistlocks in the original Sea-Land patent. The twistlock is the pointed lug extending downward from the spreader (top). The twistlock is inserted into an opening on top of the container's corner post and rotated 90 degrees, locking the container to the spreader. The bottom part of the sketch shows the container secured to the spreader and ready for lifting.

71

house flag of the Waterman Steamship Corporation of Puerto Rico, a separate operating company McLean had established. San Juan longshoremen, organized by the independent United Dock Workers Union, refused to unload the ship, and the *Bienville* sat in the harbor for 26 days while the company and the governor of Puerto Rico attempted to resolve the impasse. At the end of March the ship left, with all cargo on board, and proceeded to New Orleans.

McLean then turned to the International Longshoremen's Association, which had been handling his ships in Atlantic and Gulf ports. McLean and the ILA agreed to a contract for Puerto Rico workers that matched the agreements covering union longshoremen in Atlantic Coast ports. In late July the *Fairland*, flying the Pan-Atlantic house flag, departed Newark with a load of containers bound for San Juan, and this time they were successfully landed and routine service was established. Pan-Atlantic soon became the dominant carrier in the trade between the U.S. mainland and Puerto Rico. The market's previous leader, Bull Line, a carrier that traced its history to the 1870s, steadily lost business to the new competitor and was sold before entering bankruptcy and ceasing business in 1963.

The ILA's Puerto Rico agreement, and the union's acceptance of Pan-Atlantic's container services, did not mean the union was enthusiastic in its embrace of containerization. Less than five months later, on November 18, 1958, an estimated 17,500 dockworkers filled New York's Madison Square Garden to hear union officials denounce efforts to use automation to reduce waterfront employment. The crowd cheered as speakers warned that the industry should have to share the benefits of labor-saving technology. That issue would dominate union-management negotiations in Atlantic and Gulf ports for the next two decades.

Pan-Atlantic was not the only shipping company trying to bring mechanization to the movement of cargo between the U.S. mainland and Puerto Rico. While McLean was putting together his idea for Pan-Atlantic, a Miami-based naval architect and engineer, Eric Rath, was assembling a small fleet of World War II surplus LST landing craft that he converted into trailer ships. Starting in 1954 he operated the vessels between Jacksonville, Florida, and Miami to San Juan, with feeder operations to the Virgin Islands and Santo Domingo. In the opinion of many, if he had limited his operation to Puerto Rico, he might have succeeded. But Rath had visions of operating to Europe, and went bankrupt. His company, Trailer Marine Transport, continued to operate in bankruptcy for 17 years until Crowley Maritime stepped in to buy the business. Crowley replaced TMT's outdated equipment with large, multideck barges and made the company profitable. Today the service continues as part of Crowley Liner Services.

*   *   *

On the West Coast, one of America's most venerable liner companies, Matson Navigation Company, also was weighing the advantages of containerization and would soon pioneer the technology in its region. Matson traces its origins to 1882, when Captain William Matson sailed the three-masted schooner *Emma Claudina* from San Francisco to the Hawaiian island of Hilo with 300 tons of food, plantation supplies and general merchandise. Matson built a fleet of sailing ships that operated between San Francisco and Hawaii. The company, incorporated in 1901, had a colorful history through its involvements in the lives of the islands' leading settler families, through its role in romanticizing cruising and tropical vacations, and as Hawaii's essential transportation link to the mainland. But Matson was a business as well as an island institution, and like all other ocean carriers, it had to come to terms with the changing world of liner service in the post-war era.

Trailer Marine Transport pioneered the movement of trailers by sea between Florida and Puerto Rico, using surplus World War II landing craft. TMT was a forerunner of the Crowley Liner Services, which operates large multideck trailer barges on the route. The photo of the TMT Biscayne is from the late 1960s or early 1970s.

Like Pan-Atlantic, Matson was an unsubsidized domestic carrier. In the mid-1950s, Randolph Sevier, president of Matson, was concerned about the company's low profit margins. Labor costs were rising, productivity was stagnant and this combination was making it difficult to attract capital to reverse these trends. "We were generating plenty of revenue, but cargo-handling costs were so high that the stockholders weren't getting much return on their investment," said Stanley Powell Jr., who later became the company's president.

In 1953 Powell was put in charge of Matson's research team,

at the time a one-person office. He said he soon came to realize that the main obstacle to shipping's profitability was lack of standardization. A half century earlier, Henry Ford had revolutionized automobile manufacturing by standardizing assembly processes. By contrast, ship lines handling breakbulk cargo had to deal with a wide variety of types and sizes of commodities. Each had to be fitted into the irregular holds of ships, a costly and time-consuming process. If loads could be standardized into a container of uniform size, then machinery could be developed and operations designed to make the process more efficient.

As it delved into the question of how to improve its profitability, Matson sought help from the Arthur D. Little consulting firm. The consultants recommended that the company hire research experts who had not worked in the shipping industry and therefore could view it without preconceptions. Matson followed the advice. In 1956 the company established the steamship industry's first integrated research department, directed by Foster L. Weldon, who had spent 15 years in weapons research with the Defense Department. Before coming to Matson, he had been at Johns Hopkins University, where he was on loan to the Navy to conduct research that led to the construction of the Polaris submarine. Weldon had mastered the analytic techniques of operational research during World War II. He later said he welcomed the opportunity to apply his skills to commercial problems. "I was tired of military research," Weldon said in an interview years later. "I was tired of doing things you hope will never be used."

Weldon's approach to containerization could not have been more different from that of Malcom McLean. One man was a formally trained and highly methodical researcher, the other was a self-made trucker who was keenly intelligent but hadn't had a lick of scientific training. McLean relied on personal instinct, hard-working associates and closely guarded information; Weldon led with a formal research methodology, proceeded in an open and fully documented manner, and published his findings for all the world to see. But the two men reached similar conclusions.

It was easy for Weldon to determine that Matson's greatest opportunity for cost reduction lay in cargo-handling operations in port. Costs of loading and discharging cargo accounted for almost half of total transportation costs in the Hawaii trade. The extra time that ships spent in port reduced the number of voyages they could make and the amount of revenue they could pro-

Foster L. Weldon applied scientific analysis to the development of Matson's container transportation system.

duce. Viewed another way, the delays required more ships to handle the same amount of cargo. "Clearly, cargo handling was the area where cost-reduction measures would exert their greatest leverage and it was this fact that focused our attention on containerization," Weldon said.

Having identified the problem, Weldon looked for a solution. He began by producing a research report for Matson executives. Weldon then published a paper on "Cargo Containerization in the West Coast-Hawaiian Trade" in the professional journal *Operations Research*.

The abstract of the article said the study addressed the basic question of "whether or not the company should develop and operate a cargo-container shipping service as an integral part of its West Coast-Hawaiian shipping operations."

Weldon compared Matson's costs in a year of operation with the costs that would have been incurred if container service had been in effect. His conclusions included: 1) that cranes should be dock-mounted rather than ship-mounted, 2) that out-ports should be served by barges that could carry vehicles in roll-on, roll-off operation, and 3) that the 24-foot van would work best in Matson's West Coast-Hawaii trade.

At the end of his article Weldon took some pleasure in noting that his recommendations had already been warmly received. He wrote that Matson had "a full-scale prototype van and chassis undergoing operational tests and the company has announced a multimillion-dollar program which will result in the first large-scale scheduled van-cargo service in Trans-Pacific operations."

Weldon's article was published in February 1958. The following month, Matson's board of directors met in San Francisco and authorized the company's management to spend $4 million for the first phase of an expansion into containerized shipping. That was a substantial sum in 1958, when a new Chevrolet could be purchased for about $2,000.

Matson's investment was to be divided into several parts. For example, a maximum of $900,000 was allocated for the purchase of 350 twenty-four-foot containers; $850,000 for 275 truck chassis to carry the containers; and $600,000 for outfitting of six conventional freighters to carry containers on deck. For terminal improvements, $300,000 was allocated for dock modifications; $200,000 for four straddle trucks; $50,000 for six yard tractors and $600,000 for three shoreside container cranes – one at Alameda, California; one at Los Angeles and one in Honolulu.

On August 31, 1958, the Matson freighter *Hawaiian Merchant*

Matson President Randolph Sevier saw containerization as a way to improve profitability.

Matson Navigation Company loaded 20 twenty-four-foot containers onto the deck of the Hawaiian Merchant on August 31, 1958, at Alameda, California, for a voyage to Honolulu.

sailed for Hawaii with 20 containers on deck that the company said were "filled with everything from beer to baby food." There was little fanfare. The old piers at San Francisco, Matson's home port, could not support the weight of loaded containers and cranes and lacked adequate space for trucks to maneuver, so Matson's first containers moved through the Todd shipyard at Alameda. Operations soon were transferred to the Encinal Terminal, also at Alameda. Charles Wright, master of the *Hawaiian Merchant* at the time, said the initial voyage was uneventful. He said the only problem was in the wheelhouse, where visibility was hindered by the sun glaring on the shiny, new aluminum containers on deck. Sunglasses took care of that problem, and oxidation from the salt air eventually dulled the containers' finish.

As more containers were moved on subsequent voyages, containers were stowed two-high on deck. This was a new experience and created concerns about the ship's stability. Richard F. Andino, a Matson employee who later rose to chief executive of Delta Steamship Lines, said operations personnel estimated the weight and density of cargo, noted the cargo's placement, and checked those calculations against the ship's draft. "After that, we'd perform some experiments: We would pick up predetermined heavy weights with ship's gear and I would stand on the bridge with a sextant and check the angle of the roll of the vessel. In this way, we would determine the ship's actual stability. Finally, we'd compare that with what we had calculated during the previous two or three days of loading."

*   *   *

Although Matson and Pan-Atlantic reached similar conclusions about the benefits of shipping cargo in standardized boxes, there were substantial differences in the way they implemented

The Hawaiian Merchant's containers were stowed atop hatches between the ship's regular cargo cranes.

the new technology. After launching its service with converted tankers, Pan-Atlantic's next ships carried their own cranes designed especially for containers. This provided a quick way to start new services to ports lacking shoreside cranes. Even after containerization had become well established, shipboard cranes remained a necessity to serve regions such as Africa and South America where dockside cranes might not be available. Matson took a different approach. It decided early to build shoreside gantry cranes, which could handle containers more rapidly, did not take up valuable space on ships and could be maintained and repaired without disrupting ships' schedules.

Leslie A. Harlander, who in early 1957 had been promoted to manager of Matson's engineering department, argued against reliance on shipboard cranes. He noted that stability was a problem for vessels that were not built to carry them, and that maintenance and repair would be easier if the crane was on the dock. Like most traditional freighters, Matson ships were built with shipboard cranes designed to handle breakbulk cargo. Those cranes could also handle containers, but the process was inefficient. Matson's containers initially were handled with revolving dock cranes.

These "whirley" cranes were used only as a temporary measure to help the company begin container operations. Matson decided early that efficient operations demanded a crane specially designed to handle containers. Matson solicited bids from 11 crane manufacturers before awarding the contract to Pacific Coast Engineering Company of Alameda, California, which submitted a low bid of $238,000 per crane. Paceco, as the company was known, proposed an "A-frame" gantry-crane design with a boom that extended horizontally over the ship and was retracted to a vertical position when not in use. Even after awarding the

Gerber baby food was among the cargoes in the Hawaiian Merchant's first containers. The boxes were loaded by a dockside revolving crane.

contract, Matson engineers were worried about excessive sway of the container when it was in the air. Harlander went to work on the problem. That Christmas, he worked out a solution with an anti-sway feature that he tested with his son's electric train and Erector Set. The anti-sway system was introduced as a design change in the Paceco contract. Paceco cranes soon were installed at other ports. For years, container gantry cranes were referred to generically as a Paceco, just as photocopiers are often called Xerox machines.

Another difference between Matson and Pan-Atlantic was in the way the carriers stored containers at marine terminals. With his trucking background, McLean insisted that every container be stored on a wheeled chassis while on land so that it could be retrieved without delay. Space limitations at terminals on the West Coast and in Hawaii led Matson to stack its containers and use overhead cranes, or straddle carriers, to lift and lower the stored boxes and shuttle them around the terminal.

Matson and McLean also chose different container sizes. On the East Coast, the former trucker McLean chose the 33-foot box to fit the dimensions of his used tankers but switched to 35 feet as soon as the tankers were replaced by converted C-2 freighters. Matson chose 24-foot boxes as its standard length. The decision was based on the company's knowledge of its market. Weldon's study identified the 24-foot length as the size that would make the best use of weight and space for the kinds of cargoes that Matson carried to and from Hawaii. Also, unlike states in the East, California and several other states west of the Rocky Mountains permitted trucks to haul two 24-foot trailers in tandem.

Because neither Weldon nor Matson's executives thought of a ship as a truck, as McLean did, they were untroubled by having their ships carry breakbulk freight and containers at the same time, at least at the outset. In 1958 Matson, acting on Weldon's advice, altered the *Hawaiian Merchant* and two other breakbulk freighters so that each could carry 70 containers on deck. By the

end of 1958, Matson had in operation 600 twenty-four-foot containers, along with a few prototype refrigerated vans, and 400 chassis that fit under containers.

Earlier that year, in a report to shareholders, Randolph Sevier had said, "Matson's research report on cargo containers is not the end of the line in streamlining marine operations. It would be the first step, but a first step only. It is the key which opens the door to many new and exciting innovations in shipping."

Weldon also had glimpsed the possibilities of containerization. The study that he and his team had presented to Matson officials in July 1957 emphasized that containerization would mean a fundamental change in the way Matson conducted business. Containerization, the study said, "is not just an attractive and highly productive special service to be superposed on top of present shipping operations – it is a far-reaching innovation that has a major impact on the economics and operations of the total West Coast-Hawaiian trade."

Matson used the first high-speed, dockside gantry crane on January 7, 1959, at Encinal Terminals in Alameda, California. The crane was built to Matson's specifications by Pacific Coast Engineering Company. It was purchased in 1987 by the Port of Nanjing, China.

Stanley Powell Jr. was a rising executive at Matson when the company began studying containerization.

That impact was not lost on the International Longshoremen's and Warehousemen's Union, which represented dockworkers at Matson's ports on the West Coast and in Hawaii. In 1957, aware of the research that Matson had begun, the ILWU began debating how to deal with the fast-approaching mechanization of its members' work. At the same time, J. Paul St. Sure, chairman of the Pacific Maritime Association, which represented West Coast waterfront employers, began working to mold the PMA into a more cohesive force that could deal with the changing labor environment.

In 1960 the ILWU and the PMA signed the landmark Mechanization and Modernization Agreement. Under the M&M Agreement, employers agreed to contribute to a Mechanization and Modernization Fund that was established primarily to subsidize early retirements and mandatory retirements for workers displaced by mechanization. In return, the union agreed to lift certain work rules that would have impeded the efficient introduction of containers, and to accept new labor-saving methods. The agreement also included a statement of understanding that was unprecedented on the strife-ridden waterfront: "It is the intent of this document that the contract and working and dispatching rules shall not be construed as to require the hiring of unnecessary men." The M&M Agreement was renewed in 1965, and permitted containerization to continue to move forward on the West Coast.

The agreement did not have unanimous support among management or the ILWU. When the M&M Agreement was negotiated, Matson was the only West Coast carrier with any significant degree of containerization. On the management side, the agreement was resented by some of the other ship lines and by smaller stevedoring companies that feared they would be forced out of business by containerization. ILWU President Harry Bridges, meanwhile, had to overcome bitter opposition by a sizable faction within the union. Local 13, representing ILWU members in the ports of Los Angeles and Long Beach, voted against the agreement. Bridges defended the agreement, saying that change was inevitable and that the union's job was to secure the best possible deal for its members. "We as a union could do one of two things," he said. "We could accept mechanization and reap some of its benefits, or we could say no to it and fight it. Historically, we could put up a successful fight – we could fight progress – but how long would that do us any good?"

*　　*　　*

The Hawaiian Citizen was the first all-container ship in the Pacific. It began service in 1960 between the U.S. West Coast and Hawaii.

Matson had led the West Coast into containerization and, with the M&M Agreement in place, continued to invest in ships and equipment. In 1960 the *Hawaiian Citizen*, Matson's and the Pacific's first full container ship, was completed. It could carry 400 of Matson's 24-foot containers. By May 1963, the company reported that 70 percent of Hawaii cargo that was amenable to containerization was moving in containers, and that shipping costs in that market had been reduced by 25 percent. In 1964, Matson rolled back its rates to their 1961 level and did not raise them again for 10 years.

The impact of containerization in Hawaii went beyond transportation. Refrigerated containers made possible the shipment from the mainland of fresh eggs, butter, meat, California produce and bananas transshipped from South America. Some of these products were produced in Hawaii but local suppliers could not meet the islands' market demand. Containerization made these and other products widely available. By reducing transit time and damage, containerization also benefited Hawaiian producers of pineapple. Fresh Hawaiian pineapple, once a luxury unobtainable in most of the United States, began

Matson introduced the use of straddle cranes for handling containers in port. These refrigerated containers are being loaded on a rail flatcar.

to appear in large volume in supermarkets throughout the country. More than a decade later, Shurai Hirozawa, vice president of First Hawaiian Bank in Honolulu, said containerized shipping had proven essential to the state's modernization. "Containers have changed Hawaii's lifestyle," he said.

By 1961, 40 percent of Matson's cargo between the West Coast and Hawaii was moving in containers, and the company said current or planned expansion projects would soon increase the percentage to 65 percent. The company was profitable, and was looking toward continued expansion.

While Foster Weldon was the theorist of Matson's containerization, the executive who made it happen was Stanley Powell Jr. A 1940 graduate of the University of California, Powell worked for Matson before spending three years in the Navy. He returned to Matson in 1945 and by the mid-1950s was climbing the executive ranks in the company's financial division, where he worked closely with Weldon and his research group. By 1959 Powell was heading Matson's freight division. Three years later, he became the company's president.

Powell was a man of vision and had ambitious plans for Matson, plans that were not universally welcomed or shared. Although many shippers embraced containerization, Matson's shift to containerization was not always popular with some mem-

M&M: Give And Take

To some International Longshoremen's and Warehousemen's Union members, it was a sell-out to management. To *Wall Street Journal* editorialists, it was a "strangely one-sided pact" favoring the union.

Viewed from the perspective of 45 years, the Mechanization and Modernization Agreement that the ILWU and the Pacific Maritime Association signed in October 1960 was the deal that paved the way for containerization on the West Coast.

The M&M Agreement's chief architects were ILWU President Harry Bridges and J. Paul St. Sure, president of management's Pacific Maritime Association. Bridges and St. Sure began discussing what evolved into the M&M Agreement while Matson Navigation Company was still preparing its first move into containerization. Everyone knew that the new technology would require fewer workers. No one knew how fast or far-reaching the change would be.

Bridges recognized that change was inevitable and that the union had best strike a deal while it had leverage. The PMA saw the need to use mechanization to reduce rising costs and realized that the only way to achieve the savings was to share them with the union.

M&M allowed management to introduce mechanization and to establish manning scales with no unnecessary workers. In return the PMA agreed to preserve the existing ILWU workforce but to share mechanization's savings with them.

The PMA agreed to subsidize early retirements and to guarantee minimum pay for those still on the job. In the end, increased volume fueled by the Vietnam war provided so much work that the guarantees were not needed.

Both sides benefited from M&M. ILWU members became some of the best-paid blue-collar workers in the nation. The PMA's members were able to reduce costs. During the first five and a half years of M&M they paid $29 million to the M&M fund and saved an estimated $200 million on cargo-handling costs.

Harry Bridges, left, and Robert J. Pfeiffer, in 1961. Pfeiffer, who later became CEO of Matson Navigation, headed Matson Terminals when the Mechanization and Modernization Agreement was negotiated.

bers of Matson's board of directors. The board approved the company's initial investments in containerization, "but there were doubters," Powell recalled.

"One member of the board hired a guy to study what we had done and he said it won't work," Powell said. "He said it would [waste the ship's cubic capacity] by filling it with boxes instead of paying cargo. And he said all those boxes will create traffic jams in Hawaii. And it's too expensive. And when one guy told me I was 10 years ahead of my time, I told him we had a board of directors that was a hundred years behind the time and wanted to stay there. ...The shippers really saw the advantages of the new system quicker than anybody else. By 1964 we didn't have enough containers for the whole trade and we were overwhelmed by cargo. Nobody wanted to ship any other way, and from then on, there were no questions from the board or any other resistance."

*   *   *

Back east, McLean in 1958 moved Pan-Atlantic's headquarters from Mobile to New Jersey, and two years later, Pan-Atlantic Steamship Corporation changed its name to Sea-Land Service Inc., to "better describe the service offered." In 1962 Sea-Land began shifting its New Jersey terminal operations from its original base at Port Newark to a leased site at a new terminal that the port authority had built at nearby Elizabeth. The port authority approved construction of the Port Elizabeth terminal four months before the initial sailing of the *Ideal X*. The $150 million project required the dredging of 13 million cubic yards of material from the marsh to transform a narrow, shallow, meandering creek into a navigable channel, and the deposit of an additional seven million cubic yards of dredged material to form usable storage area for containers.

McLean was not the only one to recognize the opportunities in the former New Jersey marshes. Michael E. Maher had worked on the New York waterfront as a longshoreman while earning a law degree at St. John's University. During World War II he served in the Army Transportation Corps, assigned first to New York's port of embarkation and later to Europe, where he helped restore the shattered port at Le Havre, France. He was discharged from the Army as a major. In 1947, he founded a small ocean stevedoring company, for which he exercised his veteran's rights to purchase military surplus forklifts and hoist

cranes. When containerization developed, Maher Terminals grew with it. The family-owned company eventually became the largest terminal operator in the Port of New York and New Jersey, handling about half of the port's container traffic. By the early 21st century, the company's a terminal at Port Elizabeth and Port Newark was the largest proprietary container terminal in the United States, covering 463 acres, with an additional 150 acres for chassis, empty containers and rail transfer.

With the development of Port Elizabeth, Sea-Land moved into a new administrative building nearby. Dockside cranes were constructed and an IBM 360 computer system was installed to track Sea-Land's ships, boxes and chassis. The new container port site originally occupied 92 acres but within two decades it had grown to more than 200 acres. The port authority would continue to invest in traditional cargo-handling piers in Manhattan and Brooklyn in the early 1960s, but the days of bustling activity on Manhattan's historic West Side piers were numbered. On the West Coast, there was a similar shift in activity from San Francisco, the coast's main port for a century, across the bay to nearby Oakland, where there was ample space for containers.

In September 1962, the first ship to tie up at Sea-Land's new

The Port of New York Authority began dredging channels and filling in marshes at Port Elizabeth, New Jersey, in 1958. The Newark airport is visible at upper left, above the New Jersey Turnpike. The Port Newark terminal, where Pan-Atlantic began container operations, is at right.

The Elizabethport and its sister ships were fashioned from German-built hull sections sandwiched between bows and sterns of U.S.-built tankers. This photo was taken in 1962 when the Elizabethport's mid-body section was being towed to Todd Shipyards in Hoboken, New Jersey.

Port Elizabeth terminal was, appropriately, the *Elizabethport*, the first of a new "jumbo" class of container ships. The *Elizabethport* and its three sister ships, *Los Angeles*, *San Francisco* and *San Juan*, were converted T-3 tankers. The hulls were cut in half, the bows and sterns were saved, and the propulsion machinery in the stern was thoroughly refurbished. New mid-bodies built in a German shipyard were then towed across the ocean and welded into place between the bows and sterns. McLean continued to use the original registration number of these hulls so that they would still be considered U.S.-built and thus eligible to carry coastwise and intercoastal cargo. U.S. shipyards grumbled. They were upset at not having been given the job of constructing the new mid-bodies, and Congress quickly amended the governing legislation to prevent this kind of sleight-of-hand in the future.

The converted ships were also equipped with onboard gantry cranes so they could load and discharge their containers without shoreside assistance. The resulting ships were nearly 630 feet

The Elizabethport's first call at the new Port Elizabeth terminal in September 1962.

long and each could carry 476 thirty-five-foot containers. The *Elizabethport*'s first voyage from its namesake port was for Oakland on a voyage that initiated regular container service between the East and West coasts.

Container ships with shipboard cranes continued to be useful, especially when initiating new services to ports that lacked their own cranes, but as the number of ports with shoreside cranes increased, more ships without shipboard cranes were put in service. Gradually, container service began to cluster around major ports that were equipped with dockside cranes and had ample open space.

Carriers recognized that there were more ships than ports, and that it made sense to install cranes on the dock instead of on each ship, where they took up valuable space that could be used to carry cargo. Smaller ports continued to be served by vessels that had onboard cranes and carried fewer boxes. But while containerization was beginning to move beyond a simple model of truckload delivery, the transition was slow. Many ships being converted to carry containers still reflected choices made when they were first constructed or converted to container service. The *Elizabethport*-class ships, however, were among the last Sea-Land vessels to be equipped with cranes. As a general rule, after 1963 Sea-Land did not put cranes on ships.

McLean's company continued to expand on domestic trade lanes. In 1964, Sea-Land launched a service to Alaska from Seattle. The company had leased a terminal in Anchorage and was preparing to start service there within a few weeks when Anchorage was devastated by the powerful Good Friday earthquake. Ron Katims, in charge of Sea-Land's landside facilities, spent much of the following day listening to the radio for scraps of news about the quake's destruction. On Sunday, after attending Easter Mass, he drove to Sea-Land's new office in Elizabeth, which the staff was scheduled to occupy for the first time the next day. McLean saw Katims there and directed him to fly to Alaska immediately to provide a first-hand report on the damage.

The next morning, Katims was on a plane for Anchorage. Fires were still burning when he landed, but the port area remained usable. He quickly hired an airplane and flew to Whittier and Seward to check out those ports. "They were all destroyed...There wasn't a single port facility standing but the one that we had under contract." Katims managed to put through a telephone call to Sea-Land headquarters. "How fast can we get a ship over here?" he asked. The launch of the new service was accelerated, and a ship loaded with relief cargo – as well as chassis and other gear needed to begin operation – was dispatched from the East Coast. Sea-Land quickly established itself in the Alaska trade.

By December, the service to Anchorage had been operating successfully for eight months, but most people expected it to shut down for the winter. During winter months, the city had been considered inaccessible by ship and was served by other carriers by rail from Seward, a year-round port. McLean, however, was determined to serve Alaska's largest city directly throughout the year. Charles R. Cushing, Sea-Land's chief naval architect, said McLean's philosophy was, "You take the cargo to the marketplace, as close to the marketplace as you can. And Anchorage was the population center up there." Before starting the Alaska service, McLean directed Cushing to find a way to serve the market year-round. "Malcom sent me up there to see what I could learn about the trade up there," Cushing said. "And I talked to everybody up there, and they all said, 'You can't do it.' But nobody could ever prove why you couldn't do it. So my report to Malcom was, we can do it, and Malcom decided to do it, and everybody told him he was crazy."

The Coast Guard warned Sea-Land against trying to transit Cook Inlet in winter and said that if the company had a problem, it was on its own. But Cushing said the *Anchorage*, which Sea-Land had converted to containers after acquiring it from bankrupt Bull Line, could handle the winter weather. The *Anchorage* made it in and out of port safely, and initiated the

The Seattle was one of two ships that Sea-Land used to provide year-round service to Anchorage.

first winter service by sea to the vessel's namesake city. Competitor Alaska Steamship, carrying containers on outdated Liberty ships, soon went out of business, just as Bull Line had after Sea-Land entered the Puerto Rico trade.

* * *

During the decade in which McLean was establishing his new company, his main competitors continued to be the railroads, not other trucking companies or other coastwise carriers. This situation created some difficulties, for the railroads and coastwise carriers were both regulated by the Interstate Commerce Commission. The ICC was not in principle opposed to containerization and coastwise cargo operations – it had approved Pan-Atlantic's application to carry trailers in the coastal service between Newark and Houston. The railroads soon cut their overland rates in an attempt to keep their customers from switching to Pan-Atlantic. But when the ICC generally supported the railroads against challenges that these rates did not cover their costs,

McLean Industries Inc. stock first traded over the counter in 1955 and was listed on the New York Stock Exchange on December 2, 1960. Malcom McLean's guest that day was his first-grade teacher, Marguerite Townsend. McLean bought her 100 shares at $47. From left, James McLean, Miss Townsend, Malcom and Clara McLean.

McLean was neither surprised nor dismayed by this favoritism. He was confident that in containerization he had a winner, and that he had found a profitable niche.

As a domestic carrier, Pan-Atlantic was not eligible for federal operating subsidies that the 1936 Merchant Marine Act made available to U.S.-flag liner operators plying international routes. However, that situation was not entirely negative. Subsidized operators had to deal with government red tape and tight restrictions on the services they offered on particular trade routes. Many international carriers remained under the U.S. flag primarily to carry military cargoes and other government-impelled shipments, such as relief supplies. McLean could have targeted that cargo, but chose to wait until he was on firm footing in the domestic market.

In the early 1960s, when McLean was concentrating on domestic operations, the Department of Defense was once again addressing the always-thorny problem of military sealift. The various components of the U.S. maritime industry – the shipbuilders, the operating companies, and the labor unions – were again pressing for increased federal funding for the U.S. merchant marine. The U.S. had enormous worldwide military commitments that included major military installations in East Asia and Europe. In 1962 Defense Secretary Robert S. McNamara acknowledged that the need for military sealift was growing, but he resisted asking for additional money for merchant shipping subsidies. McNamara told the members of the House Merchant Marine and Fisheries Committee, "I do not wish to leave the impression that we have no requirement for merchant shipping. Obviously we do. But rather I do not wish to overstate the military requirement, thereby providing an umbrella under which a huge ship construction program for the merchant marine can be justified."

McLean probably welcomed this clear indication that the construction and operating subsidy programs authorized by the

1936 Merchant Marine Act would not be significantly expanded. This meant that unsubsidized U.S.-flag carriers such as Sea-Land would have a better chance to win contracts to carry freight to support overseas military installations and operations. This large and growing market, reserved for U.S.-flag ships, was waiting for McLean's kind of technical innovation. In 1966, after focusing on domestic trade lanes for 10 years, McLean was ready to bid for military cargo that would take his ships overseas.

McLean, like Graham Brush, the developer of Seatrain, clearly had his eye on particular niches in the overall market for shipping. However, the niches he served, unlike Seatrain's, were potentially huge. Seatrain operated only with railcars. Containers, however, could be used by rail or on highways. As the interstate highway system took shape after its authorization by the National Defense Highways Act of 1956, this market grew quickly. In coastwise and intercoastal trade lanes McLean was competing for freight with both railroads and interstate truckers, and he was able to beat

McLean and Ludwig: Kindred Spirits

If Malcom McLean is the father of the container ship, Daniel K. Ludwig can be called the father of the supertanker. McLean and Ludwig, two of the most successful shipping entrepreneurs of the post-World War II years, had a lively business and personal relationship that began with competition for federal ship-mortgage guarantees.

After the war, Ludwig concentrated his entrepreneurial talents on bulk shipping but he also owned a liner company, American-Hawaiian Steamship Company. For several years, American-Hawaiian competed with Pan-Atlantic and later Sea-Land for a limited pool of federal financing of ships to operate in the U.S. intercoastal trade.

Neither McLean nor Ludwig secured the financing – Sea-Land eventually used converted break-bulk freighters to start container service between the Atlantic and Pacific Coasts; Ludwig invested in other areas. But these fierce competitors formed an enduring cooperative relationship. Knowing McLean was running short of capital as he expanded Sea-Land in the 1960s, and recognizing an investment opportunity when he saw one, Ludwig negotiated the purchase of a million shares of McLean Industries stock at a discount of nearly 40 percent.

Eventually Ludwig acquired more shares and owned 11 percent of McLean Industries. When R.J. Reynolds acquired the company in 1969, Ludwig, who had paid $13 million for his shares, received Reynolds stock worth approximately $60 million.

Despite their competitiveness, McLean and Ludwig had a grudging respect for each other, a kind of combative affection. They remained friends, and for many years these two captains of industry maintained New York City residences within a block of each other – McLean in his suite in the Pierre Hotel, Ludwig in a penthouse a block away. McLean also served on the board of directors of the Ludwig Foundation in New York, surely a sign of respect and trust on Ludwig's part.

Grace Line had high hopes for the "seatainer" service to Venezuela that it launched in 1960. New Jersey Governor Robert B. Meyner spoke at the Santa Eliana's inaugural sailing from Port Newark.

them both on cost. But to do this on a continuing basis, he had to successfully manage two challenging tasks. One was to convince shippers that he could and would deliver superior service at lower costs; the other was to make sure his company had the equipment and facilities it needed to meet the growing demand for the kind of shipping services it provided.

This second task posed particularly worrisome problems, for McLean had a great aversion to putting his own money at risk when acquiring capital assets. He once told a confidant that since launching his trucking company in the 1930s, he had operated on borrowed capital. As an unsubsidized operator, where could he get the ships he needed? After the war, he had solved his problem of trucks by hiring hundreds of veterans as owner-operators, each of whom used his rights under the GI Bill to obtain government funds that were used to buy trucks for use in the McLean fleet. Was there a government program that would do something comparable for McLean's new container service when he needed more ships? McLean could launch his container business by converting into container ships some of the war-built ships he acquired when he purchased Waterman, but eventually he would need other ships as well. McLean found them in the government's large fleet of surplus ships, many of which could be converted into container ships at a manageable cost.

McLean was able to parlay this into a profitable niche. He operated in a market that was restricted to unsubsidized U.S. operators of U.S.-flag ships, and he had access to the government's huge supply of war-built cargo ships. When in 1966 McLean took containerization abroad, he had to face new competition from foreign carriers and from the subsidized U.S.-flag liner companies engaged in international trade. But by then his early years in the domestic market had given his container initiative a big head start. With Bull Line out of the picture, Sea-Land's Puerto Rico service had become highly profitable. With this base, access to ships and the prospect of military and commercial cargoes, he was convinced he could expand his operations to worldwide service by carrying on as he had before.

The first ship line to try to extend containerization to international markets, however, was not Pan-Atlantic or Sea-Land. That distinction went to Grace Line, a venerable American steamship

company, based in New York, that provided liner service to South America. After World War II the company diversified and concentrated its shipping activities on trade with Venezuela. In an attempt to stay ahead of the wave of post-war changes, Grace jumped into containerization with what it called its "seatainer" service, a system built around the use of 17-foot-long aluminum containers. Grace Line was a subsidized company under the 1936 Merchant Marine Act and was thus able to obtain federal construction funds to pay for part of the cost of converting to containerization. It obtained two surplus C-2s, lengthened them by adding 45-foot-long midsections, equipped them with shipboard cranes modeled after those installed on Sea-Land's ships, and named them *Santa Eliana* and *Santa Leonor*. Each ship could carry 476 seventeen-foot-long containers. The 17-foot length was chosen because two of them could fit on a flatbed trailer and comply with Eastern states' highway restrictions.

In January 1960, the *Santa Eliana*, the first fully containerized ship to enter foreign trade, sailed for La Guaira, Venezuela, the first of three scheduled ports of call in

Grace Line spent $6 million converting two ships and acquiring 17-foot aluminum containers for its ill-fated container service.

South America. It had on board a partial load of 176 seatainers filled with U.S. export products; the ship expected to carry a full load of coffee on its way home. However, when the *Santa Eliana* arrived in La Guaira, the Venezuelan Federation of Port Workers announced that its members would not unload the vessel. Negotiations ensued but went nowhere, as the ship sat at anchor.

Eleven months later a temporary agreement was reached, the containers were landed and the ship returned to New York, where it remained out of service until a permanent agreement had been reached. Two years later the company and the Venezuelan long-shoremen's union announced they had reached an agreement, which did not hold up. In the interim Grace Line had asked United States Lines, the leading U.S.-flag carrier on the East Coast routes, if it would be interested in a joint trans-Atlantic container service. U.S. Lines officials were still not convinced that containerization had more than a limited future. They declined the offer.

By this time Grace officials had had enough. They had nothing to show for their investment, were thoroughly disgusted, and offered to sell the two container ships to McLean, who was pleased to get them and immediately put them to use. Because the government had granted Grace Line a construction subsidy to cover part of the cost of converting its two C-2s for international liner service, McLean was obliged to pay back a pro-rated portion of these funds when he purchased these ships for domestic service between the U.S. mainland and Puerto Rico. The ships were renamed the *Ponce* and the *Mayaguez*. The latter vessel would attract international attention in 1975, while in Sea-Land's fleet, when it was seized by Khmer Rouge off the Cambodian coast and the ship and crew had to be recaptured by the U.S. Marines.

The difficulties Grace Line encountered demonstrated there was nothing automatic about success in containerization. Those who thought the new technology was too risky or too expensive to succeed were able to cite this example as evidence for such a view. Others, however, still believed containerization had only scratched the surface, and that it had a future internationally as well as domestically.

Helen Delich, the *Baltimore Sun*'s maritime editor, was among those who recognized the possiblities. Reporting in 1957 on the first voyage of McLean's *Gateway City*, she wrote that, "The shipping men invited to observe this only major change in domestic shipping in more than half a century expressed the undisputed opinion that it is the answer to many problems of expensive cargo handling and will be copied on both domestic and foreign operations."

PART TWO

Bridging The Oceans

CHAPTER FOUR

The Big Bang

"In August 1966 we received a container of Scotch in Louisville, Kentucky. After many years of importing this product via conventional methods, then sorting the cases on arrival into empty cases and broken bottles, cases that needed re-coopering and finally into saleable merchandise...it was hard to realize we had received a complete shipment – all in saleable condition."

— Wayne S. Franklin, Brown-Forman Distillers Corporation

Many tradition-bound shipping executives saw the Grace Line debacle in Venezuela as vindication of their beliefs. They remained convinced that while container shipping might benefit shippers and serve a useful purpose in coastal carriers' competition with the U.S. railroad system, it would never work internationally. Others recognized that containerization was no passing fad. By the mid-1960s, with containerized shipping firmly established on routes between the U.S. mainland and Hawaii, Alaska and Puerto Rico, several international carriers began planning to establish similar services to Europe and Asia.

Viewed from the perspective of four decades, such a move appears to have been inevitable. At the time, however, the extension of containerized shipping to international markets generated skepticism. Carriers such as Sea-Land and Matson had nearly a decade of experience in domestic markets, but operators on those routes were shielded by U.S. law from non-American-flag operators. By contrast, the Atlantic and Pacific were highly competitive international markets, home to entrenched carriers from Europe and Japan as well as the United States. These carriers, organized into tight rate-setting cartels, or conferences, were not eager to yield their market positions to new competitors using more efficient technology. There were additional obstacles. Labor unions feared the loss of jobs and often had considerable power, as Grace Line had learned in Venezuela. Port, road and rail systems posed operational challenges, especially in countries that lacked the open spaces of the United States. Important technical issues had yet to be solved. What container size should be used? Which ports were configured to

Opposite: Malcom P. McLean, 1962

handle containers? What about cranes? The biggest question – did containers benefit the shipper? – had already been answered favorably and emphatically in the United States. There were other arguments for extending containerization to international markets. The booming global economy was increasing demand for international sourcing of goods. American-flag carriers had a built-in market in military shipments to supply the still-substantial deployment of U.S. troops in Germany, Korea and Japan. There also was an increasing flow of military-related shipments to an obscure Southeast Asian nation, South Vietnam, that was rapidly gaining prominence on newspaper front pages and evening news broadcasts.

When the carriers took the plunge into international container service, it resembled horse racing's blanket finish – one in which the leaders hit the wire so close together that their heads could be covered by a blanket. Although several carriers had begun carrying containers along with breakbulk cargo, at the start of 1966 not a single ship line carried containers internationally on a vessel devoted exclusively to containers. Within two years, nearly a dozen carriers were regularly moving containers across the Atlantic or Pacific. For the participants, this moment in history was exciting and unpredictable. They were trying to integrate a new technology into a business with a long and complex history and an entrenched, sometimes burdensome set of rules and practices.

The Isaac Wright, a 1,300-ton packet ship of the Black Ball Line, which provided the first trans-Atlantic liner service in 1817.

Liner service, meaning ships scheduled to depart and arrive at scheduled intervals, was then well over a century old, having begun with the Black Ball Line's sailing ships between New York and Liverpool in 1817. It now was on the brink of being transformed by a new way of handling cargo, and there was no script that could tell anyone what would happen next.

*   *   *

Isthmian Line used plywood containers on its breakbulk ships in the early 1960s. This photo was taken in New Orleans.

Two other American carriers were the first to launch trans-Atlantic container services in 1966 using ships devoted entirely to containers. Sea-Land and United States Lines would engage in a 20-year rivalry for dominance of U.S.-flag container shipping in international trade.

U.S. Lines was one of the nation's most storied liner companies. It was created by the U.S. Shipping Board in 1921 as a government-owned company to operate German liners that the United States acquired as war reparations, the most famous being the *Leviathan*. In the 1930s U.S. Lines became part of the International Mercantile Marine, a steamship company that was founded by J.P. Morgan and which had owned White Star Lines and the *Titanic*. By the 1960s, U.S. Lines operated about 50 ships – conventional freighters, plus its two remaining passenger liners, the *America* and the *United States*.

In 1965, reports began circulating that Sea-Land was preparing to launch a trans-Atlantic service. U.S. Lines executives, meanwhile, were locked in an internal debate over adoption of containerization. The carrier's commercial leadership, including John Griffith, the general freight traffic manager, and his boss, Don Wierda, the vice president of freight, insisted that general cargo's future lay in containerization. U.S. Lines operating executives, those responsible for running the ships and loading the

Containers were carried on many breakbulk ships, such as this States Marine Lines vessel, in the early 1960s.

cargo, favored a more limited approach. They wanted to adopt a handling procedure in limited use in Norway, in which forklifts would carry palletized cargo into the ship through large openings in the ship's sides. "Both sides of the argument said, 'We can't continue to do what we were doing,'" Griffith recalled. "There was no argument about that. The question was, what technology should we adopt."

Intimating which idea he preferred, William Rand, president of U.S. Lines, rejected suggestions to hire an outside consultant. Instead, he assigned Griffith to pull together an internal group to study the issue. Griffith pursued the assignment with zeal. He took his team to visit the domestic operations of Seatrain, Sea-Land and Matson, and even to air-cargo terminals at John F. Kennedy International Airport. Today, air and sea cargo operate two mostly discrete markets, with air cargo reserved for urgent, high-value shipments. In the mid-1960s, things were different. With the introduction of the trans-Atlantic jet in 1958, air cargo was making inroads into sea freight.

Griffith made that point in a detailed report that argued U.S. Lines should switch its trans-Atlantic services to containers. He cited Trans-World Airlines advertisements comparing the costs and time of shipping machines and parts by air and sea between Chicago and Zurich. According to the TWA ad, a 435-pound shipment that took 20 days and cost $267.75 to move by sea could be delivered by air in 15 hours for $208.12. Griffith's report noted that between 1962 and 1964, U.S. exports by air increased in weight by 53 percent, while exports by ship increased only 5 percent. The report observed:

> International air cargo business was in its infancy just after World War II and consisted mainly of small amounts of light packaged goods carried in passenger aircraft. The volume of traffic increased rapidly, and in a few years, one all-cargo airline and most of the trunk airlines were flying freighters between the United States and Europe. At the outset, typical air cargoes were rush orders, sample shipments, extremely valuable goods and similar special cases, where the element of time was a factor of sufficient import to offset high air freight rates.... The situation had changed to the point where not only is the total volume of air cargo of considerable significance, but the character of air cargo is such that air transportation is in competition with ocean transportation for a wide range of the 'better' commodities.

Those commodities, he said, included electrical equipment, automobile parts, typewriters, apparel, metal goods and pharmaceuticals. Although air cargo rates remained higher than sea freight, Griffith noted that the gap was narrowing and that door-to-door costs, including packaging and insurance, sometimes made airfreight cheaper.

Griffith's 142-page report noted that several competitors were moving to containerization in the North Atlantic. Sea-Land was already operating 14 container ships on domestic routes and had 17 others planned or under conversion into container ships. The company had also sent staffers to Europe to lay the groundwork for its expected entry into the North Atlantic trade. American Export-Isbrandtsen Lines had purchased two 24,000-deadweight-ton ore carriers for conversion into container ships. Griffith cited reports of plans "to organize a consortium of European national-flag lines for the purpose of operating a trans-Atlantic conference service." Finally, he noted the "the moderate successes scored during 1964 and

Moore-McCormack Lines was an early convert to containerization on the North Atlantic. The Journal of Commerce, October 13, 1965.

Eight New Ships Planned

Mooremack Unveils Container Plan

By GEORGE PANITZ

One of the most ambitious international trade containership projects embodying firm plans for the keel-up construction of the largest and fastest new ocean vessels of this type by an American shipping company has been disclosed by the head of Moore-McCormack Lines.

According to company president William T. Moore, the proposal to build eight highly automated containerized cargo freighters has been under study by the Maritime Administration for some two months and contracts for the building of the first four ships hopefully will be signed next June.

Mooremack Plans

The Moore-McCormack plans call for ships 602 feet long, with a deadweight capacity of 13,000 tons and space for more than 1,200,000 cubic feet of cargo, and with a designed speed of 25 knots.

With facilities and equipment to handle hundreds of 10, 20, or 40-foot cargo vans by roll-on-roll-off or lift-on-lift-off methods, the vessels will also be able to accommodate conventional break-bulk, liquid and refrigerated cargo on the company's subsidized ocean trade routes to Europe and South America.

A revised version of Moore-McCormack's record-breaking C-4 Constellation Class freighters, the new group of vessels carry an estimated cost of $16,-500,000 each on designs developed by the company and J. J. Henry Inc.

Included are plans for a hydraulically operated stern ramp for the movement of military or commercial vehicles and the use of high pressure steam turbines for propulsion with refinements that will give the vessels fuel consumption efficiency close to that of diesel engines, Mr. Moore said.

Moore-McCormack, one of the nation's largest general cargo ship companies, operates the automated Constellation Class freighters currently holding trans-Atlantic speed records for cargo vessels.

The new group of containerships reportedly will have the most powerful engines now contemplated for general cargo vessels and will be able to maintain the speed now possible in the Constellation Class ships.

With equipment emphasizing speedy cargo handling and reduced port time, the ships will also feature bow thrusters to speed docking and undocking, passive tank stabilization to decrease rolling and safeguard the vessel and the cargo and hull designs to improve seakeeping characteristics.

Still in Early Stage

Containership operations, which hold the promise of the greatest advance in overseas cargo movement, are currently limited to domestic trades where they have had great success. Containerized cargo movements in international trade are still in an early stage of development and aside from specialized automobile carriers there are no ships currently in foreign commerce comparable to those in the domestic trade or in the proposed plans of Moore-McCormack and several other American and foreign ship lines.

The proposed ships of Moore-McCormack are part of a fleet replacement program which the company is building in conjunction with the Maritime Administration.

Under its operating subsidy contract with the government shipping agency, the company is required to replace all of its ships with vessels built in United States yards.

Since 1958, Moore-McCormack has put 14 new freighters and two passenger ships—the Argentina and the Brasil—into trade route services.

UNITED STATES LINES
1 Broadway, New York 10004
Telephone: DIgby 4-5800

**NEW CHALLENGER II
CONTAINERLINERS
SUPER EXPRESS
SERVICE**
**ANTWERP, ROTTERDAM,
AMSTERDAM**

Pier 62, N.R.

AMERICAN RACER (R)
(21 knots)
PHILADELPHIA _____Mar. 14
NEW YORK _____Mar. 18
AMERICAN ROVER (R)
(21 knots)
BALTIMORE _____Mar. 18
PHILADELPHIA _____Mar. 19
BOSTON _____Mar. 21
NEW YORK _____Mar. 25
AMERICAN RELIANCE (R)
(21 knots)
BALTIMORE _____Mar. 27
PHILADELPHIA _____Mar. 28
NEW YORK _____Apr. 1
AMERICAN RANGER (R)
(21 knots)
BALTIMORE _____Apr. 2
BOSTON _____Apr. 4
NEW YORK _____Apr. 8
AMERICAN RACER (R)
(21 knots)
BOSTON _____Apr. 8
PHILADELPHIA _____Apr. 10
NEW YORK _____Apr. 15
AMERICAN ROVER (R)
(21 knots)
BOSTON _____Apr. 15
BALTIMORE _____Apr. 17
NEW YORK _____Apr. 22

**HAMPTON RDS/BENELUX
DIRECT SERVICE**

AMERICAN REPORTER
(Omits Antwerp)
HAMPTON ROADS _____Mar. 14
AMERICAN LEADER
(Omits Antwerp)
HAMPTON ROADS _____Apr. 18

Atlanta ____Strachan Shpg. Co. ____JA 3-3313
Avon, Conn., James E. Johnson-OLdfield 8-6394
Baltimore ____10 Light St.____Saratoga 7-5260
Boston ____40 Broad St. ____Hancock 6-4406
Charleston ____Carolina Shpg. Co. ____RA 3-6485
Chicago ____ 140 So. Dearborn ____ 346-3381
Clevl'd____9th St. & Euclid Ave. Superior 1-0255
Detroit ___ 1240 Washington Blvd. ___ 961-5057
Jacksonville ___ Strachan Shpg. Co.___EL 6-0711
Los Angeles 523 W. 6th St. Madison 6-6767
Morehead City Shipping Co. _ — 726-6151
N. Orleans ____ Tipton Shpg. Co. ___ 524-3662
New York____US Lines 1 B'way____DI 4-5800
Norfolk_200 East Main St.__Madison 2-5303
Philadelphia ____Mall Bldg. ____Market 7-8000
Pittsburgh H. W. Oliver Bldg. Atlantic 1-0333
Rochester ____ 14 Franklin St. ____ 546-7676
S. Francisco __311-California St. _ 362-8680
Savannah—Strachan Shpg. Co.—Adams 4-6671
Toronto ____Royal Bank Bldg. ____366-2801
Wash., D.C., 1000 Conn. Ave. N.W. _223-4361
Wilmington, NC Wilmington Shpg.__RD 3-7333

American Pioneer Line
Far East See Card #241

*Ship-card advertisement for U.S. Lines'
first container service, The Journal of
Commerce, March 11, 1966.*

1965" by Waterman Steamship Corporation and States Marine Lines in carrying commercial cargo containers on the decks of their North Atlantic vessels. Moore-McCormack Lines also was carrying containers as deck cargo. In February 1966, Moore-McCormack would load 130 twenty-foot containers on the deck of one of its conventional ships departing New York for Europe in what the company announced would be a regular service. Moore-McCormack later ordered hybrid ships that had a roll-on, roll-off ramp in addition to separate holds for breakbulk cargo and containers. Such combination vessels appeared to offer the advantages of flexibility, permitting ships to handle the new containers as well as the loose cargoes that still predominated. In practice, the combination ships proved inefficient. Juggling containerized and breakbulk cargo at the same pier caused problems and delays. A ship could load or discharge its containers within hours, only to be stuck in port for days while breakbulk cargo was handled piece by piece.

The Griffith report convinced Rand of the merits of containerization. Quickly and with considerable secrecy, U.S. Lines put the *American Racer* and three other recently built breakbulk vessels into shipyards to be equipped with below-deck container cells. The ships had been designed with large hatches to permit simple conversion for carrying containers below deck.

The converted ships could carry 206 twenty-foot containers or the equivalent — 102 units in the two main hatches, and the balance on deck. On March 18, 1966, the *American Racer* departed New York for Europe with a load of containerized cargo. U.S. Lines was the first carrier to enter the North Europe market with containers carried in ships with cells designed for them. U.S. Lines also was the first carrier to adopt the 40-foot-long container, which along with the 20-footer soon became the international standard. Though the *Racer* and its sister ships also could carry uncontainerized cargo, they were used almost exclusively as all-container ships.

*   *   *

Sea-Land was close behind. Its *Fairland* departed the company's terminal at Elizabeth, New Jersey, on April 23, 1966, bound for Rotterdam, Bremen, and Grangemouth, a small port in eastern Scotland. The *Fairland* was one of the cargo ships that had been converted into a container ship that could carry 226 thirty-five-foot-long boxes. The ships also were equipped with shipboard

cranes. *The Fairland* was the first of four identical ships that Sea-Land was committing to this service. If this first voyage went well, Sea-Land planned to add Baltimore as a regular monthly stop on this route. Containerized freight for England would be sent to and from Felixstowe, a port served by small vessels that connected to Rotterdam.

By 1966 Sea-Land was riding high. Conceived as a container shipping company, it did not face the internal barriers other companies encountered in deciding between breakbulk and containers. For a decade it had been converting World War II-built ships for container service and operating them in the U.S. domestic trades. After a $4.2 million loss in 1958 caused by heavy investments in ships, cranes and related equipment, the company had been consistently profitable. In 1965, Sea-Land's parent company, McLean Industries, had net income of $12.5 million on $101.8 million in revenue. The company had been planning for some time to extend its services to North European ports, since the North Atlantic was the world's busiest and richest trade lane, but it did not want to make the leap until everything was in place. The key to success in containerization, as Malcom McLean well knew, was moving containers through the port and to the customer as quickly as possible. The fastest and most reliable way

Moore-McCormack Lines invested in North Atlantic ships that carried breakbulk, containers roll-on, roll-off cargo in various combinations. The Journal of Commerce said the hybrid ships reflected Mooremack's decision "not to try to guess the trend of events but to be ready for whatever happens."

American Export-Isbrandtsen Lines, a U.S.-flag carrier, began operating container ships in the late 1960s before falling victim to North Atlantic rate wars. These ships' wheelhouses were placed near the bow to protect containers on deck from high seas.

to do this in Europe was by truck – barge and rail would come later. Sea-Land agents had signed contracts with more than 325 road haulers before its first ship sailed to Rotterdam.

The American carriers were not alone. Many coastal European nations had long traditions of seafaring and they had no intention of sitting still as containerization rolled over them. Knowing that Sea-Land would soon be coming to Rotterdam, Holland-America Line in 1965 established a joint venture with three Swedish companies, an arrangement that was formalized in 1966 with the creation of Atlantic Container Line. Wallenius, which operated car carriers and was a leading partner in ACL, had already ordered two ships that carried a combination of containers that were lifted on and off ship and vehicles that were rolled on and off the ship on a ramp that was part of the ship's stern. Wallenius contributed one of these combination container/roll-on, roll-off ships to the consortium. Each of the other partners, Transatlantic, Holland-America and the Swedish American Line, also contributed a ship. Soon afterward, two other companies also joined ACL. One was the leading French operator on the North Atlantic, Compagnie Generale Transatlantique (CGT). The other was the famous British liner company Cunard.

ACL developed the first successful long-range vessel that combined container and roll-on, roll-off transport. Some of the consortium's members had been successful with ro-ro ships on the North Sea, and foresaw growth in trans-Atlantic shipments of automobiles and wheeled machinery that could be loaded and unloaded quickly. The combination ships proved successful and eventually were replaced with larger versions that remain in operation on the North Atlantic.

The move by large European carriers to cooperate in containerized shipping had begun even earlier. In September 1965, when Sea-Land, U.S. Lines and other American companies were preparing to bring containerization to Europe, four of the five largest British carriers joined in forming Overseas Containers Limited to establish containerized service between Britain and Australia. OCL's members were Peninsular and Oriental Steam

The American Reliance was one of the Racer-class ships that U.S. Lines used to start its trans-Atlantic container service in 1966.

Navigation Company (P&O), Furness Withy and Company, Ocean Steamship Company (also known as Blue Funnel) and British and Commonwealth Shipping Company. A rival consortium in the Europe-Australia market, Associated Container Transport, soon was formed with Ellerman, Blue Star, Ben Line, Harrison and Port Line as members.

Organizing competing carriers into consortia was a tricky exercise. Participants in these groups had worked together in rate-setting groups, but jointly managing the operations and costs of ships went considerably further. Many of the European carriers, however, realized that cooperation was needed to address the problems of steep investment requirements and rising costs. "A solution is likely to be achieved only by very close co-operation within a group small enough to act effectively but strong enough to command the necessary contacts and resources," said Sir Donald Anderson of P&O.

The development of alliances among European lines underscored the capital-intensive nature of container shipping. Before containerization, cargo-handling costs represented about half the cost of a typical trans-Atlantic breakbulk voyage. These costs were variable; if no cargo was being moved, no dockworkers were hired and no expense was incurred. Containerization substituted expensive capital equipment, a fixed cost, for the variable cost of manual labor. In container shipping, fixed costs of capital equipment represent approximately 90 percent of total

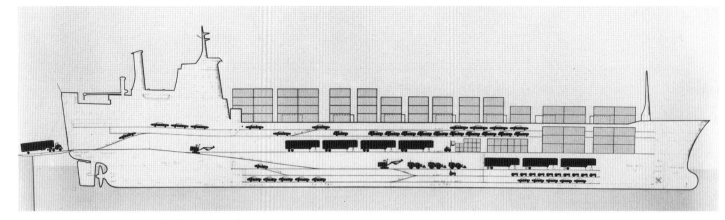

Atlantic Container Line has operated in the North Atlantic since the late 1960s with combination container and roll-on, roll-off ships. This cutaway drawing depicts the first generation of those ships, including the Atlantic Saga, at right.

voyage costs. The European carriers recognized that the demands imposed by container service, such as the need for adequate and up-to-date ships and for shoreside support for cargo collection and management, justified a pooling of resources. Because there was little room in the world of containerization for small independents, "consortia became one of the most dynamic forces in the rapid diffusion of container shipping in the late 1960s and early 1970s," noted Frank Broeze in his 2002 history of containerization.

Otto Porton, North American general manager of ACL, described the carriers' dilemma in a seminar conducted by the Federal Maritime Commission in 1967:

> Many of the lines...found themselves in the position the airlines faced when the first jets came on the market. Many of the airlines had just heavily invested in the improved DC-7 models and were suddenly confronted with the necessity to switch over from propeller-driven planes to jets. Likewise, shipowners with newly built conventional vessels found themselves in a situation where these new vessels were no longer suitable to deal with the demands for container space.

The organization of carrier consortia also highlighted an important difference between European and American shipping. European shipping companies – and later, Japanese companies – were free to form consortia and alliances. In trade lanes that did not include the United States, they also were permitted to form and participate in rate-setting liner conferences that were closed to outsiders. In the United States, such cartel-like groups of ocean carriers were permitted under a 1916 exemption to antitrust laws, but the law required them to be open to all applicants. Furthermore, with a few exceptions such as Sea-Land,

most American liner companies engaged in foreign trade after
World War II received construction and operating subsidies
provided under the 1936 Merchant Marine Act. Subsidized companies were prohibited from entering into associations with
other liner companies at home or abroad without Maritime
Administration approval. The constraints imposed by this prohibition, at a time when capital requirements for participating in
international shipping were rapidly rising, hobbled American carriers and obliged them to plead repeatedly for additional federal
support and operating flexibility. It also put them at a severe dis-
advantage when competing with the powerful consortia and
alliances that were rapidly being formed by European and
Japanese carriers.

   The American-flag carriers pushed forward on their own.
Conferences dominated by non-U.S.-flag lines could not prevent
American-flag carriers from calling at ports that traded with U.S.
ports, although they could make life difficult for the upstarts. As

Associated Container Transport was among the consortia formed by carriers to operate on the long routes linking Australia with Europe and the United States.

a longtime member of the North Atlantic conference, U.S. Lines had to convince European conference members to adjust conference tariffs to provide for pricing of containerized shipments. U.S. Lines insisted that shippers using containers be offered a discount of roughly 10 percent from breakbulk rates. Griffith said U.S. Lines told the other members of the North American Continental Freight Conference that it was prepared to leave the conference and operate as an independent if the other lines wouldn't go along. The European lines agreed, but asked that U.S. Lines use its influence to persuade Sea-Land to operate within the conference when it introduced container service to the Atlantic.

*　　*　　*

Late in 1964, Sea-Land had put together a "startup" team to go to Rotterdam and make the arrangements needed to launch container service to Europe. Scott Morrison, a young Sea-Land executive from southern Virginia with a background in trucking, was told to work on pricing and tariffs and to get Sea-Land into the rate-setting conferences that controlled most of the cargo. Morrison had been forewarned that some of the other carriers might give their Sea-Land visitors a frosty reception. He later said McLean and others had cautioned him to negotiate a deal and "not start any fights."

The warnings proved accurate. One evening Sea-Land representatives hosted a hotel reception in Rotterdam for local forwarders who specialized in beer and wine shipments. Morrison said a senior executive with Holland-America Line angrily confronted him, "red in the face and violent," and emphatically told him that containerization was not welcome. On other occasions the Sea-Landers were received more cordially. Morrison and a colleague later went to Germany to make arrangements with agents. In Hamburg they were greeted warmly and were assisted in many ways by a former U-boat captain. Their reception in Bremen was more difficult. By the time they got there a Sea-Land ship had already called at the port. Local rules required that dockworkers operate the shipboard cranes when moving boxes in port. Before the ship arrived, the German longshoremen had been trained in the operation of the shipboard cranes. However, on the Fairland's first call at Bremen, a crane operator released a box before it had been lowered all the way onto a truck chassis. The container crashed onto the truck cab, narrowly missing the driver. Once it was demonstrated that the machinery had not malfunctioned, the Germans put the incident behind them and cargo-handling resumed, but it was a sobering accident.

Morrison and his compatriots also checked out ports in southern England. In the shipping industry, London's port was considered a disaster area because of its strained labor relations, so Sea-Land decided to use Felixstowe, a private port. Sea-Land began service to Felixstowe with small vessels that shuttled boxes to and from Rotterdam. When Sea-Land applied to join the U.K. rate-setting conference, the line was rejected for the stated reason that the American carriers had brought only a feeder vessel, not a trans-Atlantic ship, to England.

The status quo was not yielding easily. Crossing the Atlantic on a Pan American flight, Morrison overheard a half-dozen "conference guys" from U.S. Lines and Cunard talking loudly about how they were "going to bury Sea-Land." Morrison quickly got in touch with a London barrister who assured him that Great Britain had antitrust laws that would apply to efforts to exclude Sea-Land from the conference. After Sea-Land had been denied membership at a subsequent meeting of the U.K. conference, a legal notice was filed. When Morrison went to the emergency meeting called soon thereafter, he recalled that "you would have thought that I walked into a freezer box." He was shunned, and after the cocktail hour, "The chairman came over to me and he says, 'Mr. Morrison,' in his heavy British way, 'would you not like to withdraw the complaint?'" When Morrison said no, the chairman "made some slanderous comment about us crude Americans, you know, we didn't play by the rules." But the tension soon dissolved, and the chairman ended up inviting Morrison to dinner. The Sea-Land representative said he assured the conference official, "We promise to abide by the rules. We don't have to cut your rates. We're not going to do anything ugly to you."

Shipcard advertisement from The Journal of Commerce listing Sea-Land's first trans-Atlantic sailings in 1966.

Change On The Waterfront

Watching containers lifted aboard one of his first ships, Malcom McLean is said to have asked a fellow observer what he thought of the newly refitted vessel. "I think they ought to sink the sonofabitch," replied Freddie Field, a high-ranking official of the International Longshoremen's Association.

Though that story may have been embellished in countless retellings, it accurately describes the reaction to containerization by the union representing Atlantic and Gulf dockworkers. When the World Trade Center was being built, Field's Manhattan ILA local filed a lawsuit seeking to have the adjacent waterfront land used for cargo handling instead of the construction of Battery Park City.

Containerization eliminated thousands of ILA jobs, but it provided higher pay for those who remained. Ship lines, which provided most of the capital investment needed for containerization, gradually took the lead role in ILA contract negotiations. Having invested heavily on ships, containers and equipment, the carriers were willing to grant higher wages and benefits to avoid work stoppages.

Thomas W. "Teddy" Gleason was president of the ILA from 1963 to 1987 and its real power for several years earlier. He resisted efforts to reduce labor requirements but negotiated a series of contracts requiring shippers and ILA employers to pay container royalties to support cash bonuses and fringe benefits to ILA members. Gleason also secured a "guaranteed annual income" for dockworkers whose jobs were eliminated by mechanization and a "50-mile rule" requiring union labor for all packing and unpacking of containers within 50 miles of a port. The 50-mile rule was struck down by the Supreme Court in 1987 and the guaranteed annual income eventually was phased out, but the ILA's container royalties survive.

Fifty years after the *Ideal X* carried its first containers, the ILA has made peace with containerization. After waterfront strikes that made the ILA the target of eight Taft-Hartley Act back-to-work injunctions between 1948 and 1971, the union has not had a coastwide strike since 1977.

Containerization has made union dockworkers among the highest-paid blue-collar workers in the United States. On the West Coast, where most general cargo is containerized, average regular and overtime pay for full-time longshoremen exceeds $100,000. With overtime and container-royalty bonuses, many ILA dockworkers also enjoy six-figure annual paychecks.

The redoubtable Thomas W. "Teddy" Gleason was the ILA's leader during containerization's early years.

Sea-Land had the last laugh; its lower operating costs permitted the company to quote conference rates, which were about 10 percent lower for containers, and still earn higher margins than its breakbulk competitors on every item. Conference rates were pegged for breakbulk costs, and all the container carriers had to do was persuade the conference to allow pricing for containers. Sea-Land also received an allocation of trans-Atlantic military cargo, which at the time was almost automatic for U.S.-flag carriers. "All we had to do was meet the rates," Morrison said. Other Sea-Land officials made the same point. "The last thing we want to do is start a rate war. We want to preserve a profit picture," said John C. Kerans, Sea-Land's European sales manager.

Grangemouth, Scotland, was Sea-Land's third port of call. The company's first ship to call there picked up a small load of Scotch whisky. Here, again, Sea-Land's preparation paid off. Importers who controlled the routing of wines and spirits shipments were centered in New York, "and they were all friends of ours from domestic service," Morrison said.

Containerization enjoyed immediate popularity with wines and spirits shippers, who had fought a losing battle with loss and pilferage of their cargoes on the docks. Before containerization, the standing joke on Manhattan's Hudson River piers was that longshoremen's wages were "twenty dollars a day and all the Scotch you could carry home." Containerization changed that. "We brought this stuff in absolutely pilfer-free, and of course, that reduced their cost by maybe 40, 50 percent," Morrison said. "Their insurance cost went to nothing." Winning over the shippers of wines and spirits was a breakthrough that encouraged others to accept containerized shipping.

In the 21st century, 40 years after containerization was introduced on international routes, it is easy to overlook the anxiety and dread that this new technology aroused among many members of shipping's tight-knit fraternity of executives. Many U.S.-flag shipping lines, restricted by subsidy rules and having sunk millions of dollars into conventional freighters and docks, resisted the switch to containerization. The same was true of the executives in charge of many of Europe's venerable steamship companies. These men were leading citizens in the continent's

Sea-Land promoted its North Atlantic service with full-page ads in the spring of 1966.

111

Rotterdam's Frans Swarttouw sought Sea-Land's container business.

ancient port cities, men of the world experienced in trade and politics. The ancestry of their maritime enterprises could be traced back through the modern era of European conquest and colonialism, back even further to the Northern European trading networks formed by the ports of the medieval Hansa, and in some cases even back to the ancient Mediterranean grain trade. In the third quarter of the 20th century, European liner companies still held pride of place in global commerce, but with the arrival of containerization, it suddenly appeared that this world would be turned upside down by a new cargo-handling technology developed by an American trucker. Of course, Europeans in the second half of the 20th century had seen more than their share of tragedy and hardship – the devastation of World War II was still fresh in their minds. Yet they had good reason to resist and regret the kind of revolutionary change in well-established routines that containerization was about to loose on an industry they considered their own. These boxes and the odd-looking ships that carried them were an unwelcome challenge, and their introduction was bound to provoke a hostile response.

But containerization also presented new opportunities, and some shippers were quick to recognize them. New markets emerged. Instead of merely reallocating the shares of cargo carried by various ship lines, containerization expanded the size of the cargo pie. In the 1950s, imported beer was rarely seen in American bars, restaurants or retail shelves. The cost of shipping had to include a hefty allowance for breakage and pilferage. The Dutch makers of Heineken beer were an early convert to containers, which they used to develop a market in the United States.

There were countless other examples. Soon after entering the trans-Atlantic market, Sea-Land introduced tank containers for transporting liquids and refrigerated containers for moving perishables. Florida oranges and grapefruits began appearing in fresh-produce markets in Europe. Texas beef producers found a new customer base in the continent's butcher shops and restaurants. Sea-Land moved container after container of offal from U.S. meat-packing plants to France, where it was used in the making of sausage. In the United States, most of that product had gone into the manufacture of dog food. Now the meatpackers had a new market where they could sell their byproducts at a higher price. "We really opened up the markets for a lot of things that never had moved," Morrison said.

One of Morrison's early assignments in Europe was to find marine terminal operators to work with Sea-Land, so he and an

Hapag-Lloyd Container Line was formed as a partnership of North German Lloyd and Hamburg America Line. Hapag-Lloyd's first container ships were the Elbe Express and the Weser Express, shown here at Bremerhaven. Two sister ships, the Moselle Express and the Alster Express, provided weekly North Atlantic service.

associate went out to find one in Rotterdam. They ended up with Frans Swarttouw, a member of a prominent Rotterdam family that owned the stevedoring firm Quick Dispatch. Swarttouw had been following the development of containerization carefully. He was so enthusiastic that in the early 1960s he wrote to McLean saying that he hoped that Sea-Land would consider working with his family's firm when establishing a base in Rotterdam, Europe's foremost port for maritime freight.

McLean remembered. When Sea-Land entered the European market, the carrier joined Swarttouw in forming European Container Terminals, a consortium that included Quick Dispatch, the Dutch National Railway, and a stevedoring firm.

When European Container Terminals' new facility was ready, McLean and Swarttouw hosted a reception for the Rotterdam shipping fraternity. To their surprise, the guests booed their hosts. McLean shrugged it off, but Swarttouw was reduced to tears. ECT, however, turned out to be an enormous success. It grew into one of Europe's largest terminals and was a pioneer of automation, eventually introducing a handling system in which containers are moved around the terminal by driverless trucks. Swarttouw went on to become chairman of Fokker Aircraft.

During its first year of operation, European Container Terminals handled 380 container or roll-on, roll-off ships. European Container Terminals and other continental terminals quickly developed as transfer points not only for trans-Atlantic shipments but for containers moving on shorter routes to and from European and

North Atlantic Activity Hits Dizzying Pace

By GEORGE PANITZ

Outlines of the revolutionary changes in ocean shipping expected to result from the growing use of cargo containers are already in clear focus in the North Atlantic trade between the United States and Europe—the world's most heavily used and lucrative sea route.

Sparked by booming economies, a nearly $18 billion U. S.-Europe trade exchange, and wide adaptability of many seaborne shipments to unitized handling, the transport concept known as containerization is in full motion on the route and moving ahead at a dizzying pace.

New ships, new facilities, new methods of handling at pierside and in the interior, new arrangements with dockers, and new approaches to cargo insurance, pilferage, documentation, freight consolidation and even rates are only some of the manifestations of the shipping revolution underway in the North Atlantic.

Merged Services

A merging of shipping services, a consolidation and sharing of terminal facilities, interchanges of containers and movement towards computerized pier operations, reductions in port calls and planning for speedier transatlantic movement are also accelerating at an incredible rate.

So great, in reality, is the impact of container movement on ship operators that every line now serving the North Atlantic route or those hoping to remain in the highly competitive service has been compelled to make long range studies of how extensive its involvement in this transport concept should be.

It is obvious, too, that many knowledgeable steamship officials are highly disturbed by the rush into containerization on this route, particularly s i n c e many of the lines admittedly have little real knowledge about inland transportation and other problems related to the new shipping system.

As the head of one line noted, the North Atlantic is afflicted with a "disease known as containeritis" that could prove to be a fatal economic ailment to many lines. Similarly, a spokesman for another North Atlantic ship line voiced fear that the route will be badly over-tonnaged shortly by containerships and cargo containers and the result may be a classic ship industry problem—a rate war.

As the ship line official put the problem—"A lot of dogs will be chasing the same bone." However, he conceded that his own company is offering container movement to its customers and that the service will have to be increased if the line is to stay on the transatlantic route.

Significantly, even some of the larger ship lines that have been leading the way in the container revolution are showing signs of misgivings about over-investment in facilities and equipment. The head of one

(Continued on Page 26A)

Containerization required heavy investment in ships, ports and equipment. The Journal of Commerce, May 1, 1967.

United Kingdom ports. The Netherlands Central Bureau of Statistics reported that during the first half of 1968, Dutch ports discharged almost 50,000 containers from oceangoing ships, and loaded more than 44,000 boxes. Of the arriving containers, only about 15,000 were from the United States, and just over 8,000 of the outbound containers were U.S.-bound. Many of the shipments moving to and from European points were in smaller containers less than 20 feet long, with loads averaging only six tons each.

U.S. Lines launched its container service to Europe with weekly calls at New York, Antwerp and Rotterdam on a 28-day round trip. In early 1966, the carrier reconfigured its Pier 62 terminal in Manhattan's Chelsea district into a semblance of a container terminal by demolishing a shed and creating parking space for trailers under the elevated West Side Highway. Four years earlier, the Port of New York/New Jersey had spent more than $20 million renovating old Hudson River breakbulk piers for U.S. Lines. That would be one of the last significant investments in port facilities in Manhattan, and coming just as the container revolution was picking up speed, it proved to be a poor investment. Within the next decade, most of the port's cargo activity would shift to New Jersey, where more land was available to load, discharge and store containers. U.S. Lines moved its New York operations to Port Elizabeth, which the Griffith report had identified as the most efficient place to handle containers in the area.

* * *

Many of the early containerized shipments to Europe by the U.S.-flag carriers were military-related, particularly on eastbound routes. The Defense Department embraced the use of containers to ship large volumes of pilferage-prone military household goods and PX supplies as well as for equipment for the U.S. military's bases in Europe. Since many U.S. troops were still stationed in Germany, Bremen and its sister container port, Bremerhaven, were major ports for military shipments.

Military supplies also helped jump-start containerized shipping in the Pacific market, where the U.S. was steadily increasing its presence in Southeast Asia as fighting heated up between a communist insurgency in the north that was threatening to bring down the post-colonial western-supported government in the south. The war in Vietnam would prove to be a transforming experience for U.S. military logistics and for container shipping in the Pacific.

Vietnam was a particularly difficult war zone to supply. Besides being 8,000 miles from the United States, South Vietnam offered no secure area where supplies could be delivered, stored and dispensed. When the United States first began its steadily growing involvement in the Vietnam conflict, Defense Secretary Robert S. McNamara offered assurances that logistical support could be provided by aircraft. Such wishful thinking was soon dispelled by harsh reality – there was no way that air freighters could supply a conflict that at its peak required the deployment of more than a half-million American soldiers. But providing sealift to Vietnam would not be easy. The docks on the narrow harbor in the midst of Saigon were as porous as the waterfronts in other badly policed ports elsewhere around the world. Military supply corps personnel joked mordantly about supplying both sides of the war.

By 1965, nearly a million tons of supplies were arriving from the U.S. every month. Fifty World War II freighters had been activated from the National Defense Reserve Fleet, and an additional 120 would be activated before the war ended. Given the situation ashore, supply corps personnel considered these ships floating warehouses rather than ocean trucks, and they kept them at anchor offshore rather than unloading them so they could return for additional supplies. Meanwhile, the U.S. involvement continued to expand, adding to the supply bottleneck at South Vietnam's ports.

About this time, Malcom McLean visited Lieutenant General Frank S. Besson, chief of the U.S. Army Materiel Command. Besson, the first four-star general produced by the Army Transportation Corps, was the most prominent U.S. military transportation officer from the end of World War II through the Vietnam conflict. He was an imaginative military logistician. During his career he had shown willingness to experiment with aerial tramways and other unconventional transportation technology, including containers, which had caught his interest as early as 1957. McLean had known Besson for years and told him that Sea-Land might be of help in Vietnam. The general was receptive to McLean's offer. The result was a contract that helped the Army gain control of its logistics problems in Vietnam,

Lieutenant General Frank S. Besson led the Army into containerization.

Destination: Saigon

By 1966, Ron Katims had worked at Sea-Land for six years and was accustomed to moving quickly. The experience came in handy when Sea-Land secured contracts to move military cargo to Vietnam.

On January 1 of that year, Katims had flown from New York to Bremen to take care of business in Germany. After his plane landed at 2 a.m., he had barely gotten to bed when the telephone rang.

"It was McLean," Katims recalled, "and he says, 'Ronnie, meet me in Beirut tomorrow morning at 10.' I told him that was impossible, so we finally agreed that I would meet him in Paris in two days. 'Be prepared to get on a plane,' he said. So I finished my work in Germany and flew to Paris. McLean met me and said to get on the plane. 'Where are we going?' I asked. 'We're going to Saigon,' he told me.

"We flew east for 33 hours – seven stops. We arrived in Saigon at 10 in the morning and it's 104 degrees in the shade. I'm dressed in a European wool suit and an overcoat and tie, and we're off to our first appointment."

McLean had arranged with the Defense Department to look at shipping facilities. He, Katims and engineer Robert Newton "Booze" Campbell spent a week touring ports, talking to military transportation officers and looking at facilities in Saigon, Da Nang, Cam Ranh Bay and elsewhere.

Before it sent ships to Vietnam, Sea-Land established itself there by organizing a trucking

Sea-Land's Ron Katims in Vietnam, 1966.

company, Equipment Inc. When military logisticians in the field urged Pentagon officials to embrace containerization, Sea-Land was ready. "We had already figured out how we were going to do it," Katims said. "We had the cranes, and we made a fixed-price bid. That shocked them, because everybody else over there was on a cost-plus basis."

Katims and his team built cranes for prefabricated DeLong piers that the military had installed. With seven ships dedicated to Vietnam service, Sea-Land carried 10 percent of the supplies destined for Vietnam during the war. The remaining 90 percent required more than 250 other ships. The Vietnam service proved lucrative for Sea-Land and laid the groundwork for the carrier's start of commercial trans-Pacific service.

Opposite: A Sea-Land gantry crane being installed on a DeLong pier in Cam Ranh Bay in 1966.

while providing Sea-Land with a lucrative stream of revenue and the opportunity to explore commercial opportunities in Asia.

Historians of military logistics sometimes note that the U.S. Army started developing containerization well before McLean came on the scene. In one sense it did, for the military's Conex box was widely used to transport items such as tools and spare parts that were subject to loss or damage in transit. These boxes could be moved from origin to destination without being opened, but as many supply corps officers noted, they almost always disappeared after being delivered. Thus while Conex boxes served

Container Express

Anyone who served in the U.S. military is likely to be familiar with the Conex container. The Conex was a reusable steel container that carried unitized shipments of small items. It was a predecessor of the larger boxes used in modern containerization.

The Conex was developed by the Army Transportation Corps and built by various manufacturers. Research on Conex, an abbreviation for Container Express, began at the end of World War II. Conex boxes were first used extensively during the final months of the Korean War.

Conexes came in two sizes. The most widely used size was approximately seven feet high and just over six feet wide and deep and had a capacity of 295 cubic feet. It could be lifted manually if no cranes or fork lifts were available.

Military planners designed the boxes to be stacked three high and handled by conventional lifting gear on land or ship. They also were designed to fit in tween-deck spaces of breakbulk ships, and on 2.5-ton military trucks and stowed crossways on railcars. Its commercial counterpart

was the similarly sized Dravo Transportainer.

Although the military used Conex boxes extensively, they did not form the basis of a system of containerized transport. Many of the boxes made one-way trips to battle areas where they were used as command posts, living quarters, tool sheds and even pillboxes. More than 200,000 were built. Although the military began using standard commercial containers in the 1970s, many Conex boxes are still in use.

the Army well, they did not form the basis for a well-coordinated system for moving goods.

Bringing containerization to Vietnam presented special problems, starting at the ports. There were only a couple of deepwater ports, and piers would have to be built to handle containers. Fortunately, another member of Besson's early container team, Colonel L.B. "Slim" DeLong, had addressed the pier problem in the 1950s, when he developed a new kind of pier that could be quickly assembled in remote locations. The DeLong pier was a movable barge large enough to serve as a berth for an oceangoing ship. It operated on the same principle as a jack-up oil rig. It was equipped with legs that extended through holes around the perimeter of the barge's deck. Once the barge was

The Bienville at a DeLong pier in Vietnam in the late 1960s. The ship, one of McLean's original C-2s, also helped launch Sea-Land's North Atlantic container service.

moved into position, the legs were placed in the holes and were driven into solid footing below the water, and the barge was adjusted to a proper height for use as a wharf. The DeLong pier proved to be a workable idea in the difficult circumstances encountered in Vietnam. Until its effectiveness had been demonstrated, however, some Pentagon officers were skeptical. Lieutenant General Jack Fuson, a military historian, said Besson, DeLong and McLean worked out the arrangement, but that Fuson "later learned that this sophisticated installation had not been easy to sell and the deal nearly collapsed several times, surviving only because of Besson's persistence."

*   *   *

McLean secured two important contracts with the Army. In 1966 he signed a two-year contract for over $12.5 million for Sea-Land to carry Army freight from the West Coast to Okinawa. The Okinawa service, which began July 11, 1966, was expanded the following April to include the Philippines. In 1967, Sea-Land signed a second two-year contract, for $70 million, to carry freight to Vietnam. Six container ships would provide scheduled service, departing Seattle or San Francisco and arriving every 15 days at Cam Ranh Bay and Da Nang in Vietnam. A seventh container ship would operate in shuttle service between these two ports and the ports of Saigon and Qhi Nhon. In 1966 military cargo provided only 10 percent of Sea-Land's revenue. In 1968 it was up to 31 percent. This steady business was especially valuable in the 1960s, when the International Longshoremen's Association and U.S. seafarers' unions engaged in frequent strikes that idled commercial ships for as long as several months at a time. The longshoremen didn't hold up ships delivering military cargo, so McLean avoided much of the costly downtime that plagued other American-flag ships during these years. Sea-Land struck a deal for Japan's Mitsui O.S.K. Lines to serve as the U.S. company's agent, and soon added feeder services from Japan to Korea and Hong Kong. The company worked out accommodations with the trans-Pacific rate-setting conferences, just as it had done in Europe.

By mid-1968, the Defense Department estimated that the Military Sea Transportation Service had saved more than $200 million on transportation costs to Vietnam by using containerization. Other U.S.-flag carriers, including American President Lines, Pacific Far East Line and States Marine, were carrying containers to Vietnam on conventional ships, but Sea-Land was the only carrier that was sending all-container ships to Vietnam.

As containerized cargo to Vietnam increased, container sizes emerged as a point of bitter controversy among U.S.-flag carriers. Containerization pioneers Sea-Land and Matson had developed unique standards (35-foot lengths for Sea-Land, 24 feet for Matson). Subsidized U.S.-flag carriers, most of which still had little or no presence in containerization, lobbied for regulations to prohibit the Defense Department from shipping cargo in containers that did not meet the standard lengths of 10, 20, 30 or 40 feet that had been recently established by the International Organization for Standardization.*

At a congressional hearing, Malcom McLean testified that the Maritime Administration and the ISO's U.S. standards committee "either knowingly or unknowingly [had] been led into acceptance of standards that, in fact, are nothing but a disguise for a conspiracy to destroy competition." McLean quoted Transportation Secretary Alan Boyd as saying that the issue of container size had not been settled and said that while Boyd "endorsed standards in principle, he in fact felt the marketplace would be the determining factor in size."

*The industry's standard measure of comparison of container sizes eventually became the TEU, or twenty-foot-equivalent unit, a term coined in 1972 by London-based maritime journalist Richard F. Gibney. One 20-foot container is one TEU; a 40-foot box is two TEUs or one FEU (40-foot-equivalent unit).

How Large Is The Box? It Depends.

What's the ideal container size? There's no consensus answer. Since containerization's early days, the shipping industry has struggled to balance standardization with customer needs.

Malcom McLean's first containers carried on converted T-2 tankers were 33 feet long. When those ships were replaced by freighters with underdeck stowage of containers in 1957 and 1958, he switched to 35-foot lengths, the maximum allowed by Eastern states' highway laws. On the West Coast, where double trailers were permitted on California highways, Matson Navigation Company opted for 24-foot lengths. Alaska Steamship Company also used 24-foot boxes.

Other lines tried different sizes. Grace Line used 17-foot lengths on its ill-fated container service to Venezuela. Seatrain tried 27-foot boxes in a 1960s trans-Pacific service. Neither of those sizes gained wide acceptance.

The Federal Maritime Board endorsed the principle of standard-sized containers as early as 1958 and directed its Office of Ship Construction to begin studying the issue. Three years later the American Standards Association established standard lengths of 10, 20, 30 and 40 feet and standard heights and widths of eight feet. The International Organization for Standardization tentatively adopted the ASA standards in late 1965.

Ten-foot boxes were impractical, and few 30-foot boxes were built, leaving 20 and 40 feet as the most popular lengths. The standard height soon became eight feet, six inches. "High-cube" boxes, mostly nine feet, six inches high, later were introduced despite regulatory resistance in Japan, whose national-flag carriers had invested heavily in standard boxes.

Sea-Land eventually switched to standard sizes, although 35-foot boxes were used in the early 1980s. Matson still uses 24-foot boxes, which are not interchanged with those of other carriers, in its Hawaii service.

As highway restrictions were eased, carriers eventually added larger boxes to gain economies of scale. American President Lines introduced the 45-foot container in 1984 and the 48-footer in 1986. These boxes, however, were built with posts centered at 20 and 40 feet so they could be stacked with regular-sized containers. Even larger boxes followed. In 1991 Malcom McLean's final shipping venture, Trailer Bridge, introduced high-cube 53-foot containers on its new service between the U.S. mainland and Puerto Rico.

Early container handling at Hong Kong required improvisation. U.S. Lines used wharf cranes to transfer containers between the ship and barges or feeder vessels on the other side.

After the hearings, Congress approved legislation backed by Sea-Land and Matson that prohibited government agencies from discriminating against carriers whose containers deviated from ISO standards. Commenting on the dispute, Helen Delich Bentley wrote that the campaign to prohibit government shipments in non-ISO standards appeared to be motivated by competition, not by a desire for efficiency: "It was the general feeling of both Sea-Land and Matson, as expressed at the Congressional hearings, that a deliberate attempt was being made by the subsidized lines, instigated by foreign interests who did not want to compete against the pioneers and by sharp operators, to hurt the two lines by demanding the ten-foot modular."

*　　*　　*

The race to extend container services to the Pacific produced a close finish involving several lines, just as it had on the North Atlantic. Sea-Land and U.S. Lines were in the vanguard along with Matson, which made an aggressive but short-lived expansion into the trans-Pacific market. Japanese carriers also were in the first wave.

U.S. Lines' American Astronaut made its first call at Japan's Port of Kobe on October 11, 1968.

At U.S. Lines, John J. McMullen, who had taken over as president in 1968, asked John Griffith to go to Asia and oversee the launch of the company's Pacific container service. The shift toward containers by U.S. Lines had continued to gain momentum after the company's introduction of its Atlantic container service. Early in the construction of 11 Lancer-class breakbulk ships at Sun Shipbuilding, McMullen ordered the design changed to fully cellular container ships.

U.S. Lines launched its Pacific container service in 1968, with port calls at Honolulu, Hong Kong, Kobe and Yokohama. In Asia, U.S. Lines encountered a mixed bag at the ports that would be served by the container service. "The big issue was terminals. That was the major problem," Griffith recalled. Government restrictions and space limitations required adjustments. Containerization could be introduced relatively easily at certain ports, Griffith found, but not others. Also, because a limited number of container ships would be available for the service, direct calls at certain ports would have to be dropped to maintain a weekly service.

U.S. Lines used mini-liner ships as feeder vessels to secondary ports in the company's fledgling trans-Pacific service.

Compared to other Japanese ports, containerization at Kobe was launched relatively easily. There, three container terminals had been built – two for Japanese lines, which were the first to begin container service between Asia and Europe, and one for non-Japanese carriers. Sea-Land had been pursuing the concession for the non-Japanese terminal, and Griffith said he arrived in Japan two weeks before the deadline to submit bids. U.S. Lines got its bid in, and to everyone's surprise the terminal was awarded jointly to U.S. Lines and Sea-Land. The two companies worked amicably, agreeing to separate parking areas, repair shops and terminal gates and offices.

Yokohama was a different story. It had a single large common-user terminal and authorities would not allow a separately operated terminal as they did in Kobe. U.S. Lines ended up renting about 10 acres of the common-user terminal. To establish its borders, the carrier bought a cache of 50-gallon oil drums, painted them red, white and blue and lined them up around the perimeter and linked them together with a white chain. U.S. Lines built movable gates and offices, forming a "de facto" private terminal.

In Hong Kong, Griffith recalled, "There was absolutely nothing there. Some operators had makeshift arrangements, but there was no way to get a container terminal." To establish its operations, U.S. Lines loaded and discharged containers along a traditional wharf. Because no space was available there for container storage, the company shuttled boxes by barge to a parking lot on the other side of the harbor. British-built cranes, with booms long enough to extend over the ship, were used to transfer cargo between ship and barge, or between the ship and feeder vessel. Customers could pick up cargo for local delivery at the parking lot. Cargo for Asian ports not served directly would be transferred to or from feeder vessels or temporarily stored alongside the shed.

In introducing container service, U.S. Lines faced a quandary. What to do about its customers in ports not being served directly by the container ships? Customers in Taiwan, the Philippines or Korea would not appreciate the uncertainty and potential problems of having to use a second carrier to move their cargo to and from the main port. Griffith, who was given considerable autonomy to launch the Pacific service, devised a solution. Instead of relying on third-party carriers, U.S. Lines would, from the beginning, establish its own feeder network in Asia.

The opportunity came from an unlikely source. George Livanos of Ceres Shipping was building a fleet of 50 small ships in Japan, known as mini-ships or mini-liners, to carry dry bulk cargoes such as grain. During construction, four of these were modified to handle containers, were fitted with cranes, and had their bridges elevated to provide visibility over the containers. Although slow – their Caterpillar diesel engines could push the ships through the water at a maximum of only 10 knots – they served their purpose. Importers and exporters in Manila, Pusan, Kaohsiung and Keelung would be given a U.S. Lines bill of lading that would provide a single rate and the assurance that the steamship line would be responsible for the cargo from the origin to destination ports. This was the first in-house feeder network operated by a container line. Three feeders operated from Hong Kong to Manila, Keelung and Kaohsiung. The fourth operated between Kobe and Pusan.

*   *   *

Opportunities in the Pacific market also caught the attention of Matson Navigation, which had pioneered the use of container ships between the U.S. West Coast and Hawaii. In 1964, Stanley Powell Jr., the company's president, recommended to his board of directors that Matson build on its experience and expand into international routes. The recommendation, which came more than two years before Sea-Land and U.S. Lines launched container service to Europe, was an indication of Powell's belief in the future of containerized shipping.

Matson was owned by four of the Hawaiian merchant compa-

The Pacific Banker helped Matson launch its trans-Pacific service between the U.S. and Japan in 1967.

nies established by the island's early settlers. On January 20, 1964, the U.S. Department of Justice filed a civil antitrust lawsuit, charging that control of Matson by the four companies – Alexander & Baldwin, Castle & Cooke, C. Brewer & Company and American Factors – constituted an illegal restraint of trade. To settle the lawsuit, three of these companies sold their shares to the fourth, Alexander & Baldwin, which later became Matson's sole owner. This rearrangement gave the company's officers, and especially Powell, greater control over the company's direction. He steered Matson in the direction of further containerization, which he saw as a springboard for growth:

> Matson has now emerged from its long period of transition from a diversified company to one principally in the transportation business. The time has come to explore possible areas of expansion in the field of transportation so that operational risks, now confined to one area of the Pacific, can be more diffused. In the development of the ocean freight container system, now serving Hawaii so well, Matson has also forged a high degree of technical and managerial know-how in its staff of able and experienced people. This is an additional reason to undertake a program of expansion.

Powell envisioned an "intermodal system" that would reduce by days the movement of goods between Japan and Europe. Fast container ships would carry products across the Pacific and the Atlantic, and unit trains running coast-to-coast would speed containers across the continent. "He had this idea of a two-ocean container ship fleet, linked together overland, across the continent by a unit train," said Robert J. Pfeiffer, who later would become Matson's chief executive officer. "Of course, he was at least 10 years before his time." In 1968, Matson attempted to acquire U.S. Lines to provide a trans-Atlantic link. Matson also tried unsuccessfully to buy U.S. Freight, a company that had forwarding rights from coast to coast.

Matson's move into international service was in the Pacific. In 1966 the Maritime Administration approved Matson's request that it be allowed to operate an unsubsidized freight service linking the U.S. West Coast, Hawaii and the Far East. The permission was needed because Matson would be operating in the protected domestic market while also competing against subsidized U.S.-flag lines in the international market.

The expansion to Asia appeared to be well-timed. Matson knew how to build and operate container ships, and Japanese liner companies – which represented potentially stiff competition – had not yet seized the initiative in this new cargo-handling technology. Furthermore, Japan, Korea, Taiwan, the Philippines and Hong Kong were manufacturing products such as televisions, watches, and clothing that were ideal for containerized shipping. Matson's ships could also carry U.S. military cargo on their westward routes.

In November 1965, Powell and Norman A. Scott, Matson's executive vice president, traveled to Japan to lay groundwork for a possible trans-Pacific service and to seek potential Japanese partners. "We made a number of calls on the chief executives of the six principal Japanese firms, and talked to them about our general plans of coming into the trade, and told them we had container facilities on the West Coast," Scott said. "We thought it made a lot of sense to try to couple those up with other operators, in exchange for coupling up new facilities in Japan that would serve us and other Japanese lines." Matson and Japan's Nippon Yusen Kaisha agreed to share port facilities. NYK's president, Yoshiya Ariyoshi visited the United States to see Matson's operations.

To initiate its service, Matson sent two C-3 breakbulk freighters to a Japanese shipyard for conversion into container ships and ordered two new container ships from the Bremer-Vulkan shipyard in Germany. In April 1966, Matson leased

Matson was first with container service to Japan.

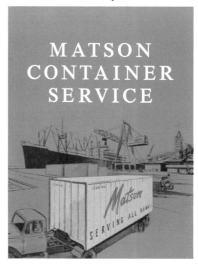

acreage for a container port in Oakland, where its San Francisco Bay container operations would be centralized.

Matson's container service to Japan began in September 1967, after the first ship conversion in Japan was completed. The first container ship service to Japan proved successful. In addition to commercial shipments, Matson carried military shipments to Japan and Korea, where the company established a feeder barge service from Kobe to Inchon. The Korean service was preceded by nearly two years of negotiations over things such as a Korean government requirement that a road tractor be imported with each container chassis. When Matson's first containers were brought into Inchon, they were sent off in truck convoys with a guard riding shotgun on each vehicle to deter bandits.

Service also was extended to Hong Kong, Singapore and Keelung and Kaohsiung, Taiwan. Each of those countries presented startup problems but they were nothing compared to what Matson encountered in the Philippines. R.S. Kernan, the Matson executive in charge of Southeast Asia, said that when Matson's *Pacific Trader* approached Manila, its officers discovered that local longshoremen had hired two tugboats, placed machine guns on deck and threatened to open fire if the vessel docked. Kernan said he told the ship's master to turn back rather than risk the loss of life. The dockworkers' union later relented and Matson's ships were allowed to call at Manila.

Despite Matson's success and Powell's international ambitions for the company, Alexander & Baldwin was showing reluctance to support the ship line's expansion into new markets. The parent company's board was uneasy about exposure to the cyclical international shipping market. Their uneasiness was fueled by several developments. Matson and other carriers were facing competition from Japanese liner companies that jumped into container shipping more quickly than expected. Five Japanese carriers, coordinating their operations, initiated service to the U.S. West Coast in September 1968. They soon grabbed a substantial share of the market's cargo, much of which was directed to them by affiliated Japanese trading companies.

Adding to Alexander & Baldwin's concerns were the maritime industry's strained labor relations with seagoing

The Journal of Commerce, May 9, 1966. Japanese carriers coordinated their entry into containerization.

Mitsui O.S.K. Lines began service between Asia and the U.S. East Coast with the New York Maru in September 1972. The ship had capacity of 1,884 TEUs.

and longshore unions. The International Longshoremen's and Warehousemen's Union struck West Coast container terminals on March 17, 1969, demanding that all containers except those filled by shippers be packed and unpacked by longshoremen instead of Teamster warehousemen. A federal court ordered the longshoremen back to work, but the situation remained volatile. At the end of its next contract in 1970, the ILWU would strike for 134 days, with an interruption for a federally imposed cooling-off period under the Taft-Hartley Act.

Alexander & Baldwin replaced Powell as the shipping line's president in April 1970 and suspended Matson's Far East service the following summer. Under Powell, Matson had boldly ventured across the Pacific, but within three years it had pulled back from international service and returned to the safety of its primary niche within the protected domestic trade between the West Coast and Hawaii.

Matson's withdrawal left four container ships under construction, two in Germany, and two in the Bethlehem Steel yard in Sparrows Point, Maryland. Sea-Land happily acquired the two ships being built in Germany shortly before they were completed. Sea-Land was then in the process of converting from its 35-foot boxes to the recently-established international standard 40-foot box, and Matson had designed its ships to carry 24-foot boxes, so several adjustments had to be made to the vessels' design. The

German-built ships could not be used in U.S. domestic markets, which the Jones Act limited to U.S.-built vessels. But because Sea-Land by then was operating container ships on international as well as domestic routes, it had no trouble deploying them.

Interviewed years later, Norman Scott, who became an executive at American President Lines, spoke regretfully of Alexander & Baldwin's decision to withdraw from international service:

> In spite of all the obstacles and problems, we were doing fine. I always felt we were like guys trying to cross a creek by stepping from one stone to the next, and that we got part of the way across. But then, the directors of Alexander & Baldwin got frightened when faced with the prospect of committing the money to continue the operation while the projections for near-term financial results didn't seem to be too favorable. And just like the guy who sort of hesitates to continue when he is in the middle of the stream and steps back, they too pulled back instead of pressing forward. I think, if they'd had the courage to continue, we'd have succeeded.

Matson's Robert Pfeiffer was more succinct: "Stanley Powell correctly foresaw the development of containerization in the Pacific. Unfortunately he didn't get the support of some influential directors of Alexander & Baldwin."

*　　*　　*

Although containerized shipping was introduced to the Pacific market by American carriers, Japanese liner companies were close behind. From the start, the Japanese carriers' entry into containerization was a collaborative project. In 1964, the nation's shipping and shipbuilding industries underwent a reorganization orchestrated by Japan's Ministry of Transport through a national Council for Reorganization of Shipping and Shipbuilding Industries. Liner shipping was concentrated in the nation's "Big Six" carriers – Nippon Yusen Kaisha (NYK), Kawasaki Kisen Kaisha ("K" Line), Mitsui O.S.K. Lines (MOL), Yamashita-Shinnihon Steamship Company, Showa Line and Japan Line.

As *Containerisation International*'s Jane R.C. Boyes observed two decades later, "The 1964 reorganization could hardly have been better timed." When containerization emerged, Japanese carriers were prepared to seize the opportunity to establish themselves quickly. Under the administrative guidance of the Ministry

Opposite: Matson had four ships under construction when it ended its trans-Pacific service. Sea-Land acquired two of them. Alabama Shipbuilding and Drydock Company in Mobile completed them and installed cell guides to accommodate 35-foot and 40-foot containers instead of Matson's 24-footers.

Japan's Nippon Yusen Kaisha launched its trans-Pacific container service in September 1968 with the 752-TEU Hakone Maru.

of Transport, they took a careful approach, usually operating through consortia or joint services that spread the risk. Using this joint approach, the Japanese carriers soon spun a complex web of routes that covered much of the world.

Japanese shipping officials had studied the formation of Atlantic Container Line with keen interest. But unlike the European shipowners who formed a jointly held consortium company in the form of ACL, the Japanese lines elected to retain their individual identities by creating consortia with other lines. Between 1968 and 1972, Japanese carriers created or became partners in nine consortia. Five of these groups – four in the U.S. trade and one on an Australian route – consisted exclusively of Japanese-flag lines. The other four groups, two for Australia and one each serving North Europe and the Mediterranean, included non-Japanese partners.

U.S. law required Federal Maritime Commission approval for cooperative agreements among carriers serving American ports. On July 3, 1968, the commission approved a request by Yamashita-Shinnihon, Mitsui O.S.K., Japan Line and "K" Line for a "space-charter agreement," a tool that eventually would become common. The agreement detailed how the lines would share ships, coordinate sailings and interchange empty containers while retaining separate marketing, cargo booking and bills of lading.

Japanese carriers began negotiating for port leases at U.S. West Coast ports in 1966 and signed lease agreements early in

1968. In September of that year, only a few months after Matson, Sea-Land and U.S. Lines had entered the Pacific trade, NYK and Showa led the Japanese lines into containerization with the start of a service between Japan and California ports. Within weeks, another trans-Pacific service was launched by the consortium of Mitsui O.S.K., "K" Line, Japan Line and Yamashita-Shinnihon.

A year later, NYK, Mitsui O.S.K, "K" Line and Yamashita-Shinnihon began moving containers to Australia. The following year all six of the Japanese lines joined in a service between Japan and the U.S. Pacific Northwest. By 1972, all but Showa were cooperating in a joint service to the U.S. East Coast. That same year, NYK and Neptune Orient Lines became partners in the Trio consortium between Asia and Europe and in the Med Club consortium between Japan and the Mediterranean ports of Genoa, Marseilles-Fos and Barcelona.

* * *

During this period, Sea-Land continued to press its early advantage. Sea-Land's international expansion during the 1960s was carried out with the model it had used from the start — converted ships that the company had picked up inexpensively and refitted to handle containers. Naval architect Charles R. Cushing was first exposed to containerization in 1958, when he sailed on Pan-Atlantic's *Gateway City* as a mate while attending the Massachusetts Institute of Technology. After graduation in 1960, he answered a *New York Times* ad for a mechanical engineer at the company, still named Pan-Atlantic.

Cushing began working at the company's offices, which were located behind a partition in a cargo shed at the Port Newark terminal from which the *Ideal X* had sailed four years earlier. His drafting table was adjacent to that of Ron Katims, a recent civil engineering graduate of Cornell University who left a job with the New York Housing Authority to join Sea-Land. A year later, Cushing was named the company's chief naval architect. During the next eight years, he oversaw the conversions of 42 ships for the rapidly growing company.

Sea-Land's ship conversions took many forms, including the insertion of mid-body sections, but all had the basic objective of creating maximum container ship capacity, at minimum cost, as quickly as possible. Used freighters and tankers were converted to container ships, with container slots crammed everywhere they

Loads Of Trouble

Not everyone enjoyed reduced cargo damage in the early days of containerization. It took time for some shippers to learn how to safely pack or "stuff" a container to withstand the stress of sea transportation.

Within a year after containerization went international, cargo underwriters reported an unexpected flurry of claims for ruined cargo. Many shippers wrongly assumed that they could stuff a marine container the same way they loaded a highway trailer.

Poorly braced cargoes can smash through container walls, ruining the shipment and endangering the ship and its crew, especially if hazardous cargo is involved. Adding to the problem, the fact that containerized cargo is out of sight encourages unscrupulous shippers to intentionally misdeclare a box's contents to obtain a lower freight rate. No ship's master can state with certainty what his ship is carrying. This ignorance can be deadly. Highly toxic chemicals, radioactive cargoes, explosives and flammable gases are regularly transported in containers.

When such cargoes moved only on breakbulk ships, safe stowage practices were determined by the crew's seamanship skills and by insurance underwriters. In recent years this responsibility has passed largely to government authorities. The U.S. Coast Guard founded the National Cargo Bureau in 1952 to develop uniform standards for cargo stowage. The National Cargo Bureau published its first guide to safe stowage of containers in 1967

Unsafe stowage of hazardous cargoes in containers is a continuing problem worldwide.

and has updated it several times to reflect new hazards and stowage techniques.

The International Maritime Consultative Organization, now renamed the International Maritime Organization, issues international recommendations and rules for the safety of seafarers, ships and the environment. The IMO also has established the International Maritime Dangerous Goods Code, which sets regulations for the international transportation of dangerous goods.

would fit, in three to six months. The vessels' steam-turbine engines were left in place, and McLean didn't worry about changes that would reduce fuel consumption or crew sizes. Sea-Land was still competing against less-efficient conventional ships and McLean realized he didn't have to seek additional advantages by spending his limited funds to replace engines. "If he had a buck to spend, he was going to spend it on containerization, not on trying to squeeze a few extra barrels out of the fuel bill, or trying to automate the ship," Cushing later recalled. McLean "was constantly expanding, expanding, using other people's money. He was trying to get as much container space afloat, in service, as he could for his limited dollars. And so he wasn't looking to build fancy."

McLean had become adept at turning the dross of surplus vessels into the gold of container shipping. As an unsubsidized operator, Sea-Land was able to take advantage of opportunities unavailable to U.S.-flag carriers that received operating and construction subsidies under the 1936 Merchant Marine Act and were ensnared in the accompanying red tape.

One such opportunity emerged in 1961, with a new government "Trade-In/Trade-Out" program. Rather than proposing complex deals that required assessments of the value of used ships, the costs of building in U.S. shipyards and the expense of federal ship-mortgage guarantees, the government offered to accept any U.S.-flag vessel in exchange for one in the government's fleet of ships left over from World War II. The program was created to clear the backlog of mothballed ships while stimulating shipbuilding. It was not designed specifically to provide hulls that could be converted into container ships, but McLean seized the opportunity. In early 1964, the Maritime Administration used the program to allocate 18 surplus C-4 troop ships to seven U.S. companies, with one requirement being that those companies not be recipients of federal operating subsidies. Sea-Land qualified for and received six of the 18 ships.

Before the Trade-In, Trade-Out program was ended in 1969, a total of 120 ships had been swapped out of the reserve fleet. By 1968, Sea-Land had converted 10 former troop ships – large, fast, well-built ships that were among the best in the reserve fleet – into container ships. Lengthened with the insertion of mid-bodies, two could carry 622 containers each; the other eight could carry 360. The vessels for which they were exchanged were ready for the scrap yard – Liberty ships, a Delaware River ferryboat, a New York excursion boat and a railroad ferry. It was all legal and above board, and had such a program not existed, the container revolution might have been stalled by the cost of building new ships.

*   *   *

The Sea Chest, made of heavy corrugated cardboard, was used to stow small items in breakbulk ships in the 1950s. The boxes could be stacked three high in a ship's hold.

The American Legion was one of the 1,200-TEU Lancer-class ships that U.S. Lines ordered in the late 1960s and early 1970s.

By the end of the 1960s, the supply of World War II freighters suitable for conversion was dwindling and most shipping lines realized that containerization was around to stay. Some conventional ships were still being converted to containers and, despite their proven shortcomings, some vessels were still being operated as combination container/breakbulk vessels. But it was clear that containerization was destined to supplant much of the world's general cargo fleet. A boom ensued in construction of container ships by U.S., Japanese and European companies. In August 1967 the Maritime Administration reported that 80 container ships with capacities of at least 9,500 deadweight tons were under construction or on order – 31 by U.S. owners and 49 by owners from other countries. In addition, nine ships were being converted to container ships by U.S. owners.

After entering containerization with the *American Racer* and its sister vessels, U.S. Lines quickly introduced its Lancer-class vessels. The Lancers had service speeds of 22 knots and container capacities of 1,200 TEUs. Although conceived as breakbulk vessels, their plans were quickly reworked and the Lancers were the first vessels to be built as container ships from the keel up. The first Lancer was delivered in 1966 and entered the trans-Atlantic trade. On its first call at the British port of Tilbury, the *American Lancer* discharged about 300 containers stowed with 4,000 tons of cargo in 13 hours, using 13 men to move 4,000 tons of cargo that on a conventional ship would have required 120 dockworkers. Later, the Lancers also were deployed in the Pacific.

Not to be outdone, Sea-Land began preparing for even faster ships – its first container ships to be built from scratch. McLean directed his designers to begin work on ships that could sail at 33 knots. John Boylston, who became chief naval architect at Sea-Land after Charles Cushing left to form his own firm, worked on the design of the new ships, designated the SL-7s. When Boylston joined Sea-Land in 1965, he had never seen a container ship. But he had sailed on general-cargo ships while a cadet at the Merchant Marine Academy at Kings Point, N.Y., and decided then that there must be a better way to ship cargo. When cargo was loaded and discharged a piece at a time, he later recalled, damage rates were so high that he used to wonder

Not All Boxes Were Steel

The overwhelming majority of marine containers in use today are made of corrugated steel. But in the early years of containerization, carriers also used boxes made of aluminum or plywood and fiberglass.

Plywood/fiberglass boxes were used by several ship lines in the North Atlantic. These boxes had standard steel corner posts for lifting and stacking.

Aluminum was the most popular alternative to steel. The first containers that Malcom McLean sent to sea were made of this material, which was lightweight and allowed more freight to be packed into a container that was carried by truck.

Eventually steel became the material of choice for containers. Welded steel containers proved to be more watertight than aluminum boxes, which were prone to popped rivets. Besides being more durable, steel containers were cheaper to build and repair.

Lightweight aluminum and fiberglass were used on the walls of many early marine containers. The yellow Delta Line boxes were made of fiberglass and plywood, with steel corner posts.

sometimes why people even bothered to ship things. Boylston recognized the advantages of containerized shipping, and saw Sea-Land as an opportunity to get in on the ground floor of a developing industry. After graduating in 1961, Boylston sailed for three years as an engineering officer. Then he enrolled in the University of Michigan and earned a second bachelor's degree, in naval architecture, and joined Sea-Land.

Boylston said McLean approached him with an idea to build eight ships that would circle the world every 56 days, calling at a handful of ports. When Boylston worked out the speed the ships would need, he discovered that some port-to-port segments would require 30 knots. He reported his findings to McLean, who asked how large the ship would be. Boyston squared the speed and estimated it would be 900 feet long. "Would that carry 750 containers?" McLean asked. Boylston assured him it would. McLean told him and his supervisor, Warren Leback, Sea-Land's vice president of operations, to go ahead. The ships, designed by the New York naval architectural firm of J.J. Henry, eventually were 947 feet long and built to sail at 33 knots – a full 50 percent faster than most other container ships in service at the time. Boylston said McLean wanted a 10 percent margin to ensure that the vessels could achieve the needed 30 knots.

*　　*　　*

Malcom McLean shares a word with Andrew E. Gibson, U.S. Maritime Administrator under President Nixon.

onstruction in the late 1960s and early 1970s of larger purpose-built container ships at a time when many World War II-built conventional freighters were still trading on international routes, was a sign that container shipping was entering a new era. It would be an eventful period of highs, lows and drastic change.

Before U.S. Lines could fully deploy its new Lancers, the company became a target of corporate raider Walter Kidde, who was determined to gain control of the company. He succeeded in early 1968, but soon regretted his success. A year later, after retiring the *United States*, the company's last passenger liner, Kidde tried to charter the U.S. Lines container fleet to Sea-Land, but the Federal Maritime Commission and the antitrust division of the Justice Department refused to approve the deal. Sea-Land and U.S. Lines would remain rivals.

In the same year that Sea-Land's planned charter of U.S. Lines ships was scuttled, the R.J. Reynolds Tobacco Company purchased Sea-Land. The company was based in Winston-Salem, N.C., home of McLean Trucking. Reynolds held about a third of the U.S. cigarette market and was becoming nervous about potential liability exposure following publication of the 1964 Surgeon General's Report on the health consequences of smoking. McLean Industries appeared to be an attractive potential acquisition. Reynolds acquired Sea-Land in a $530 million deal that exchanged one new Reynolds preferred share, valued at $2.25, for each McLean common share.

Malcom McLean was kept on as president of Sea-Land under a five-year contract that paid him $100,000 a year. He also would receive roughly $8 million a year in dividends, $125 million in cash, his Reynolds stock, and a seat on the Reynolds board of directors. McLean, who received a total of $160 million in the deal, agreed to the sale when his company's stock price was near its peak. He said he did so because it would allow Sea-Land to grow more rapidly and with less risk. According to several who worked with him, he also was looking for additional financing for the SL-7 program, which would eventually cost $250 million for the eight ships.

Sea-Land's SL-7s, which entered service in 1972 and 1973, were the fastest container ships afloat. Each was powered by two steam-turbine engines that generated a total of 120,000 horsepower.

The sale of Sea-Land marked the end of an era. For the company's staff, it was a transition from Sea-Land's early go-go days to life as a subsidiary of a large corporation. Ron Katims offered an example of the change in corporate culture. As the executive who oversaw Sea-Land's landside equipment, Katims frequently ordered more cranes than could be immediately used. In its early years, Sea-Land was constantly expanding, and there was always a new port where the cranes could be put to good use. When McLean decided to jump into a new market, he was delighted when Katims could install cranes and get port facilities into operation ahead of the competition.

"I used to buy all the cranes for the company…and I always used to keep about two cranes ahead of the program," Katims recalled. "I had no authorization to buy them, I didn't know where they were going to go, but…I'd make the commitment that we were going to buy. After '69, I kept doing the same thing, and I had one of the Reynolds guys come to me at one point and tell me that if they caught me doing that again, I would be fired. That's when I knew that…it was going to be tough for me to work in that culture, because, to me, being ahead of it and planning ahead was what you were supposed to do."

During the following years, many still-young veterans of Sea-Land's early days struck out on their own or took executive positions with other companies that were going into containerization

The Mayaguez Incident

Sea-Land's container ship *Mayaguez* was passing through the South China Sea on May 12, 1975, when the ship and its 39 crew members were seized by the Khmer Rouge, 61 miles off the coast of Cambodia. U.S. President Gerald Ford declared the seizure of the unarmed merchant ship an "act of piracy." When negotiations failed to win the quick release of the ship and crew, he ordered military action.

Marines recaptured the ship, which was towed back to international waters by a Navy frigate. U.S. forces carried out a helicopter assault on a Cambodian position, unaware that the ship's crew had been released unharmed. The incident cost the lives of 41 U.S. servicemen – 15 Marines killed in combat, three others who later were killed in Cambodia, and 23 U.S. airmen who died in a helicopter crash.

and recognized Sea-Land as the market leader. The ex-Sea-Landers found a ready market for their talent and knowledge. From the start, McLean had paid careful attention to hiring and training. "Good people lift you up, bad people lift you out," he was fond of saying. In the company's early years, each new applicant was interviewed by Malcom's sister Clara, the company's corporate secretary and a no-nonsense enforcer of office rules such as clean desktops at the end of the day.

Sea-Land developed an intensive management training program and was among the first shipping companies to use a staff psychologist to screen applicants. Among the traits most highly valued in prospective new hires were aggressiveness, initiative, intelligence and the ability to work without direction. "A generation of transportation executives went to 'McLean Tech' in the sense that he trained them all," Katims said. "McLean trusted people with talent, and let them do their jobs without breathing down their necks. Micromanagement was never his style."

Sea-Land's rapid expansion, first in the United States and later internationally, provided its staffers with varied experience and opportunities for rapid advancement that weren't available in many of the industry's more traditional companies. "It was an exhilarating time," said George Marshall, who left the trucking industry to help establish Sea-Land's operations in Japan and other Asian countries and later became a top executive at Mitsui O.S.K. Lines. "It was great because you were working with people who conceived the whole concept of containerization. Sea-Land was so far ahead that no one else was in second or third place."

CHAPTER FIVE

Full Circle

*"Traditional container operators will eventually succeed
in convincing their colleagues from the developing countries
of the economic advantages of large container ships and their joint
deployment. Third World shipowners will then profit from
the rather costly experience of the container 'pioneers'."*

— Karl-Heinz Sager, 1981

Chang Yung-fa said he had just signed the contracts in September 1972, when he "had that uncanny feeling that something was amiss." Only four years earlier, he had founded Taiwan-based Evergreen Marine Corporation with a single second-hand freighter. Now Chang had just acted to upgrade the company's fleet by contracting for the construction of two breakbulk ships. But after studying maritime publications and watching industry developments, he suddenly decided he had made a huge mistake. He contacted his shipbuilder and bankers and said that instead of building more breakbulk ships, he was switching the order to container ships.

"There was no grand scheme," Chang recalled years later. "I saw the trend. The container wave was not stopping." At the time, few paid attention. Evergreen was an obscure carrier that only recently had ventured beyond its home region by establishing routes for its breakbulk ships between Taiwan and the Middle East and the Caribbean. In the United States and Europe, hardly anyone had heard of Chang or Evergreen. In less than a decade, that would change. As Evergreen ordered more ships and developed new routes, the Taiwanese line would come to symbolize the globalization of containerized shipping.

By the early 1970s, containerization had been established for 15 years in U.S. domestic services and had been adopted internationally by carriers from the United States, Japan and Europe. By the 1970s it was apparent that containerization had turned the shipping business upside down.

Entrenched carriers that had sunk millions of dollars into breakbulk ships suddenly found that their investments had turned into liabilities as they tried to compete with wholly containerized operators. Old-line carriers were rushing to update their fleets and catch up with the early leaders. Upstart carriers such as Evergreen were

Opposite: U.S. Lines' Jumbo Econships, which became Sea-Land's Atlantic class of ships, dominated news of liner shipping in the 1980s.

entering the market, often as lower-cost independent carriers that operated outside rate-setting cartels.

The century-old liner conference system was showing strains as carriers struggled to get a grip on costs and rates. Although the conference system still held sway over most major trade routes, new and efficient competitors were undermining the ability of established carriers to set rates collectively. Historically, any significant improvement in operating efficiency has been accompanied by lower rates. Containerization was no exception. It changed the industry's economics as drastically as the switch from sail to steam had done a century earlier.

Instead of having to worry only about operating ships from port to port, container ship lines suddenly found themselves having to invest heavily in containers and chassis that were out of their control for weeks or months at a time. Computer systems to track equipment were still in the early stages of development. As carriers took on responsibility for inland transportation of containers by rail and truck, they assumed liabilities and costs that many maritime-oriented executives did not understand and could not control.

Other changes also were unfolding. Unsubsidized American-flag carriers Sea-Land and Matson had pioneered containerization in the U.S. domestic markets. When containerization was extended to international routes, other American-flag carriers such as U.S. Lines entered the fray. These long-established carriers received operating subsidies, that helped offset the higher costs of operating U.S.-flag ships. For years, the primary competition for U.S.-flag carriers was fleets operated by carriers based in developed nations, primarily in Europe. Now new container ship operators were popping up throughout the world. Maritime publications were filled with headlines about government-controlled shipping lines that had entered competition with privately owned companies. As low-cost Asian carriers joined the container revolution, the gap widened between the costs of U.S.-flag lines and their overseas competitors. At the same time, the government restrictions on how and where subsidized lines could operate was becoming an increasingly difficult problem for the American carriers.

*   *   *

Taiwan's Chang was not burdened by those impediments. He had the good fortune to enter the scene at a time when his small country's economy was finally recovering from World War II and when the shipping paradigm was changing. Taiwan and other Asian countries were growing economically. Abetted by the development of efficient containerized shipping, these nations found receptive markets in the United States and Europe for their exports of manufactured goods.

Chang took advantage of his opportunities, much as Malcom McLean had done in the unsettled U.S. trucking environment of the 1930s and with the surplus war-built ships in the 1950s. In some ways, Chang and McLean had similar careers. Both men rose from humble beginnings and learned the transportation business through hands-on experience. Both weathered early setbacks and defied conventional wisdom in building their successful companies. Finally, at crucial times for their businesses, both enjoyed the support of an understanding banker.

Chang, the son of a seafarer, was born in 1927 and as a teenager worked as an office clerk for a Japanese steamship company. He later spent 15 years at sea, working for several shipping companies and rising to the captaincy of a 2,000-ton freighter. In 1961, he and two partners founded a small shipping company, New Taiwan Marine. He left four years later to join two brothers in another shipping venture, Central Marine. After a disagreement with his partners, Chang struck out on his own. On September 1, 1968, he founded Evergreen Marine. He later said a friend had suggested the name because it symbolized vigor, prosperity and perennial life, and "depicts the company as a beautiful island much like Taiwan."

Although Chang's previous shipping ventures had been short-lived, he had learned the basics of running a steamship line. His years at sea had given him a thorough understanding of ship operations and costs. Equally important, he had earned the confidence of bankers at Japan's Marubeni Corporation. As Chang built his company, Marubeni's Koyoshi Hosaka would serve a role similar to the one that National City's Walter Wriston served for McLean at Pan-Atlantic and Sea-Land. Hosaka and Wriston shared a willingness to take risks on visionary but unproven enterprises, and to rely on their assessment of an entrepreneur's skills, character and market opportunity. Chang and Hosaka first met during Chang's first shipowning venture, when Hosaka was a section head in Marubeni's vessel division, which made small loans to help Chang and his partners get started. They formed a close relationship that proved crucial a year after Evergreen's founding, when a fire on one ship and an engine breakdown on another put the fledgling carrier in precarious financial condition. In his autobiography, *Tides of Fortune*, Chang told of approaching Hosada

Chang Yung-fa in 1975.

with trepidation after those setbacks and asking for the equivalent of US$300,000 to pull Evergreen through its crisis. Hosada listened to the Evergreen owner, and made a surprising recommendation. Instead of $300,000, Hosada suggested, Chang should borrow $600,000 to provide a cushion of working capital. Chang took the larger amount, and repaid the five-year loan within a year. Three years later, when Chang decided to stake his company's future on containerized shipping, Hosada helped persuade other Marubeni officials to provide the necessary financing.

Chang needed all the help he could get. His Japanese bankers were cautious and skeptical of his plan to enter containerized shipping. Evergreen was doing well in its niche markets as a breakbulk carrier, the Marubeni officials pointed out. The bankers grilled Chang, asking him how a small carrier such as Evergreen could hope to succeed as a solo operation. They reminded Chang that Japan's six largest carriers had felt it necessary to join forces to launch their container operations. With Hosada's backing, Chang persuaded the bankers to approve his financing. The loan expanded a relationship between Marubeni and Evergreen that would prove profitable for both companies in the years to come.

The Japanese bankers' skittishness was understandable. Chang was going against the established order with which Marubeni and other Japanese lenders were familiar. Cooperation was the rule among Japanese carriers. Although they maintained separate organizations, they sought to share ship capacity among themselves or with non-Japanese conference lines. Under the Ministry of Transport's supervision, the Japanese carriers were careful to avoid competing with each other in these arrangements. They also tended to be staunch members of rate-setting cartels.

*   *   *

The conference system was encountering severe pressure, largely because of containerization. Conferences that included breakbulk and container lines had an increasingly difficult time reconciling the sometimes conflicting interests of these two groups. Pure container ship operators had different cost structures from breakbulk operators, and hybrid carriers had yet another set of costs. In the United States, some carriers were introducing services that offered ocean and inland service under a single rate. This produced friction with carriers that preferred

The Ever Spring at Port Newark, New Jersey, in 1975. Evergreen's first container ship had a capacity of 646 TEUs. The ship later was lengthened to carry 866 TEUs.

to operate port-to-port. The emergence of upstart non-conference lines and government-controlled carriers added yet another element to the mix.

Although barriers to entry were still low enough to allow the emergence of new carriers such as Evergreen and Switzerland-based Mediterranean Shipping Company, containerized shipping had become a high-stakes game that required heavy capital investment. Ships were growing larger. Individual operators such as Sea-Land and U.S. Lines ordered new vessels and European and Japanese lines continued to pool their resources, forming consortia that provided more frequent sailings and wider coverage than the carriers could have provided individually.

The first European container-shipping consortium was Atlantic Container Line, but others soon followed. The multinational Trio Group, operating between Asia and Europe, was formed in 1972 by five lines – Japan's NYK and Mitsui O.S.K., Germany's Hapag-Lloyd and Britain's Ben Line and Overseas Containers Limited, itself the container-operating arm of four British shipping companies. The Trio Group's name reflected its tri-national membership, comprising carriers based in Britain, Germany and Japan. Trio operated on the space-charter system that the Japanese carriers had pioneered. Members maintained separate ownership and management of ships and containers and marketed their services independently while sharing space on ships and at terminals where the vessels called.

The Trio Group had five lines as members in 1972. The consortium's largest ships, furnished by OCL and Hapag-Lloyd, had capacities of 3,000 TEUs each – four times more than the conventional freighters they replaced. For more than a decade, these European carriers' ships in the Trio consortium were the largest container ships afloat. The ships' service speeds of 26 knots provided transit times of 21 to 23 days between Europe and East Asia. In terms of productivity, each vessel of the Trio group replaced six or seven conventional ships. The ratio of time a ship spent at sea to the time it spent in port went from 60/40 to 80/20.

Membership Of The Trio Group, 1972		
COMPANY	COUNTRY	PARTICIPATION
Overseas Containers	Britain	5 ships, approx. 3,000 TEUs each
Hapag-Lloyd	Germany	4 ships, approx. 3,000 TEUs each
Ben Line	Britain	3 ships, approx. 2,800 TEUs each
Nippon Yusen Kaisha	Japan	3 ships, approx. 1,950 TEUs each
Mitsui O.S.K.	Japan	2 ships, approx. 2,000 TEUs each

Besides offering a way to share capital expenses and operating costs, consortia were designed to limit the downward pressure on freight rates caused by an oversupply of ships. In the late 1960s, when carriers began rushing to build and convert ships to handle containers in international trade, there were widespread warnings that carriers were expanding too rapidly. Carriers were warned that they would face the same overcapacity and rate wars that had accompanied the switch from sail to steam a century earlier and that had led to creation of the conference system. In a May 1967 analysis of the rapid development of container shipping on the North Atlantic, *The Journal of Commerce* reported that "even some of the larger ship lines that have been leading the way in the container revolution are showing signs of misgivings about over-investment in facilities and equipment."

These concerns intensified during the 1970s. While ship lines were rushing to start or expand their container ship fleets, the global economy was jolted by a series of major shocks, including the end of the Bretton Woods currency agreement that had existed since shortly after World War II and the worrisome rise of price inflation. The most significant economic development of the decade, however, was the jump in energy prices. After the Six-Day War in 1967, Arab members of the Organization of Petroleum Exporting Countries began using this marketing cartel as a vehicle for achieving their political goals. When the conflict known as the Yom Kippur War broke out in 1973 and foreign assistance helped Israel withstand Egyptian and Syrian forces, the Arab members of OPEC retaliated by imposing an embargo on oil exports to the United States, Western Europe and Japan. The resulting jump in oil prices affected consumer demand in importing nations and caused transportation providers' fuel costs to soar.

*   *   *

No company involved in containerized shipping felt the oil price shocks more acutely than Sea-Land, still the market leader. The Lancer-class ships of U.S. Lines had been introduced to compete with Sea-Land's fleet of converted World War II cargo ships. Under McLean, Sea-Land had begun planning its response – a new fleet of even bigger and faster ships. These were the SL-7s, each of which would carry nearly 2,000 TEUs and steam at 33 knots. With the company's acquisition by R.J. Reynolds, Sea-Land had ample cash to build the super-fast ships. Eight were constructed in three European shipyards – two in Germany and one in the Netherlands. The first SL-7 was put into service in October 1972.

The SL-7s were planned and built in an era when oil was cheap and plentiful. In the years preceding the OPEC oil embargo, crude-oil prices fluctuated within a narrow range between about $2 and $2.50 a barrel. Prices for ship's bunker fuel, which consists largely of what is left after crude oil has undergone catalytic cracking into various products, were so low as to be almost incidental. That situation soon would change. The effects of the embargo were immediate and drastic. By 1974, the embargo had driven the price of oil up to four times what it had been before the war.

The Sea-Land McLean, which entered service in 1972, was the first of eight SL-7s.

Increased fuel prices radically altered the economics of operating the SL-7s. The new ships had been competitive when running at 33 knots, despite their enormous consumption of bunker fuel. After the OPEC oil embargo, the ships quickly became uneconomical, even when operated at 26 knots. In 1981 they were sold to the U.S. Navy for $268.4 million, less than two-thirds their original cost. Though the SL-7s had turned into a white elephant for Sea-Land, they were a bargain for the Navy, which kept their fast engines but adapted their cargo spaces to handle roll-on, roll-off cargoes. The converted SL-7s became part of the Navy's expanded fast-supply fleet.

After oil prices soared, Sea-Land had moved swiftly to build a new fleet of 12 diesel-powered container ships known as D-9s. The design requirements for these ships called for a service speed of 21 to 22 knots, a hull size that would allow them to transit the Panama Canal, and diesel propulsion that could be controlled directly from the ship's bridge, thereby reducing the vessel's requirement for engine-room manning. Sea-Land contracted with two Japanese shipbuilders and a Korean shipyard for construction of the vessels, all of which were in service by the end of 1980. Their construction cost was $396 million, $29 million less than Sea-Land had paid for eight SL-7s a decade earlier. Each of the D-9s could carry about 10 percent fewer containers than the SL-7s, but because they relied on diesel power instead of the high-speed, steam-turbine engines of the SL-7s, they sharply reduced Sea-Land's fuel costs.

As Sea-Land's war-built fleet aged and the carrier's ambitions became global, the company abandoned most of the domestic routes on which it had launched containerization. In 1978 Sea-Land terminated its U.S. coastwise and intercoastal services, except for its services to Puerto Rico and Alaska. By then Reynolds, now renamed RJR, was looking for ways to bring the rambunctious Sea-Land operation under control. Under McLean, Sea-Land had developed an entrepreneurial culture in which department heads were given broad latitude. In 1974, on the advice of a consulting firm, RJR shifted Sea-Land's financial management from the company's New Jersey headquarters to Winston-Salem and put the chairman of RJR's finance committee in charge of the company. A centralized cash management system was also put into place. This was not the way McLean wanted to see his company run, and he said so. He resigned his position as RJR director in 1977.

*   *   *

McLean was an entrepreneur to his core and had been bored as an RJR director. "I am a builder, and they are runners [managers]," he said of his fellow directors. "You cannot put a builder in with a bunch of runners. You just throw them out of kilter." After selling Sea-Land to RJR, McLean invested in several non-maritime businesses, including a large hog-farming operation in North Carolina and the Diamondhead residential development on the Mississippi Gulf Coast. Although McLean was out of shipping after leaving the RJR board, the containerization pioneer was not yet finished. A year after resigning as a director of Sea-Land's parent company, he cashed in much of his RJR stock and acquired U.S. Lines for $160 million.

McLean accepted the prevailing wisdom of the early 1980s that oil prices would continue to rise.

Despite its entry into containerization in the late 1960s, U.S. Lines was a company in need of rejuvenation. The carrier was still based at its historic address of 1 Broadway, across from New York's Battery Park, in a limestone building emblazoned with coats of arms of some of the ports that its great passenger liners once served. U.S. Lines still operated the Lancers it had built in the late 1960s and early 1970s, but it also had a large number of conventional breakbulk vessels, some of which were periodically chartered to the military. One shipping periodical described it as a "proud...down-at-the-heel shipping company with a fleet of first-generation container ships too small for the trades they served and costly to operate." McLean, however, saw U.S. Lines as a company that could be rebuilt into a competitor with more modern rivals in Europe, Asia and the United States.

One of McLean's last initiatives at Sea-Land had been development of the SL-7s. Sea-Land had hoped to use the fast ships to create new markets for time-sensitive cargoes and to seize business from slower competitors. There was logic to the plan, but the SL-7's edge in speed was quickly canceled out by the OPEC-driven surge in oil prices, which jumped again during the second oil shock in 1978 and 1979. Some oil-industry analysts predicted that crude prices would more than triple to $100 a barrel within the next few years.

Having guessed wrong on oil prices with the SL-7s, McLean

decided to go in the opposite direction with U.S. Lines. He began developing plans for construction of a fleet of large, comparatively slow but fuel-efficient vessels that would circle the globe, loading and discharging cargo at ports along the way. These vessels, dubbed Jumbo Econships, would carry approximately 4,400 TEUs, 50 percent more containers than any other ship.

Henry Gilbertson, an executive under McLean at Sea-Land, said that after years on the sidelines, McLean was eager to make another mark in shipping. "He wanted to make one more run at leapfrogging ship technology," Gilbertson said. Since his early days as a struggling trucking operator, McLean had always looked for an edge through transportation technology. That motivation pushed him to enter containerized shipping, to develop specialized containers for liquids and refrigerated cargoes, and to build the SL-7s, whose speed he hoped would expand the market for containerized cargo and enable Sea-Land to secure a bigger portion of it.

McLean was fond of saying that shipper loyalty was worth only two cents per hundred pounds of cargo — that even a customer who had an established relationship with a carrier would jump to a competing transportation provider for a two-cent difference in rates. With a modern fleet that used less fuel than its competitors, he reasoned, U.S. Lines would be able to grab market share from competitors and earn a handsome profit.

*   *   *

The Econships would be built and operated without government subsidy. For its other vessels, however, U.S. Lines continued to receive subsidies to help offset the higher costs of employing American crews and complying with U.S.-flag requirements. Sea-Land's ships also flew the U.S. flag and were eligible for programs that gave U.S.-flag carriers preference in the carriage of military and other cargoes purchased or financed by the government. But Sea-Land, which had started in the unsubsidized domestic trade and developed internationally at a time when it enjoyed a technological edge over its competitors, did not participate in the subsidy programs established by the 1936 Merchant Marine Act.

By remaining unsubsidized, Sea-Land enjoyed more freedom in its operations. Subsidies were tied to contracts under which carriers agreed to provide service on specified "essential trade routes" to and from the United States. Subsidized carriers had to seek Maritime Administration approval to revise schedules, start new services or increase capacity. Rival carriers, subsidized and

The American New York was the first of 12 Jumbo Econships that U.S. Lines ordered from South Korea's Daewoo Heavy Industries.

unsubsidized, routinely objected to those requests. The result often was protracted regulatory squabbling and litigation that entangled subsidized carriers in expensive red tape. W. Bruce Seaton, chairman of American President Lines, a subsidized line, recalled that era: "If we wanted to change a dinky little trade route, we had to go through a long, long, involved system with the Maritime Administration with advocates or challengers, usually Sea-Land. And I don't blame them; if I'd been in their shoes, I'd have done the same thing."

Among the conditions for receiving a subsidy was a requirement that a carrier build its ships in U.S. shipyards. By the early 1980s that requirement placed subsidized lines in an impossible situation. Despite construction subsidies provided by the 1936 Merchant Marine Act, U.S. shipbuilders had become uncompetitive for construction of oceangoing commercial vessels. American-flag operators were finding it virtually impossible to compete internationally with U.S.-built ships that cost far more than their non-U.S. competitors paid. To encourage U.S.-flag carriers to update their fleets with more-efficient ships, the government granted a two-year moratorium during which subsidized carriers could build ships in foreign yards and still receive operating subsidies for them.

McLean jumped at the opportunity. On April 12, 1983, U.S. Lines ordered 12 container ships from South Korea's Daewoo shipyard.

The Adrian Maersk was the first of nine container ships that entered the Maersk fleet in 1975-1976. This photo was taken in the Panama Canal.

The new ships weren't the only element in McLean's plan. To help pay for the new vessels, McLean persuaded the government to accept a deal under which U.S. Lines would forgo years of future subsidy payments in exchange for an accelerated smaller payment. After ordering the Econships, McLean purchased $300 million worth of containers and equipment. As part of his strategy to capture the world's trade and to provide feeder services that would keep the Econships full, McLean acquired two subsidized niche U.S.-flag carriers, Moore-McCormack, which operated primarily between the U.S. East Coast and Africa, and Delta Steamship Lines, which served the U.S./South America trade. The Moore-McCormack and Delta routes would be used to feed the Econships on their round-the-world route.

The Econships were scheduled to circle the globe every 84 days, providing weekly sailings from ports they served. The big ships were designed for fuel efficiency, with service speeds of 18 knots, compared with the 21 or 22 knots of most competitors' ships. McLean said that even with their slower speeds, the ships' operating efficiency would enable U.S. Lines to "suck up cargo like a vacuum." Richard Gibney, in a *Container Briefing* analysis in February 1987, wrote that, "Rightly at the time, McLean calculated that the scale benefit of 4,500 TEU coupled to ultra-economical power plants would give U.S. Lines a cost advantage which, with every rise in the price of oil, could only get better."

Notwithstanding the conventional wisdom about oil prices, McLean's bold gamble was widely questioned. Some predicted the Econships would flood the market with excess capacity and cause rates to plunge. Sir Ronald Swayne, chairman of Britain's OCL, said in December 1982 that he had tried to talk McLean out of his plan. "A number of us have done our sums on this and looked at it very closely and we think it is absolutely crazy," Swayne said. He said McLean was counting on high utilization rates to generate economies of scale that would cut per-unit costs by 35 percent, but that the planned round-the-world service would have to overcome fierce competition and high costs for repositioning containers, among other obstacles. Filling the big ships, Swayne said, would require "the most incredible marketing skill or cutting rates to the absolute bare bone." He added: "I very much hope the whole project does not come off."

Others also noted the heightened competition that McLean would face. In the early days of containerization, Sea-Land had competed primarily with less-efficient breakbulk carriers. By the mid-1980s the world's main trade routes were served by efficient carriers with modern fleets of container ships. In some cases, the latecomers had been able to profit by learning from the experiences and mistakes of the pioneers. The American, European and Japanese carriers had been joined by upstarts from other regions. Hong Kong's Orient Overseas Container Line and Singapore's Neptune Orient Lines were developing sizable container operations, as were established European carriers such as Denmark's Maersk Line.

*　　*　　*

Maersk had been in shipping since 1904, when Captain Peter Maersk Moller acquired a second-hand, 2,200-deadweight ton steamer, the *Svendborg*. Over the years, the A.P. Moller Group had developed into an enterprise with interests in oil and gas exploration and production, air travel, retailing and manufacturing, including two Danish shipyards. The group's shipping interests were diverse and encompassed not only liner shipping, but tankers, dry-bulk and specialized vessels, and an array of support vessels for offshore oil supply, towing, anchor-handling and firefighting.

Maersk took delivery of its first all-container vessel, the 1,800-TEU *Svendborg*, in 1973. The ship, named for the small vessel that Peter Maersk Moller had used to start his company, had an unusual early history. Before its construction was completed, the ship was chartered to a partnership that was dissolved before the ship was delivered. Then the vessel was chartered for a year, laid up for a period, and then brought back into service several times as a temporary replacement for other vessels that were being rebuilt.

The Danish carrier did not establish a full container service until 1975. But when Maersk took the plunge, it went all the way, placing a $340 million order for nine 26-knot container ships that were delivered in 1975 and 1976. Within a year, container ships were handling the majority of the cargo that the ship line carried.

In the years that followed, Maersk quietly and steadily expand-

Maersk's first large container ship construction program was reported in The Journal of Commerce, June 29, 1973.

The 1,800-TEU Svendborg, shown at Sydney, was Maersk's first container ship. It bore the same name as that of A.P. Moller's first ship in 1904.

ed its presence in container shipping. The company developed a fuel-efficient fleet through a combination of new ships and conversions of older vessels that were lengthened – "jumboized" in shipping parlance – by the insertion of mid-body sections. By pulling ships out of service one at a time for lengthening, Maersk was able to expand its capacity with minimum disruption to schedules. When this activity had been completed, the result was a modern fleet that had been developed inexpensively. The company preferred to operate its own ships instead of joining consortia or chartering space from competitors. Maersk developed such a reputation for service that *Containerisation International* said the Danish carrier was "sometimes dubbed the 'Rolls-Royce' of the container market by its rivals." By 1985 the line had spent well in excess of $1 billion developing its container-carrying fleet. In 1985, its fleet had shipboard capacity of 59,317 TEUs, fourth among the world's carriers, behind Evergreen, U.S. Lines and Sea-Land.

*   *   *

Other carriers were also ready to resist McLean's attempt to seize their markets. In response to higher oil prices, numerous lines ordered diesel-powered ships, slowed the speed of their ships or sent their vessels into shipyards for engine replacements or overhauls that improved fuel efficiency. After the 1973 jump in fuel prices, the 3,000-TEU Hapag-Lloyd and OCL ships in the Trio consortium were operated at 23 knots instead of their maximum 26. The ships then underwent extensive modifications to their steam-turbine engines and hulls to reduce fuel consumption by 25 to 30 percent. Sea-Land's fuel-guzzling SL-7s had become uneconomical, but the D-9s were efficient to operate. Later, rather than make large investments in new ships, Sea-Land opted to insert mid-body sections into the D-9s, like Maersk and other carriers had done with their diesel-powered ships. Sea-Land was able to expand the capacity of the D-9s by more than a third for a total outlay of only $76 million, a bargain price of slightly more than $6.3 million per ship.

In the space of a decade, Evergreen had used its low costs and finely tuned pricing to vault into the upper ranks of the world's container ship operators. Now Chang countered McLean's ambitious expansion plan with one of his own. In the spring of 1982, while McLean was preparing his Econship venture, Chang announced plans to order 16 container ships for his own round-the-world service. The Evergreen ships would have capacities of about 2,100 TEUs, less than half that of U.S. Lines' Econships, but were several knots faster. They also had much lower crew costs; Evergreen's new ships would carry 16-man crews, compared with the 21 Americans required for the Econships.

The Taiwanese carrier's new ships would operate in a two-way, round-the-world service with a call at each port every 10 days. As new ships were brought in, Evergreen planned to upgrade the service to weekly. The service was launched in July 1984. Like U.S. Lines, Evergreen started building up its regional services to feed cargo into the main east-west routes. With lower costs, the Taiwanese carrier was prepared to go head-to-head with its American rival.

U.S. Lines and its ships with their distinctive red, white and blue stacks had been famous in shipping decades before Chang had acquired his first second-hand ship. A few years earlier, upstarts such as Evergreen would have been no match for a company such as U.S. Lines. By the 1980s, however, the competitive picture had changed. Liner shipping was becoming a free-for-all.

When Chang broke into the Middle Eastern and European markets in the 1970s, he had to compete with tightly organized

Sea-Land to Increase Size of 12 Ships

By TIM NEALE
Journal of Commerce Staff

NEW YORK — Sea-Land Corp. has announced that it will increase the total carrying capacity of 12 of its containerships by 37 percent.

The $76 million "jumboization" program involves the company's D-9 class vessels, which were built in 1980 and which are deployed in Sea-Land's trans-Pacific and trans-Atlantic services. Each of the vessels will be cut in half and a new mid-body inserted, increasing their total carrying ~~~~ 904 40-foot ~~~ ~ 40-

Sea-Land's announcement did not rule out the possibility of ordering new containerships, which has been rumored for months. Mr. Abely said, however, that the D-9 jumboization program represents an investment of $19,100 per 40-foot slot, "considerably less than the cost of comparable new construction."

The capacity of the D-9s has been increasing ever since they were introduced as part of a shift from steam turbine to the more fuel-efficient diesel-powered engines. Origin~~ ~~~ ~~~ a capacity of 839 40 ~~~

Sea-Land "jumboized" its D-9s by lengthening their hulls. The Journal of Commerce, October 18, 1984.

Evergreen's Chang Yung-fa launched two round-the-world services in the 1980s.

conference lines that did not take kindly to independent operators such as Evergreen. Chang recalled that the conference lines did not necessarily allow new lines to join. He said the Far Eastern Freight Conference, representing carriers in the Europe-Asia trade, was especially hostile:

> It was strong and, frankly, ruthless, and a very restrictive cartel. If a shipper was disloyal – that is, used an independent – and then wanted to come back to a conference carrier, the customer was at their mercy; there were no guarantees that the freight would move. They could turn down the booking, and the shipper could be blackballed, scrambling for space at any price. There was so much acrimony and betrayal.

Independent carriers had long struggled with the perception that their service was less reliable than that of the more established conference lines. By the 1980s the gap was closing fast. Besides Evergreen, other new carriers, generally operating outside conferences, were springing up.

Although many still considered the service of non-conference lines to be inferior, *Containerisation International* reported in 1985, "Now this is no longer the case. Evergreen is well-known in the markets it serves, although its level of service may lack some of the fine-tuned features of a Maersk Lines, for example, it generally compares well with those of its major rivals." With lower costs, Evergreen held an advantage similar to the kind that Sea-Land had once enjoyed over old-line breakbulk carriers.

*   *   *

The late 1970s and 1980s were difficult years for many shipping lines. Recurrent rate wars contributed to the failure of several well-known carriers, including Pacific Far East Line, States Line, Prudential Lines and Hellenic Lines. Besides the unsettled global economy, carriers were still struggling to understand the costs of containerized shipping. McLean discussed that issue on December 9, 1982, when he made a rare speech at a seminar at the Merchant Marine Academy at Kings Point, New York. McLean warned that poor cost controls led to poor pricing decisions that undermined rates for all carriers. "The entire industry depends on survival from proper pricing," he said. McLean told his audience, which consisted primarily of carrier representatives, that shippers had benefited from rates that were lower than when containeriza-

The Sea-Land Independence, a diesel-powered D-9, passing the Bayonne Bridge in the Port of New York and New Jersey.

tion was introduced to international routes 15 years earlier. "You haven't hurt the shipper," he said. "You have helped him in every way under the sun." Asked how the growth of intermodalism would affect carriers, he replied, "If you can't count, it will get worse; if you can count, it will get better."

Executives at other ship lines expressed similar views. In an October 1982 speech to the annual convention of the Propeller Club of the United States, William B. Hubbard, senior vice president of American President Lines, lamented carriers' propensity to underprice their services:

> The shipper today has available fast, dependable liner service at substantially less in real terms or equivalent dollars – even 30 percent, 40 percent, even 60 percent cheaper than the cost available when containers first began to be a factor in the Pacific trade in 1967.... In plain English, we don't make or keep enough money. The reason, in part, is our own doing.

*   *   *

By the time the first of U.S. Lines' Econships entered service in June 1984, McLean faced an external problem that was beyond the ability of anyone in the shipping industry to solve. After several years of almost universal predictions that oil prices would continue to rise, bickering among the OPEC cartel's members had caused the price of oil to suddenly collapse. When McLean planned his round-the-world service, there were widespread predictions that crude oil prices, then about $30 per barrel, would soon rise to $50 a barrel. Instead, by 1985 they had plummeted to about $10. The plunge in oil prices hurt U.S. Lines in two ways. First, lower fuel prices negated the advantages of the company's slower but fuel-saving Econships and threw a lifeline to competitors that operated less-efficient ships. Second, the collapse in oil prices reduced shipments to the Middle East, the world's primary oil-producing region, and left the Econships largely empty on an important leg of their eastbound round-the-world service.

A third strike against U.S. Lines was a sudden softening of freight rates on many trade routes. As competition intensified in a chaotic shipping market, carriers fought to maintain market share. With conferences unable to prevent their members from undercutting the cartels' pricing, rate wars broke out on several regional segments of the Econships' round-the-world circuit and on their feeder routes.

On routes to and from the United States, the rate-cutting was encouraged by carriers' reaction to the Shipping Act of 1984. The law legalized shipper-carrier contracts, although it required that the contracts' essential terms be filed with the Federal Maritime Commission so that "similarly situated shippers" could demand identical terms. The spread of negotiated contracts encouraged deal-making between shippers and carriers that pulled rates down. Equally important, the 1984 act permitted carriers to undercut conference tariffs by filing their own rates as an "independent action." This further weakened discipline within rate-setting conferences. Cartel members would agree on common tariffs, then use their right to independent action to provide their customers with lower-cost deals that undercut conference rates. Shippers enjoyed a buyer's market in containerized cargo.

U.S. Lines was not immune to the effects of this difficult environment for carriers. The company had projected that its big ships would generate an average of $12 million in revenue per round-the-world voyage. By mid-1986, low freight rates had reduced per-voyage revenue to between $10 million and $11 million. Some of the sharpest drops in rates came on the important trans-Pacific route. When the Econships entered service in 1984, they produced $9.5 million in revenue on their trans-Pacific voyages alone, but that figure had dropped to $6 million.

After posting $62.5 million in pretax profit for the fiscal year ending September 30, 1984, U.S. Lines began struggling under

a combination of high debt and low freight rates. A $3.7 million loss in the first quarter of 1985 was followed by a $10.9 million second-quarter profit. After that, McLean's company produced a steady stream of red ink, with losses of $15.3 million, $43.6 million, $71.2 million, $62.5 million and $77.4 million during the next five quarters.

The company struggled to fill its big ships with enough cargo to keep the company afloat. *Container Briefing*'s Richard Gibney wrote that, "From mid-1985 on, U.S. Lines' sales staff were sent out to the market with an impossible mission: 'You must get X amount of freight at rate Y so that we can achieve Z revenue.'… The U.S. Lines sales force was obliged to offer container space at an average of about $1,140/TEU door-to-door in the first quarter of 1986, at a time when management knew that the carrier's mainstream total costs were running at over $1,500 per loaded TEU." Making matters worse, rumors spread about the line's financial condition, causing many shippers to divert bookings to competitors.

Even as the losses mounted, McLean was undaunted. Speaking at his company's 1986 annual meeting, he emphasized the efficiency of the Econships. "We have unquestionably the

During the winter of 1986-87, six of U.S. Lines' 12 Jumbo Econships were laid up at Hudson River piers in Manhattan. The rest were tied up at other ports.

best, the cheapest fleet in the world. It is even competitive with Evergreen...If we stick in there and work hard, we will survive this rate depression and come out of it and make some money. We are going to lose a little more this year. We will get back on the track by the end of this year or in 1987."

U.S. Lines didn't survive that long. On November 24, 1986, the company filed for bankruptcy protection. The Econships were laid up, with six of them ignominiously moored at New York's Hudson River piers, near where the famed passenger liners *United States* and *America* had once docked. Others sat idle in Singapore, Hong Kong and Tacoma, Washington.

The story of the Econships ends with a melancholy irony. With U.S. Lines now on the sidelines in bankruptcy court, Sea-Land was an obvious bidder for these new but laid-up behemoths. In 1984 RJR had spun off Sea-Land as an independent company, a move that led to a good deal of internal turmoil in Sea-Land and attracted the unwelcome attentions of a Dallas corporate raider, Harold Simmons, who began maneuvering for a hostile takeover. Charles Hiltzheimer, a veteran Sea-Lander who had been president of the carrier before RJR reorganized it as a separate company, resigned when Sea-Land was spun off and he was not kept on as president. Simmons quickly snapped up Hiltzheimer as an adviser who knew his way around Sea-Land. U.S. Lines also valued Hiltzheimer's experience and appointed him president of the bankrupt company, the hope being that he could interest Sea-Land in buying U.S. Lines' container ships. That, in the end, is what happened. Sea-Land made a low but successful bid for the 12 Econships, and for other U.S. Lines container ships. After purchasing the Econships for about $13.4 million apiece, Sea-Land, by now a CSX Corporation subsidiary, began operating them early in 1988 as its "Atlantic Class" in the North Atlantic. To increase their speed, three of the ships were shortened, reducing each ship's capacity to 3,400 TEUs. Nearly two decades later, the former Econships are still in operation.

Malcom McLean made no excuses for the failure of U.S. Lines. "I've made a lot of money in this business and I've lost a lot of money," he later said. Five years after the U.S. Lines bankruptcy McLean would return to shipping by founding Trailer Bridge, which operates 53-foot trailers between cities on the U.S. mainland and Puerto Rico, using roll-on, roll-off barges. With McLean Trucking, Sea-Land and Trailer Bridge, he is said to be the only person to have founded three companies that went on to be listed on the New York Stock Exchange.

Sea-Land operated the Econships after acquiring them in a bankruptcy sale. To increase their speed, three of the ships were shortened, reducing their capacities to about 3,400 TEUs each.

CHAPTER SIX

Bombay To Boston

*"We're not just ocean. We're origin to destination,
raw material to finished product."*

— W. Bruce Seaton

For decades, the North Atlantic was the world's busiest trade route for general cargo, and New York and London were the capitals of world shipping. Large quantities of manufactured goods and other cargoes moved between the developed nations of North America and Europe. Beginning in the late 1960s, a growing share of this trade began to move in containers. Trade on other shipping routes, including those to and from Asia, was dominated by shipments of basic commodities that were not swept up in the first wave of containerization. That began to change in the late 1960s.

Containerized shipping reached the Pacific market just as Asia's economies were starting to stir. Japan's postwar reconstruction was largely complete and the nation's export-oriented policies encouraged Japanese manufacturers to produce higher-value goods for international markets. Containerization provided an efficient way to transport the increasing volume of Asian exports to the United States and Europe. Japan was not the only Asian country that was industrializing. China would not become a global economic power for years to come, but East Asia's "Little Tigers," led by South Korea and Taiwan, were industrializing rapidly, using efficient containerized shipping to expand their export trade. In 1978, U.S. trade volume with Pacific Rim nations surpassed U.S. trade with Europe. In shipping, Asia was becoming the place to be.

American President Lines, based in San Francisco, had long been a fixture in the Asian market but was slow to take full advantage of it. APL's history in the trans-Pacific market dated to 1867 when a predecessor, the Pacific Mail Steamship Company, began the first regular steamship service to Hong Kong and Yokohama. But when containerization came to the Pacific, APL acted cautiously. APL at first viewed Sea-Land's and Matson's

Opposite: W. Bruce Seaton led APL into full-scale containerization and the industry into larger ships and double-stack container trains.

container initiatives as an innovation suitable only for the protected U.S. domestic trade. Grace Line's failure in its Venezuelan
initiative had clearly demonstrated that containerizing international trade routes raised special problems. Therefore APL, like
many other lines, limited its initial foray into containerization to
modifying its standard freighters to carry a relatively small number of boxes. APL's Searacers, two conventional ships that APL
ordered in 1958, were equipped to carry a few containers along
with breakbulk cargo. However, when these combination ships
were delivered in 1961, they demonstrated yet again that containers and breakbulk mixed poorly. Carrying containerized and
uncontainerized cargoes on the same ship created inefficiency
and delays in loading and discharging cargo. Hesitant to commit
to containerization, APL lagged as Sea-Land, U.S. Lines and
Japanese carriers seized the advantage in its primary market.

APL's hesitancy was partly due to the carrier's management
history. The company did not have the agile, forward-looking orientation that would have embraced the new technology. APL was
created shortly before World War II, when the Maritime
Commission purchased near-bankrupt Dollar Line, renamed it
American President Lines and operated it as a government-owned
enterprise. The company was spun off as a publicly traded company in 1952 and acquired in 1956 by Natomas Company, an oil and
gas exploration and production company that was founded in 1853
and was active in gold-dredging in the years after the California
Gold Rush. Natomas was headed and largely owned by a highly
successful oil entrepreneur, Ralph Davies, who installed George
Killion as APL's president. Killion, however, developed a passion
for movie-making, became a director of Metro-Goldwyn-Mayer,
and paid little attention to APL, which remained an independent
company with its own board of directors. In the meantime
Natomas acquired two other shipping lines, American Mail Line
and Pacific Far East Line, and operated them as separate companies as well. All three shipping lines were drifting, rather than
actively planning for the future, when containerization transformed ocean shipping.

Like other subsidized U.S.-flag carriers, APL was restricted in
its ability to add or alter its services. It watched helplessly as
Sea-Land leveraged its Vietnam military contracts to establish
itself on commercial routes in the trans-Pacific market.

APL had long had an around-the-world service, which was
especially well-known in the passenger trade, the part of shipping
that most interested Davies. When containerization appeared on

The California, the first Pacific Mail steamer, began service between Panama and San Francisco in 1849.

the horizon, the company sent two vice presidents on a round-the-world trip to examine the advisability of introducing containerization on this service. They visited 26 ports in 16 countries, but because APL had not yet developed a strategy for containerization, little was done.

By 1970 Davies was struggling with cancer and was planning to turn his companies over to his successors. Pacific Far East Line had been sold by this time, but in an attempt to give APL and American Mail Line the strong leadership they needed, Davies hired Norman Scott as Natomas' vice president for transportation. Scott, a U.S. Naval Academy graduate, had made a name for himself with Matson, but when Matson pulled back from its ambitious attempt to provide container service across the Pacific, Scott began looking for opportunities elsewhere. In the same year Davies also hired W. Bruce Seaton as Natomas' vice president for finance. Seaton had spent many years in the oil industry managing international inventories and financial transactions. Both men were soon appointed to the boards of Natomas and APL, and in 1973 Scott became president of APL, which in the same year was merged with American Mail Line.

Like other oil and gas producers, Natomas was riding the 1970s wave of rising energy prices. Its executives also were spending an increasing amount of time trying to figure out what

The President Lincoln, above, was one of five breakbulk ships that American President Lines built in 1967-68 and converted to container ships in 1972. The President Grant, right, is shown before its conversion.

to do with the company's under-performing shipping subsidiary. APL's profitability was inconsistent, and margins were well below those that Natomas enjoyed in oil and gas exploration and production. The parent company began considering a sale of APL if it could get a good price. First, Natomas hired outside consultants to study the shipping market and examined the tax and legal implications of selling or liquidating the company. The consultants delivered their reports in 1977. One of the consulting groups, Temple, Barker & Sloane, delivered a surprising conclusion – that APL could be highly profitable if it tightened up its management and operations, extricated itself from its money-losing round-the-world and Atlantic/Straits routes, and concentrated on container service in the trans-Pacific market. The consultants' report presented a clear challenge to Natomas and APL.

When Scott retired in 1977, there was no clear successor. Dorman Commons, the president of Natomas and chairman of APL's board, asked Seaton, who had served on APL's board for five years, to run the shipping company on a temporary basis. Seaton was a critic of the poor profitability of APL and of the shipping industry in general, and had been one of the strongest advocates of selling APL. He said, though, that he would take over the shipping line on the condition that he could return to the energy side of Natomas if he wished. Commons agreed and gave Seaton free rein to fix APL's problems. It was a decision that would have far-reaching impact. Seaton never went back to the oil business, and APL was never to be the same. Neither would the rest of the container-shipping industry, which would adopt several of the innovations Seaton introduced in the years to follow.

*   *   *

Seaton was 52 years old when he was named president of APL. A business administration graduate of UCLA, he later worked for an accounting firm and became a certified public accountant. He spent 13 years with Douglas Oil and four years with Occidental Petroleum, where he specialized in international currency management. At APL, Seaton immediately began applying to the line's trans-Pacific container operations the lessons he had learned in the oil industry. Analyzing APL's operations, he realized that the business of moving containers around the world was essentially a matter of logistics, much as the business of producing, transporting and refining oil was for an energy company. "Logistics is simply the process of efficiently and effectively moving raw materials or products around so as to maximize customer satisfaction and minimize cost," Seaton said. APL had already taken steps in this direction. Seaton later recalled that an APL executive, Henry Koslowski, "had the foresight to see that containers were highly amenable to logistics, not only analytically, but for control and operations, too."

Seaton also recognized that managing the logistics of container shipping required an automated way for a carrier to track its boxes and determine the costs of routing them in different ways. Oil companies were beginning to tap the emerging power of computers.

APL converted three former LASH barge carriers to container ships.

"They developed computer simulations and refinery simulations that would tell them how to maximize the finished product extracted from the raw material, and then how to move it through the system," Seaton said in an interview years later. He said it was apparent that container shipping had to be managed the same way:

I realized that if we were going to use logistics to manage containers it absolutely had to be automated. There was no way you could move what today would be 100,000 containers through multiple options where you had to make choices and have any kind of a decision-making process. We already had numerous people in the field who were making day-to-day decisions on how to move a customer's box, and they were doing it kind of by history, or by rote, and they had a high potential for dysfunctionality and bad mistakes...And we had to look at alternative values, multiple variables, and how you correlate multiple variables...You're looking at multiple locations – South Asia and North America – and you have various routes you can take, and various means of transportation, and various terminals. And you have a time factor, and a utilization factor for ships, boxes, trucks, and trains...How can you make a marginal analysis so that you can tell some guy in Bombay to look at the alternatives for getting a box to Boston, which may involve 10, 15 decisions and 50 to 70 variables?

The next step was electronic communications. Shortly before leaving the Natomas oil business to become president of APL, Seaton stopped at Singapore and was astonished to learn that the APL office manager had just spent six hours making a telephone call to Calcutta. "Here's the guy running all of Southeast Asia taking six hours to get a call through to Calcutta!" Seaton recalled. "And I said, 'Jesus, what'd I get myself into?' I'll tell you, the oil industry didn't operate like that." APL quickly developed electronic mail to link its offices and provide instant communications.

The most revolutionary changes that Seaton instituted at APL were to concentrate the company's efforts on containerized shipping in fast-growing trans-Pacific trade and to extend APL's control of its system inland over the North American rail system.

By the late 1970s containerization had taken hold in the trans-

Pacific market. Goods such as cameras from Japan, toys from Taiwan and garments from the Philippines lent themselves to shipment in containers. APL began replacing its older vessels with larger, faster container ships. When Pacific Far East Line, by now an independent company, went bankrupt in 1977, APL acquired its four barge-carrying LASH ships and converted them to 1,856-TEU container ships. Because these ships were U.S.-flag, APL was able to acquire and convert them with a minimum of red tape and without financial assistance from the government. APL soon acquired other container ships and, with oil prices rising as a result of the second of the 1970s oil shocks, began designing large ships that would be powered by fuel-efficient diesel engines instead of steam-turbine propulsion.

*   *   *

While APL updated its fleet, it paid even more attention to issues on land. For centuries ship operators had provided port-to-port services, leaving inland transportation to be arranged by forwarders or importers or exporters working with trucking companies or railroads. That was changing as container shipping gained in popularity. Container ship lines had practiced intermodal transportation since the earliest days of containerization, before the name intermodal was given to the coordinated use of sea and land transportation. Railroads, meanwhile, had been moving in fits and starts toward expanded piggyback transportation of trailers and containers. But the combined use of ship and rail transportation for containers remained disjointed and confusing to service providers as well as customers.

In 1967, when carriers were rushing to establish containerized shipping in the North Atlantic market, *The Journal of Commerce*'s maritime editor, George Panitz, presciently observed that "many of the lines admittedly have little real knowledge about inland transportation and other problems related to the new shipping

Barges As Boxes

Barge-carrying ships were touted as a form of containerized shipping during the late 1960s and early 1970s.

The most popular barge-carrying ship was the LASH, an acronym for Lighter Aboard Ship. Small barges, or lighters, were lifted on and off the ship by a gantry crane that traveled the length of the ship and stacked the barges in open hatches. About 30 LASH ships were built between the late 1960s and early 1980s.

Lykes Bros. Steamship Company had a different "sea-barge" carrier, the Seabee, which used larger barges that were lifted by the ship's submersible elevator instead of a crane. The Seabees, which operated between the Gulf of Mexico and Northern Europe and the Mediterranean, carried containers on their top decks.

Many LASH ships also were adapted to carry containers as well as barges, but they could not handle containers as efficiently as a regular container ship. Barge carriers worked best on trade routes that had inland waterways at each end. They were poorly suited for other markets, such as the trans-Pacific trade route, where Pacific Far East Line went bankrupt operating them.

APL Sets Int'l Precedent With 45-Foot Box Order

By CHARLES F. DAVIS
Journal of Commerce Staff

American President Lines has placed an order for 733 45-foot containers, thereby setting a precedent in the worldwide intermodal transportation industry which is presently dominated by 20- and 40-foot units.

The Oakland, Calif.-based ship line last June made known that it had asked for bids from U.S. and overseas container manufacturers for the new type of container, having earlier put into service on its trans-Pacific route a prototype for structural tests.

The contract has been awarded Nippon Fruehauf of Tokyo, according to a company spokesman. Delivery of the containers is scheduled for the first quarter of 1982.

The new type of container will have a cargo capacity of 3,035 cubic feet, approximately 27 cubic feet more than the standard 40-foot unit.

In announcing APL's projected new boxes last June, Richard J. Hill, the ship line's vice president for operations and project manager, said that because handling and transportation costs are mainly determined on a unit basis rather than the size of the container, the larger boxes are expected to bring about a significant savings.

He stressed, however, that the new units are not expected to replace the standard 20- and 40-foot units and will initially will be carried on an on-deck stowage basis only.

The company also noted that the new boxes have been designed to be carried by existing standard intermodal rail cars, having an overall length of about 89-feet, in both the container-on-flatcar and trailer-on-flatcar modes and also can be handled by standard 40-foot container-handling gear.

The new boxes are to be built of aluminum, with steel end-frames and are designed for a payload of 64,300 pounds. They are expected to operate on interstate highways with 50,000 pounds.

APL, in asking for bids on the new type of box, also asked for tenders on several hundred 45-foot chassis, also the first of their kind.

The Fruehauf Division of the Fruehauf Corp., a U.S. firm, has been awarded a contract to build 405 units and 41 will be built in Taiwan by Luo Chang Machinery Enterprises. A number of existing 40-foot chassis will also be converted to the 45-foot length, APL states.

The ship line had earlier announced that the three new C-9 class containerships being built by Avondale Shipyards have been built with a hull configuration which can be altered to accommodate the 45-foot boxes along with the standard 20-foot and 40-foot containers.

APL led the industry into larger containers. The Journal of Commerce, November 18, 1981.

*Intermodalism gave rise to three kinds of "bridge" movements: Landbridge referred to intermodal movements of freight that combined a sea voyage and rail transportation across a land mass, followed by a second sea voyage (for example, Tokyo to Los Angeles to New York to Rotterdam). Minibridge described transportation by sea and land to or from a point on the opposite coast (Tokyo/Los Angeles/New York). Microbridge referred to shipments between a port in one country and an inland point in another (Tokyo/Los Angeles/Omaha).

system." More than a decade later, that observation remained accurate. Many shipping lines still lacked a clear understanding of what happened to their containers after they were turned over to the railroads and their primitive tracking systems.

That became apparent to Seaton and his team six months after he took over at APL. A series of blizzards in the winter of 1977 closed rail lines over much of the United States, and the railroads were unable to tell APL or other ocean carriers where their containers were. Seaton said APL officials realized that they needed to extend the company's tracking procedures inland. "The question we kept asking was, how do you control the delivery of the customer's product from origin to destination? And so when I realized we needed to have a rail system to get us from Bombay to Boston – that was our standard challenge – I realized we had to have some control over that system. I said, 'We've got to control our own fate.'"

Although containerized shipping naturally lent itself to the coordinated use of ocean and inland transportation, ship lines and railroads still had not learned to work cooperatively. Part of the reason was regulatory. Although ocean carriers had begun quoting combination ocean-rail rates, the legality of combined rates for ocean pricing was in doubt in the United States. The Justice Department contended that multimodal rate-setting was illegal. The Federal Maritime Commission said it wasn't necessarily legal, but that it wasn't necessarily illegal either. Ocean carriers had to endure long delays before the commission approved combination rates.

Seatrain, the company that Graham Brush had established to carry railcars on ships, was a pioneer in the meshing of ocean and rail transportation of containers. Seatrain had acted to simplify the pricing of intermodal shipments in 1972 when it introduced "mini-landbridge" or "minibridge" service* that provided shippers with a single bill of lading with a combined rate for sea and rail service. Seatrain had quit carrying railcars on ships during World War II, but under different ownership it later operated container ships on several routes, including the trans-Pacific. Seatrain's minibridge service moved cargo from Asia to New York, transferring containers at West Coast ports to specially chartered railroad flatcars for the cross-country trip. Minibridge service survived regulatory challenges by rival carriers and Gulf ports, which correctly feared the loss of Asian cargo that moved via the Panama Canal, and by the Justice Department, which contended that conferences' antitrust immunity did not extend to the setting of combination sea-rail rates.

Simplified pricing alone was not enough to solve service problems. APL addressed that issue by leasing railcars, acquiring its own inland terminals at key cities, and working with railroads to develop a system for renting trains that ran on predetermined schedules. The APL Linertrain debuted in 1980. After more than a century of operating as a ship line, APL now was running its U.S. domestic rail system. To avoid being caught short of railcars, APL leased its own. The company also acquired its own ramps at key transportation hubs and expanded its electronic tracking and documentation system throughout the United States and into Asia. As it took charge of its rail service, APL began selling empty backhaul space to domestic shippers. APL's intermodal department worked out a three-way agreement with the railroads and Transway, a truck forwarder, that improved equipment utilization and added another stream of revenue.

The time was ripe for initiatives that combined rail, ocean and truck movement of containers. Though various forms of "bridge" services had been introduced by Seatrain, Sea-Land and other container ship lines in the 1970s, the development of these services had been slowed by questions about the legality of multimodal rate-setting by ocean carriers. That issue was not settled until the enactment of the 1984 Shipping Act. That law said ocean carriers belonging to conferences could set rates jointly for services that extended inland, although that they could not collaborate with the inland carrier to set rates. The 1984 act cleared the way for ocean carriers to develop integrated services that offered sea and rail transportation as a package.

U.S. railroads, meanwhile, were beginning to awaken from a long period of decline. The Staggers Act in 1980 had loosened

Seatrain's first minibridge service in 1972 carried 120 forty-foot containers by rail from Asia to the U.S. East Coast. On hand for the first train were Seatrain's Arthur C. Novacek, right foreground, and Santa Fe Railway's G.W. Wallace.

the Interstate Commerce Commission's stifling economic regulation of the railroad industry. Railroads had considered intermodal traffic to be incremental business, secondary to their bread-and-butter cargoes of grain, coal and other bulk materials. As rail service gradually improved, more shippers began to use intermodal transportation instead of purchasing their transportation service from separate providers.

Seaton directed William B. Hubbard, APL's new operations head, and Donald Orris, the company's director of intermodal operations, to hire more inland-transportation specialists. The days of separate land and sea organizations were disappearing fast. "Bombay to Boston means we control it from Bombay to Boston," Seaton said. "We don't hand it over to the railroad and say, 'Hey, tell me when you get it.' In Boston we don't hand it over to a transshipment shipping company. We really control that whole movement."

Sea-Land and Southern Pacific Railroad had introduced double-stack railcars, low-slung railcars that carried containers stacked atop each other, in 1981. Stacktrain technology used train space more efficiently and reduced damage. Because the double-stack cars had a lower center of gravity, containers did not sway as much while in transit. During the late 1970s and early 1980s, railcar manufacturers continually improved designs and eventually produced articulated models that were linked into units of five railcars, each of which carried two containers, for a total of 10. If the containers had been carried piggyback on truck chassis, only six could have been accommodated in the same railcar length. Stacktrains permitted nearly double the number of containers to

The Journal of Commerce,
July 27, 1984.

APL's 1st Double-Deck Train Arrives in NJ

By TIM NEALE
Journal of Commerce Staff

The first of American President Lines' new cost-saving rail cars, each of which can carry two ocean containers, one on top of the other, arrived Thursday in Kearny, N.J., just outside New York City.

The design of the cars was called a major breakthrough for intermodal transportation. It allows APL to put twice as many containers on its cross-country "linertrains," which move cargo between the line's West Coast ports of call and East Coast markets.

Instead of 100 containers, each linertrain can now take 200 containers. And because the new cars are made of lighter materials than traditional rail flatcars, the double-stacked linertrains can be pulled with virtually no increase in locomotive power and no increase in crew size.

The double stacking is made possible by a "well" in the center of each of the new rail platforms. The bottom of each well sits a mere

nine inches off the ground, which gives the double stacked cars a low enough profile to clear all overpasses and tunnels along the major east-west rail routes.

Development of the cars was a group effort, involving not only APL, but the Budd Co. of Philadelphia, which proposed the idea, the Thrall Manufacturing Co. of Chicago Heights, Ill., which is building the cars, and the three railroads involved in pulling APL's linertrains across the United States — Conrail, the Chicago and North Western and the Union Pacific System.

Representatives of APL and Conrail said in Kearny on Thursday that the new design would result in substantial cost savings for all of them and would help them capture a greater share of the substantial trade between the U.S. East Coast and the Far East.

However APL's senior vice president-operations, William B. Hubbard, said the savings would not necessary translate into lower rates for shippers.

"I don't anticipate that will happen," he said

in response to questions. The idea behind the new double-deck cars is to help keep APL profitable by lowering operating costs, not to reduce freight charges for shippers. Rates in the trans-Pacific trades, while better than last year, are still below 1972 levels, he said.

APL has taken delivery of three sets of the new 100-platform trains and has another set on order. The first three sets cost a total of $8.8 million, and they are capable of carrying about 25 percent of APL's eastbound minibridge traffic.

Mr. Hubbard estimated that minibridge services have captured about 22 percent of the cargo moving between the Far East and the U.S. East Coast, and he said APL has slightly less than half of that business.

The wells of the new rail platforms are long enough to accommodate two 20-foot containers or a single 40-foot box. APL's 45-footers are too long for the wells, but they can go on top, with a slight overhang on each end of the container on the bottom.

An APL Stacktrain passing through East St. Louis, Illinios, across the Mississippi River from the Gateway Arch.

be hauled by the same length train, with the same train crew, and with only a marginal increase in fuel costs. Most of the early double-stack railcars were included in regular trains with boxcars, flatcars and other types of cars.

In 1984 APL took the stacktrain concept a step further, when it began operating the first scheduled trains made up entirely of double-stack cars. Other ocean carriers and railroads quickly followed. Stacktrains proliferated in Western states, where there were fewer clearance restrictions on tunnels and bridges. Eventually, Eastern railroads also found it necessary to raise clearances in tunnels and bridges to handle the new railcar technology. By the early 1990s, scores of stacktrains were operating on U.S. and Canadian railroads.

Stacktrains hastened the shift in the world's trade axis toward Asia. The rapid increase in efficient rail-water services provided an easier way for Asian-made goods to be delivered to U.S. markets. Growth in these shipments turned the adjacent California ports of Long Beach and Los Angeles into the fastest-growing U.S. container ports. In 1987 Long Beach surpassed New York-New Jersey as the busiest U.S. container port.

Most of this growing trans-Pacific trade came from Japan and

The Port of Los Angeles in 1983.

Asia's "Little Tigers." In the 1980s China still had not emerged as an important factor in international trade. That would change, as Sino-U.S. political relations warmed, Chinese leaders adopted policies that encouraged exports, and China gained admission to the World Trade Organization in 2001. Sea-Land established the first U.S. container service to China in 1980, a year after Lykes Bros. Steamship Company had negotiated permission to resume U.S.-flag breakbulk service to China for the first time since the communist takeover in 1949. The first U.S. port call by a state-owned China Ocean Shipping Company ship came in 1979, and was not by a container ship but by a bulk carrier that loaded corn in Seattle. Cosco would later grow into one of the world's largest container lines.

*   *   *

The shift in trade patterns was emphasized by APL's announcement in 1986 that its next generation of ships would be "post-Panamax" vessels – those too large to pass through the Panama Canal. Since the canal's opening in 1914, most of the world's ships had been designed to fit the canal's locks, which were 110 feet wide, 1,000 feet long and 39.5 feet deep. By building ships that were too wide for the canal, APL recognized that it was limiting the routes where the vessels might be employed in the future. The decision was widely questioned, but Seaton was undeterred. APL was committed to the trans-Pacific market and the use of intermodal rail service, and he said it made no sense to design its ships to fit the dimensions of a canal that they would never use:

> The economics of going to post-Panamax were overwhelming. There was also a strategic aspect to the decision, too. We said we were going to maximize North America to Asia, and we're going to move those boxes on an inland basis through the rail system, which we knew was slightly more costly than the canal. But we also knew we could knock four or five or six days transit time off, too. One of the things we did very consciously was not go after market share, even though we were the market share leader in the Pacific for many years. What we were looking for was margin and customer service. And we were constantly saying, how can we get there on time? How can we minimize transit time and how can we maximize information to the customer? And once you look at it this way, you realize that all the canal does is add transit time. And once you make this basic strategy decision, who the hell cares what size the ship is?

APL's first post-Panamax ships entered service in 1988. These ships were designed to carry 4,300 TEUs, close to the capacity of U.S. Lines' former Econships, but their wider, less elongated hulls permitted the APL ships to sail at 24 knots. After their early skepticism, competing lines also began ordering similar vessels. The rapid increase in container ship sizes paralleled the increase in tanker sizes during the late 1960s and early 1970s, when owners built ever-larger crude carriers in an effort to gain economies of scale and reduce costs. The wider hulls provided more efficient operation and the larger vessels did not require larger crews. Steam-turbine-powered ships the size of the old *Ideal X*

APL's C-10s were the first container ships that were too wide to fit through the Panama Canal.

carried crews of as many as 50 men. APL's first post-Panamax ships had 21-member crews. The much larger but highly automated post-Panamax container ships built during the 1990s would operate with as few as 12 crew members.

In 1994 Orient Overseas Container Line of Hong Kong and Hanjin Lines placed orders for ships with capacities just under 5,000 TEUs. The 5,000-TEU and 6,000-TEU marks were crossed soon afterward. During the next two years, P&O Containers, Maersk Line, NYK, China Ocean Shipping Company, Hyundai Merchant Marine, Hanjin Shipping Company, Evergreen, OOCL and Neptune Orient Lines ordered post-Panamax container ships with capacities of more than 5,000 TEUs. Even larger ships would follow.

Ranking container ships on the basis of reported capacity is an inexact science. Because of stowage and stability considerations, a ship almost never carries its full allotment of containers. On trade routes where ships carry large quantities of dense, heavy cargo such as canned goods, a ship reaches its maximum cargo weight before it fills its available cubic capacity; on routes where cargoes are dominated by lighter cargoes, such as electronic products, the opposite happens. Further complicating the picture is the way carriers report the capacities of the ships they build. Some ship lines are proud of the size of their new ships and emphasize their large carrying capacity. Other carriers, worrying that the perception of too much capacity would be used against them in freight-rate negotiations, have adopted a policy of refusing to disclose precise TEU capacities, or of intentionally underreporting the size of their ships.

Orient Overseas Container Line was the first carrier after APL to build post-Panamax container ships. The 4,950-TEU OOCL California entered service in 1995. The above-deck cell guides on its stern help prevent containers from being knocked overboard.

There is no question, however, that the average size of container ships increased rapidly after the mid-1990s. By the start of 2006, carriers were operating 396 ships with capacities of at least 5,000 TEUs and were awaiting delivery of an additional 365 of that size. China Shipping Container Lines, which during the late 1990s emerged as one of the world's largest container ship operators, was preparing in 2006 to take delivery of what was believed to be the first ship with capacity of more than 10,000 TEUs, or 5,000 forty-foot containers. Malcom McLean's *Ideal X* carried fifty-eight 33-foot containers (or 95.7 TEUs) on its initial voyage. By 2005, carriers were reported to have orders pending for construction of 178 ships with capacities of at least 7,500 TEUs each. There were reports that carriers had placed orders for ships with capacities of 12,500 TEUs, a far cry from the *Ideal X*.

CHAPTER SEVEN

Reshuffling The Deck

"You have to be truly global because you never know where the next bonanza-region is to develop."

—Gianluigi Aponte
Mediterranean Shipping Company

Containerization began shaking up the established order of shipping from the moment Malcom McLean sent his first containers to sea. As the industry matured and expanded, the changes continued. Illustrious names faded or disappeared, new companies appeared and startup carriers grew into global leaders. To say that the container shipping industry had reached maturity by the 21st century is not to say that it had become static. The second quarter-century of the container revolution was marked by rapid growth and restructuring of container ship lines. For their customers, it also was a time of change. Shippers learned to integrate containerized shipping into their global supply chains and business strategies, and to take full advantage of it. Low transportation costs continued to create new markets by reducing distance as a factor in distribution.

During much of the 1980s and 1990s, chronic oversupply of container ship capacity kept carriers' rates and profits low and produced intense competition for cargo. U.S. Lines was only one of many ship lines that ceased operations or were merged into other companies. But there also were success stories. Carriers such as Mediterranean Shipping Company, Cosco, China Shipping Container Lines and CMA CGM were not in the first wave of containerization but were among the largest container carriers by 2006. Meanwhile, illustrious names such as P&O and Sea-Land disappeared, and established companies like Maersk and Hapag-Lloyd grew into global leaders.

Containerized shipping was an American invention, and many U.S. policymakers and industry leaders thought that it would give U.S. shipping a technological advantage in international liner service. This momentary hope soon passed as other nations began offering container services at costs the Americans could not match. Rising costs, restrictive government subsidies and

Opposite: Denmark's Maersk is the world's largest container line.

the decline in military shipments following the end of the Cold War contributed to a decline in the U.S.-flag presence in international container services. American President Lines changed its name to APL Limited and was acquired by Singapore's Neptune Orient Lines. Lykes Bros. Steamship Company entered bankruptcy and was purchased by Canada's CP Ships. The South American services of Crowley Maritime Corporation were sold to Germany's Hamburg Süd. Farrell Lines was purchased by P&O Nedlloyd, a British-Dutch company formed in a 1996 merger of P&O Containers and Nedlloyd Lines. By 2000, the only U.S.-flag liner ships in international service were 47 vessels covered by a subsidy justified on the basis of military needs. The link between a nation's merchant fleet and its naval strength, a theory developed by Admiral Alfred Thayer Mahan in his 19th century classic, *The Influence of Seapower on History, 1660-1783*, had been largely abandoned. The nations that emerged as leaders in containerization included countries such as Denmark and Switzerland, not world powers that possessed great navies.

As the industry grew, it became increasingly dispersed. Containers, cranes and ships could be and were built in many countries, and ship ownership and operation became global as well. So did container terminals, which came to be dominated by multinational operators, many of which were connected with ship lines. Containerization accelerated the decline of the traditional national-flag merchant fleets. Many nations that had long prided themselves on their traditions of maritime service were forced out of competition while new entrants pushed their way upward. As maritime historian Frank Broeze noted, "From the late 1970s container shipping broke out of the confines of trade between fully-developed economies with modern transport and information technology infrastructures, and cascaded rapidly to the lesser-developed sections of the world economy."

Shipping has always been cyclical, but containerization posed new challenges. Growth in ship sizes and in the geographic breadth of containerization increased the industry's capital requirements. This, coupled with rising expectations by customers, led carriers to cooperate more closely in the operation of ships and marine terminals. European carriers had pioneered this collaboration with the formation of Atlantic Container Line, Dart Container Line and other consortia that featured joint ownership by member lines. Ownership by multiple carriers eventually proved unwieldy and fell out of favor. By the 1990s most of the European consortia had broken up, and ACL had evolved

Top 10 Container Ship Lines

1983			2005		
RANK	COMPANY	FLEET CAPACITY IN TEUs	RANK	COMPANY	FLEET CAPACITY IN TEUs
1.	U.S. Lines	88,028	1.	Maersk Sealand	1,642,035
2.	Evergreen	69,728	2.	Mediterranean Shipping	757,580
3.	Sea-Land	61,002	3.	CMA CGM	496,257
4.	Hapag-Lloyd	53,636	4.	Evergreen	469,537
5.	Maersk	51,250	5.	Hapag-Lloyd	413,175
6.	Nedlloyd	51,186	6.	China Shipping	343,449
7.	Overseas Containers	43,986	7.	APL	332,093
8.	Mitsui O.S.K.	33,349	8.	Hanjin/Senator	318,150
9.	OOCL	32,717	9.	Cosco	311,644
10.	NYK	30,959	10.	NYK	303,862

From *Containerisation International*, May 1983; BRS-Alphaliner 2005

from a consortium into a company under a single owner, the Grimaldi Group of Italy.

Instead of jointly owned consortia, the 1990s brought a flurry of operating alliances similar to the model established by Japan's "Big Six" lines when they adopted containerization three decades earlier. Alliance members retained control of their vessels but coordinated their schedules and shared space on ships and at port terminals. Initially there was speculation that many of these alliances would quickly yield to mergers. That happened in a few cases, but multicarrier alliances proved more durable than many had expected. Carriers embraced them because they enabled lines to broaden their services while minimizing investment in ships and equipment. Shippers did not seem to mind; they liked the wider choices that resulted when carriers pooled their fleets. Because the participating lines did not use alliances to coordinate pricing, the arrangement was permitted by antitrust regulators in Europe or the United States.

Several global alliances emerged in the 1990s, many based on 10-year agreements. The largest were the Grand Alliance, comprising Hapag-Lloyd, NYK, Hong Kong's Orient Overseas Container Line, P&O Nedlloyd and Malaysia International Shipping Company; the New World Alliance of Hyundai, APL and MOL; and the CKYH, whose members were Cosco, "K" Line, Yang Ming and Hanjin. As alliances spread, their members expanded the concept to include side deals with members of other alliances. A member of one alliance would exchange space with a member of another alliance. It was a way to put surplus capacity to use and to gain a foothold in a new market without the expense and risk of adding ships. On the negative side, alliances could be cumbersome for participants. They required lengthy negotiations and frequent meetings to determine port rotations, capacity allocations and other details.

For some lines, alliances were not worth the trouble. The 1990s were marked by the expansion of independent lines such as Taiwan's Evergreen, Switzerland-based Mediterranean Shipping and Israel's Zim, which preferred to operate without partners or limited their involvement with other carriers to short-term or regional alliances. Their independent status provided them with flexibility that enabled them to react more quickly to market opportunities and to expand their market share. If they wanted to adjust their port rotation quickly, they could do it without asking for another line's concurrence. This style of operating, coupled with the decline of rate-setting conferences, shook up the established order of container shipping.

*   *   *

Gianluigi Aponte founded family-owned Mediterranean Shipping Company.

Mediterranean Shipping Company exemplified the independent newcomers. The company, based in Geneva, founded in 1970 by Gianluigi Aponte, a former Italian ferryboat captain and a graduate of the Italian Maritime Academy at Sorrento. By 2003, he had built MSC into a container ship line that was second only to Maersk Sealand in ship capacity. Aponte launched MSC two years after Chang Yung-fa launched Evergreen. Like Chang, Aponte started with a single breakbulk freighter, which he bought with $5,000 of his own money and $275,000 in credit. Aponte began operating the vessel on irregular "tramp" service. When the 1973 Arab-Israeli war closed the Suez Canal, he bought a second ship and began service down the Atlantic Coast of Africa, around the Cape of Good Hope, up to the Red Sea and back around to Europe. Just as Chang had at Evergreen, Aponte decided his company's future was in container ships. He acquired his first container ships in 1970 and by 1984 had converted to full container ships on the Europe/South Africa route. The following year he entered the U.S. market with the 300-TEU *MSC Sun*. The ship docked at the Global Terminal in Jersey City, New Jersey, on a rainy winter night with 100 containers and a crew frazzled by a difficult trans-Atlantic crossing that caused the ship to arrive two weeks late. It was a rough start but it was a beginning. MSC's direct service to U.S. ports replaced connecting-carrier agreements in which the carrier exchanged cargo with other lines that called at ports Mediterranean Shipping did not serve. MSC had connecting-carrier agreements with Pacific Europe Express on the U.S. West Coast and with Trans Freight Lines and U.S. Lines on the East Coast. Unlike a space-charter agreement, which committed a line to pay for capacity even it if was not used, the connecting-carrier agreements allowed MSC to pay only for the space it used.

In its early days, MSC positioned itself as a non-conference carrier, offering rates below those of established lines. With a small sales staff, it relied heavily on bookings from non-vessel-operating common carriers, intermediaries that purchased ship capacity from vessel operators and then resold it at a profit to shippers. Aponte could offer lower rates because his costs were lower. He used cheap, second-hand vessels and exercised a frugality instilled by his experience growing up in war-ravaged Italy. One of his early ships arrived at New York with a hatch filled with water after a hull plate came loose at sea. Instead of spending time and money to put the ship into a U.S. drydock for repairs, Aponte ordered all the cargo removed and the ballast added to the vessel's stern so that the ship's bow was exposed. Then, after securing the necessary approvals, a contractor welded a new plate into place.

MSC expanded rapidly through the 1990s, adding services mainly in niche markets, such as trade routes between South Africa and Australia, between Australia and the west coast of South America and between the U.S. East Coast and South America. Despite its name, the Geneva-based company did not regularly serve the Mediterranean market until 2002. The company continued to emphasize low costs and cooperation with

Mediterranean Shipping relied on second-hand ships until the mid-1990s.

Nippon Yusen Kaisha has been among the world's top container lines since 1968.

cargo intermediaries. It remained family-owned, avoiding the pressures and scrutiny that accompany a public stock listing, and it continued to eschew alliances with other carriers. "A partnership makes the decision process much more difficult and intricate because everybody has to defend their own interest first," Aponte said in a 2003 interview.

MSC's desire to control its operations extended to port facilities. In 1998, MSC entered a joint venture with Hutchison Port Holdings to open a transshipment hub at Freeport, Bahamas, 65 miles off the Florida coast. Freeport soon became a relay point for cargo moving on east-west routes through the Panama Canal. By 2003 the company was involved in a dozen transshipment terminals throughout the world. In the late 1990s, with customers demanding faster service and costs of older ships rising, MSC began acquiring new vessels as well as used ones. The company soon was operating some of the largest container ships afloat.

* * *

As Asia's economic importance grew, so did the container ship lines based in the region. After being among the first to adopt containerization, Japanese carriers remained in the top ranks of container ship lines. Over the years, Japan's six large carriers were consolidated into three surviving lines, NYK, MOL and "K" Line, each of which had services spanning much of the globe. The Japanese carriers were key participants in the main multi-carrier alliances established in the 1990s. The Japanese carriers also provided extensive North American intermodal services.

Evergreen continued its expansion, acquiring Italy's Lloyd Triestino and establishing new services under the name of Evergreen or affiliated companies such as Hatsu Marine. Korea's Hanjin Shipping and Hyundai Merchant Marine, each a part of their country's business conglomerates, or chaebols, were among the Asian carriers that became global in scope. The Hanjin Group was founded in 1945 by Choong Hoon Cho, who built the group into a holding company that included Korean Air Lines

China Shipping Container Line has said it plans to be one of the three largest container lines by 2010.

and Hanjin Heavy Industries, one of the world's biggest ship-builders. By 2002, Hanjin Shipping was the world's fifth-largest shipping company.

Beginning in the 1990s, no Asian carrier expanded more rapidly than China's two largest container ship lines, Cosco and China Shipping Container Group. By 2005, both of the government-owned companies were among the world's highest-volume container ship carriers and were planning to continue their rapid growth. Cosco's chief executive, Captain Wei Jiafu, predicted in 2004 that Cosco, then the world's seventh-ranked container ship operator, would be among the top five by 2010. China Shipping, which ranked 11th in 2004, set an even more ambitious goal of becoming one of the world's top three container carriers by 2010.

Cosco was founded in 1961 as China Ocean Shipping Company. The company did not enter container shipping until 1978, when the 200-TEU *Ping Xiang Chen* sailed from Shanghai to Sydney, Australia. The company began container service to the U.S. West Coast in 1982. Like many other new market entrants, Cosco relied on low rates to become established. During the 1990s it developed into a mainstream operator in the trans-Pacific and Europe-Asia markets. Cosco was the only Chinese liner shipping operator until 1986, when the market was opened to others. By 1995, the number of carriers in the Chinese market had increased to 150, mostly small domestic carriers, and China's government decided that the time had come

Cosco grew rapidly after entering the trans-Pacific container trade in 1982.

Captain Wei Jaifu, Cosco's chief executive.

to make its state-owned carriers more efficient. The Chinese government's five-year plan for 1996 through 2000 decreed that Chinese shipping companies "shall keep up with the pace of the world's advanced level" in management. Cosco later joined Yang Ming, "K" Line and Hanjin in a global alliance and, despite its ownership by China's Ministry of Communications, began to emphasize the need for "a proper investment return." Under Wei, who was appointed chief executive in 1998, Cosco listed the stock of seven of its subsidiaries on Chinese and overseas stock markets. The listings were part of the government's plan to list all of its large state-owned companies on global stock exchanges to make them more efficient and competitive with non-Chinese companies. Cosco Pacific became a component of Hong Kong's Hang Seng Index in 2003, and Cosco Singapore became part of the Straits Times Index in Singapore in 2004. Wei announced that the company's plans included a listing on the New York Stock Exchange.

China Shipping was established in 1997 after the Ministry of Communications decided that the nation needed a second major carrier to handle its booming export growth. Another motivation was to improve the performance of the companies that were merged into China Shipping. Like Cosco, China Shipping was a maritime conglomerate that encompassed tankers, bulk carriers and other ships as well as container ships. Virtually overnight, under chief executive Li Kelin, it began ordering huge ships and establishing itself as a contender in the global container market. Following the course set by China's Ministry of Communications, China Shipping listed 40 percent of its stock on the Hong Kong Stock Exchange on June 16, 2004. The largest investor in the company was Hong Kong tycoon Li Ka-shing. Although China Shipping and Cosco were described as friendly competitors, both companies' main goals were to compete with and eventually surpass large non-Chinese carriers in China's main international markets. China Shipping used part of the proceeds from its initial public offering to finance orders for large container ships, including what were reported to be the first vessels with capacities of 10,000 TEUs.

*   *   *

The lineup of European carriers was changed by a series of mergers beginning in the mid-1990s. After years of losses, France moved to privatize Compagnie General Maritime, the famous French Line, which had racked up years of losses under government ownership. The buyer was Jacques Saade, who merged the company into his Compagnie Maritime d'Affretement in 1996 to form CMA CGM. Saade, part of a family that had a history in shipping and finance, fled to Marseilles from Lebanon with his family in 1976 to escape that country's civil war, and founded CMA two years later. Like MSC's Aponte, he avoided broad alliances with other carriers and kept his company privately owned. Saade preferred the flexibility offered by short-term, regional vessel-sharing agreements. He quickly built the merged company into a global carrier. CMA CGM embarked on a large-scale shipbuilding program and by 2006 ranked fourth worldwide in container ship capacity.

Jacques Saade heads Marseilles-based CMA CGM.

Saade's acquisition of CGM came only months after the merger of Britain's P&O Containers and Netherlands-based Nedlloyd Lines. Other mergers in the 1990s included a series orchestrated by CP Ships, which was incorporated in Canada but was managed from London. Under chief executive Ray Miles, CP Ships acquired a series of niche-market carriers – Cast, Lykes, Contship, Ivaran, TMM, Italia and Australia-New Zealand Direct Line. CP's strategy was to maintain the acquired lines' brand

Container shipping is thoroughly international, encompassing companies such as (opposite) Hong Kong's OOCL and France's CMA CGM and (clockwise from left) Germany's Hapag-Lloyd, Denmark's Maersk and Japan's MOL and 'K' Line.

names in an effort to maintain customer loyalty and market share. The result was a hodgepodge of data systems and sales staffs known for their stack of business cards, each displaying the name of a different CP Ships company. In 2005, CP Ships was acquired by Germany's Hapag-Lloyd in a $2.1 billion deal.

The modern Hapag-Lloyd was created in 1970, three years after the amalgamation of the North Atlantic liner services of Hamburg-America Line (Hapag) and the North German Lloyd, a Bremen-based carrier. Both of Hapag-Lloyd's predecessor companies traced their history to the mid-19th century. Hamburg-America was founded in 1847, North German Lloyd in 1856. In November 1967, each of the companies ordered two 736-TEU, 19-knot container ships and merged their inland sales offices and container-coordination services. The new vessels entered service between October 1968 and March 1969 as part of the first wave of container ships in the North Atlantic. Hapag-Lloyd was among the members of the Trio consortium between North Europe and Asia. The German carrier remained prominent on that route after Trio's breakup. The Hamburg-based company later was a participant in the Grand Alliance. Its acquisition of CP Ships provided Hapag-Lloyd with several north-south routes to go with the German carrier's primarily east-west services.

*　　*　　*

None of the wave of mergers and acquisitions that began in the mid-1990s had the impact of two by Denmark's Maersk, which by the end of the 20th century was the world's largest container ship line. In 1999 Maersk's parent A.P. Moller Group paid approximately $800 million for the international services and most non-U.S. terminals of Sea-Land Service, then the third-largest carrier. Maersk and Sea-Land had begun working together in 1991 when they started one of the first trans-Pacific vessel-sharing agreements. In 1996 they expanded that cooperation into a global network of coordinated services. Sea-Land was still a leader in containerization, but its days of unchallenged supremacy had ended years earlier. Competition had stiffened and Sea-Land's fleet was aging. Sea-Land's parent company, CSX Corporation, was showing increasing impatience with Sea-Land's difficulty in meeting the corporate directive that each subsidiary earn at least its cost of capital. After the acquisition by A.P. Moller in 1999, Sea-Land's international operations were folded into Maersk Sealand (the unhyphenated version of the Sea-Land

Maersk ships from Asia call at the company's 400-acre terminal at Los Angeles.

name would disappear in February 2006, when the carrier was renamed Maersk Line). Sea-Land's domestic services between the U.S. mainland and Puerto Rico, Alaska, Hawaii and Guam were retained by CSX and later became an independent company, Horizon Lines. CSX also retained many of Sea-Land's terminals, which eventually were sold to Dubai's DP World.

In 2005 came an even bigger merger of two industry giants. Maersk, still the world's largest container ship line, again acquired the number-three line. This time it was P&O Nedlloyd, which was sold for $2.9 billion. The acquisition left Maersk with approximately 20 percent of the world's container ship capacity – nearly as much as the combined total of the next three carriers, Mediterranean Shipping, Evergreen and CMA CGM. Maersk's acquisitions of Sea-Land and P&O Nedlloyd underscored the increasing consolidation and globalization of container shipping.

Maersk was a latecomer to containerization but quickly become a market leader. The Danish carrier continued to expand through careful planning and a willingness to act boldly when circumstances warranted. By the end of the 1990s it had built a large, modern fleet with a transportation and logistics network that covered virtually the entire world. Besides liner shipping, the company known in the shipping industry as "Big Blue" had interests in trucking, terminals, leasing and logistics services. Other A.P. Moller companies were active in petroleum, tankers and shipbuilding.

Maersk Mc-Kinney Moller became A.P. Moller's top executive in 1965 and guided Maersk Line into containerization.

Germany's Hamburg Süd grew into a leading container line on north-south trade routes. This photo was taken at Santos, Brazil.

Though it participated in rate-setting cartels in most of its markets, in its early years Maersk had generally avoided consortia and alliances while cultivating a reputation for efficient service. But as its need for global coverage increased, Maersk surprised the industry by entering vessel-sharing agreements with P&O Containers in 1990 and Sea-Land the following year. Journalist Elizabeth Canna wrote in 1991, "A decade ago few would have predicted Maersk's transformation from a lone-wolf operator to a team player. But as Moller/Maersk gears itself to compete in a rapidly changing transportation arena, there are bound to be more surprises yet to come."

Maersk's acquisitions of Sea-Land's international services, P&O Nedlloyd and South African regional operator Safmarine solidified the Danish company's position as the world's largest container ship line. The aquisitions also generated efficiencies at sea and in port and inland operations, which were becoming an increasingly important part of the industry. To meet demand and achieve economies of scale, carriers had been building large ships to operate on high-volume routes. Maersk's large fleet and supporting network would allow it to operate independently on most routes, without having to seek the concurrence of alliance partners. As one analyst commented after Maersk's acquisition of P&O Nedlloyd, "The merged company will enjoy the critical mass of an alliance, and the ability to differentiate itself by simply being the only carrier big enough to operate entirely on its own."

*　　*　　*

A 'K' Line ship being loaded at Tokyo.

While container lines were consolidating, their customers were learning to take advantage of the opportunities provided by the global expansion of container shipping. As rate-setting conferences weakened, ship capacity increased and competition among carriers intensified, freight rates fell. Meanwhile, companies began emphasizing logistics and just-in-time supply chains. Logistics was a familiar term in the military, where the word had its origins, but it was virtually unknown in the commercial sector until the 1980s. Military logisticians managed the supply of materiel and viewed their supply chain as an end-to-end undertaking. On the commercial side, transportation usually was considered a discrete activity. Typically a company's manufacturing division made a product, and told the transportation staff, known in many companies as the traffic department, to arrange delivery. In a heavily regulated transportation environment, companies employed staffs of tariff clerks who consulted loose-leaf volumes of bound tariffs to determine published rates based on route, weight and commodity classification.

Integrated logistics became widely used first in Europe, where forwarding companies had long controlled the planning and execution of multiple links in the supply chain. Its adoption in the United States came more slowly. The military pioneered its use. Because the U.S. military was exempt from economic regulation, its logisticians were free to negotiate their own costs with transportation providers. Their commercial counterparts, by contrast, had to pay the posted tariffs of trucking companies, railroads and shipping lines. With transportation costs largely uncontrollable, there was little opportunity for creativity in supply-chain management.

That changed in 1980 with the economic deregulation of U.S. surface transportation. The Staggers Act and the Motor Carrier Act freed shippers to negotiate with railroads and trucking companies instead of paying fixed tariffs. Transportation suddenly became not only a controllable cost but a potential source of competitive advantage. A savvy company could negotiate contracts that permitted it to integrate transportation with the company's broader supply-chain requirements. As inland transportation rates plummeted following deregulation, logistics costs as a percentage of U.S. GDP declined from 16.2 percent in 1981 to less than 10 percent in 1999.

In the maritime sector, containerization increased pressure for changes to the 1916 Shipping Act, which granted antitrust immunity for liner shipping conferences. Container shipping lines wanted to be able to offer shippers a through transportation service with a single rate from origin to destination. Although carriers had begun quoting through rates, the law was unclear about whether carriers could do so without risking prosecution under antitrust laws. This prevented shippers from taking maximum advantage of intermodal shipment of containers.

After five years of study and hearings, Congress approved the 1984 Shipping Act. The act eased restrictions on cooperation among carriers by ending carriers' obligation to prove that agreements they entered with each other were not "detrimental to the commerce of the United States" or "contrary to the public interests." The 1984 act also permitted shippers to band together into associations that could negotiate rates with carriers. Shippers and ocean carriers were permitted to negotiate contracts for rates and services, but the essential terms of contracts had to be publicly posted so that "similarly situated" shippers could demand the same terms. This provision caused many companies to limit their use of contracts because they did not want competitors to find out details about their business.

Fourteen years later, the Ocean Shipping Reform Act of 1998 permitted contract terms to remain confidential. This freed shippers to negotiate contracts tailored to their international logistics needs. Shippers quickly began negotiating international transportation contracts with container shipping lines. The Federal Maritime Commission later permitted non-vessel-operating common carriers to negotiate confidential contracts with cargo owners. By this time, the NVO ranks had been joined by the logistics units of UPS, FedEx and other large providers of supply-chain services, all attracted by strong growth in container trade volume.

Many of these companies operated their NVO units as a vehicle to provide companies with third-party logistics – a catchall term describing providers of outsourced logistical services. The third parties' development was aided by computer technology. Ship lines first used computers to manage their containers – early container terminals kept track of their boxes with cards in slotted metal racks or on large magnetic boards. As computers

NVOs: Evolution Of The Breed

Containerization created openings for many new businesses. One of them was a new kind of transportation intermediary with an unwieldy name: non-vessel-operating common carrier.

NVOs emerged in the 1960s. They were authorized by the Federal Maritime Commission to develop land-sea connections that vessel operators could not provide on their own. NVOs provide intermodal service, assuming liability and providing bills of lading, even though they use the ships of vessel operators.

Over the years, many NVOs became cargo consolidators by hiring non-union labor at off-dock locations to combine multiple shippers' cargo into containers. The International Longshoremen's Association complained about the loss of jobs, and agreed with its waterfront employers to a "50-mile rule" in their contract.

This contract clause gave the ILA the sole right to pack and unpack carrier-owned containers filled with multiple shippers' cargo within 50 miles of Atlantic or Gulf ports. NVOs challenged the rule and after protracted litigation, the Supreme Court declared it illegal in 1987.

The court ruling lifted a legal cloud over NVOs. Many quickly expanded beyond container consolidation and started booking full container loads. They bought ship space from vessel operators at wholesale rates and sold it to shippers at retail rates, profiting on the spread.

This put the NVOs in competition with vessel

operators who sold their space directly to shippers, and caused friction among carriers. Established container ship lines with large sales forces resisted being turned into wholesalers of space and avoided NVOs where possible. But newer carriers relied on NVOs to supplement their smaller sales staffs.

By the mid-1990s NVOs had become a substantial presence, booking a third of the container volume in some markets. Many expanded into the growing field of third-party logistics, the business of planning or managing companies' supply chains.

This development was aided by a Federal Maritime Commission decision in 2005 to allow NVOs to sign confidential contracts with shippers. That action effectively reversed a provision that longshore unions, still smarting over the outcome of the 50-mile case, had persuaded Congress to include in the 1998 Ocean Shipping Reform Act.

improved and became more powerful, they were used to automate documentation and handle other tasks. A thriving subindustry of technology providers developed to help companies manage freight rates, customs filings, warehousing, contracts with carriers and optimum inventory levels.

By substituting information for inventory, companies could use containerized shipping to move goods through their supply chains more quickly. This was a key to the success of such large retailers as Wal-Mart Stores, a company whose growth paralleled the spread of containerization. Wal-Mart, founded in 1970, grew in

East And West

In the more leisurely pre-container era, breakbulk ships did not operate on precise schedules and routinely waited for days to be loaded and discharged. In the just-in-time environment that containerized shipping has made possible, such delays are intolerable. This was vividly demonstrated in 2002, when a lockout of International Longshore and Warehouse Union members closed U.S. West Coast ports for 10 days. The shutdown quickly rippled through corporate supply chains, resulting in empty store shelves and idle assembly lines.

The West Coast port shutdown, which came during negotiations on a new contract, followed several years of strained labor-management relations and intermittent slowdowns by longshore workers. The ILWU eventually agreed to a new contract allowing the introduction of more labor-saving technology in exchange for increased pay and fringe benefits, but the work stoppage encouraged U.S. importers to seek alternatives.

Los Angeles and Long Beach continued to handle more than 40 percent of U.S. containerized imports. But to provide themselves with an alternative to the West Coast, shippers increased their use of Panama Canal routings from Asia to U.S. East Coast ports.

That was not a perfect solution. The added container ship traffic strained the canal's limited capacity. Canal transits by full container ships accounted for 20.6 percent of all canal traffic in 2005, compared with only 7.4 percent in 1986. Tolls also were rising sharply as Panamanian authorities began planning for a larger set of locks that they hoped would permit larger vessels to transit the canal.

Facing restrictions at the Panama Canal, some carriers began planning to put their large new ships into service on Suez Canal routes. Meanwhile, to attract Asian business moving via the Panama and Suez canals, East Coast ports such as Savannah and Norfolk began encouraging the development of large import distribution centers similar to those clustered near Los Angeles and Long Beach. At the distribution centers, imports in mostly 40-foot marine containers are transferred to larger 48- or 53-foot highway trailers for delivery to stores or inland warehouses. These near-dock distribution centers have become an established and growing part of many companies' import supply chains.

Scores of ships backed up outside the ports of Los Angeles and Long Beach during a 10-day lockout of West Coast longshoremen in 2002.

barely two decades to become the world's largest company in revenue and the largest U.S. importer of containerized goods. By 2000, the company's supply chain was so efficient that the big-box retailer was able to sell most of its goods before it paid vendors for them. This would have been impossible without efficient containerized shipping.

*　　*　　*

As regulatory, technological and operational changes made it easier for companies to develop global supply chains, the container shipping industry expanded in scale and scope. The influx of larger ships helped extend containerization's reach into less-developed nations in South America, Africa and other regions.

Just as steamships did not supplant sailing ships on many out-
of-the-way ports until well into the 20th century, container shipping took time to find its way to the farthest corners of the world.
Many of the ships displaced by large new vessels were years away
from retirement age and were redeployed to other routes, bringing those areas into the economic mainstream. Ports in developing nations went through learning curves like those their counterparts in industrialized nations had encountered years earlier.
Container-handling facilities had to be built. Ports such as
Santos, Brazil, endured years of strained management-labor relations as cargo-handling was mechanized and the need for workers was reduced.

Consolidation of ocean carriers and increases in ship sizes
have fueled a consolidation of marine terminal operators. In the

Sea-Land developed this multistory container terminal in the mid-1980s in space-starved Hong Kong.

breakbulk era, investment requirements for stevedoring were minimal. Ships usually carried their own cranes, and cargo handling required more muscle than mechanization. The main expense was labor, and that cost was variable – if there was no ship in port, no dockworkers had to be hired. Containerization changed that equation. Terminal operators suddenly needed expensive cranes and other container-handling equipment. As volume grew, automated systems for tracking and documentation had to be acquired. The increasingly capital-intensive nature of container handling required deeper pockets than small, local stevedores could muster.

Companies such as Hong Kong's Hutchison Port Holdings, Singapore's PSA Corporation, Dubai's DP World and Denmark's APM Terminals emerged as global terminal operators. Some of the big operators, such as APM, a sister company of Maersk Line, have corporate ties to ship lines. Others formed partnerships or joint ventures with ship lines or other terminal operators to spread their investment costs, ensure a steady stream of cargo and meet customers' demands for wider coverage.

Even before the construction of the first ships that were too large for the Panama Canal, ship lines had been moving toward hub-and-spoke networks resembling those that airlines use. In the early days of international container shipping, carriers had used North European ports to transship containers between high-volume Atlantic services and smaller ports in the Baltic region and the United Kingdom. As ships became larger, hub-and-spoke networks grew in popularity. Singapore became the hub for Southeast Asia and vied for Hong Kong as the world's busiest container port. Regional hubs also emerged at other ports, such as Algeciras, Spain; Kingston, Jamaica; Gioia Tauro, Italy; and Freeport, Bahamas.

Japan, South Korea and Taiwan led Asia into its eventual role as the world's manufacturing workshop. As labor costs increased in those nations, assembly and manufacturing shifted southward. Thailand, Indonesia, China and the Philippines became

Top 15 Container Ports

RANK	PORT	TEUS IN 1,000s	RANK	PORT	TEUS IN 1,000s
1976			**2004**		
1.	New York/New Jersey	1,720	1.	Hong Kong	21,980
2.	Kobe	1,245	2.	Singapore	20,600
3.	Rotterdam	1,225	3.	Shanghai	14,560
4.	Hong Kong	1,029	4.	Shenzhen	13,620
5.	San Juan	875	5.	Busan	11,440
6.	Oakland	603	6.	Kaohsiung	9,710
7.	Seattle	575	7.	Rotterdam	8,280
8.	Tokyo	470	8.	Los Angeles	7,320
9.	Bremen/Bremerhaven	466	9.	Hamburg	7,000
10.	Long Beach	449	10.	Dubai	6,430
11.	Baltimore	423	11.	Antwerp	6,060
12.	Hamburg	411	12.	Long Beach	5,780
13.	Melbourne	386	13.	Port Kelang	5,240
14.	Yokohama	342	14.	Qingdao	5,140
15.	Keelung	339	15.	New York/New Jersey	4,480

From *Containerisation International* yearbook, 1978; *The Journal of Commerce*, July 11, 2005. Some figures are estimates.

manufacturing centers. Intra-Asia routes became some of the world's busiest as companies shuttled materials and manufactured products between Asian ports. An example was athletic shoes: Soles were produced with high-tech manufacturing processes in Japan and shipped to Thailand, where the upper parts were sewn on by cheaper labor. The completed product then was loaded into a container, put on a feeder ship to Singapore, and then transferred to a larger ship for delivery to North America, Europe or Japan. Variations of this process became common. Singapore's container volume increased six-fold during the 1980s to six million TEUs, then nearly tripled during the following decade.

The southward shift of Asian manufacturing soon was reflected in new services between Southeast Asia and the U.S. East Coast via the Suez Canal. Singapore's Neptune Orient Lines established the first of these services in 1991, with Japan's NYK sharing space on the ships. Although the Suez route to North America was launched with fanfare, most Asian shipments to North America continued to move across the Pacific, especially after the mid-1990s, when China began its relentless ascent toward dominance in many sectors of manufacturing.

*   *   *

Containerization has transformed the world's ports. Clockwise from above are Hamburg, Long Beach and Singapore. Opposite: Hong Kong.

Maher Terminals was in Port Newark, when Malcom McLean loaded his first containers. Today Maher is the New York-New Jersey port's largest terminal operator.

Fifty years into the modern era of containerized shipping, the future of ocean-borne trade appears to be centered on China, whose manufactured exports have soared since the nation was admitted to the World Trade Organization at the end of 2001. The statistics are astonishing. In 1978, China's imports and exports totaled $20.6 billion, the equivalent of 13 percent of its GDP. In 2004, three years after China's admission to the WTO, China's total foreign trade was 56 times higher at $1.1 trillion, representing 70 percent of the country's GDP. In 1975, China accounted for only 0.66 percent of world trade. By 2004, China's imports and exports accounted for more than 6.5 percent of world trade.

Cheap, efficient containerized transportation made this possible. Most of China's manufactured exports move to overseas markets in containers. China's expansion also has relied on imported components. Although its trade surpluses with the United States attract more attention, in recent decades China has run up increasing trade deficits with most of its trading partners. About half of China's exports consist of goods produced with imported materials, many of which are shipped in containers.

By the start of the 21st century, U.S. containerized imports were dominated by mass retailers such as Wal-Mart, Home Depot and Target Stores and other companies that had turned to China as the source for much of their merchandise. This structural shift in trade patterns developed so rapidly that it strained the transportation system's ability to handle it. To encourage its export growth, China invested heavily in port facilities. The first phase of a $1.7 billion port at Yangshan, on China's coast near Shanghai, began operation in 2006. The Yangshan development will be able to handle 25 million TEUs a year when completed by 2020 and is expected to enable Shanghai to become the world's busiest container port. The Chinese ports of Shenzhen, Qingdao, Ningbo, Tianjin and

New-Age Terminals

Dockworkers at modern container terminals are more likely to use a computer keyboard than a cargo hook. Today's sprawling ports combine grit and noise with high-tech automation.

Early container terminals were little more than truck parking lots with a couple of gantry cranes at the dock. At the entrance gates, clerks with clipboards kept track of the containers that trucks hauled in and out.

The clipboard hasn't disappeared, but its days appear numbered. Computers play an increasingly important part in the intricate process of transferring containers between the ship's hold and a highway truck or double-stack railcar. Workers use computer software to determine how boxes are stowed on a ship, the sequence in which they are removed, where to store them in the terminal, and whether the documentation is correct. Truckers schedule pickup and delivery appointments on automated systems. In a few ports such as Rotterdam, containers are shuttled around the terminal on driverless carts that automatically follow the proper path.

Container terminals have become bigger as well as smarter. Most early terminals were rudimentary and small, covering only a few acres. Gantry cranes reached across only 13 rows of containers, the maximum that could be stowed on decks of ships transiting the Panama Canal. Modern cranes stretch over as many as 22 rows of containers. Larger ships

Marine terminals are turning to computer technology to speed the flow of cargo. Here, workers oversee traffic activity at APL's Los Angeles terminal.

also require deeper navigation channels, additional land for container storage and handling, and more rail tracks for intermodal trains.

When land was plentiful, ports and terminal operators preferred to store all containers on wheeled chassis for quick retrieval. Space constraints later forced ports to stack containers – as many as seven high for empty boxes. The boxes are retrieved by rubber-tired gantry cranes that straddle the container stacks and roll on strips of reinforced concrete.

Technology is considered the key to squeezing more productivity from limited acreage at terminals. Operators have begun investing in radio-frequency identification, global satellite positioning, optical scanner recognition and other means to speed cargo handling and reduce mistakes. Acceptance of these and other technologies continues to be an issue between U.S. dockworkers unions and employers.

Xiamen are among the world's top 30 container ports in volume, primarily on the strength of Chinese exports.

The U.S. and European ports on the receiving end of these shipments have struggled to expand their capacity quickly enough to keep pace with the growth. Between 2002 and 2005, U.S.-China container volume increased by an average of 34 per-

China opened the first phase of its Yangshan port in early 2006. When completed in 2020, it will have berths for 52 ships.

cent a year, causing congestion and delays at many ports in the United States and Europe. Ports, carriers and inland transportation providers have little choice but to invest in expansion, because the growth in volume shows no signs of stopping. The World Bank projected that the value of China's world trade will reach 17.66 percent by 2010 and 22.2 percent in 2020, which would make it the world's largest economic entity. Containerized shipping helped create this "bonanza-region."

PART THREE

Changing World

CHAPTER EIGHT

The Box And Adam Smith

*"There was not much new technology involved in the idea of moving
a truck body off its wheels and onto a cargo vessel… But this humdrum
innovation roughly quadrupled the productivity of the oceangoing freighter…
Without it, the tremendous expansion of world trade in the last forty years –
the fastest growth in any major economic activity ever recorded –
could not possibly have taken place."*

—Peter F. Drucker

Containerization's impact on the global economy has been enormous, even though the core innovation itself appears to be so simple that it hardly deserves to be called a new technology. In an era bedazzled by space travel, satellites, global communications, digitization, cloning and life-annihilating weaponry, containerized shipping hardly commands center stage. Shipping containers are so common that they rarely attract attention – unless an international trade development hits the news, and television crews use a container port to illustrate the story. But despite its low-tech appearance, containerization has contributed to economic, social and political changes that are global in scale.

Contemporary globalization and containerization grew up in tandem. Globalization is an elastic, somewhat vague term that refers to a world tightly connected by its economics, communications, finance, culture, trade, language, transportation and manufacturing. Although containerized shipping did not by itself produce the global economy of the 21st century, it was a core building block. There were others. One was the General Agreement on Tariffs and Trade, the multilateral trade framework that emerged from the embers of World War II and lowered trade barriers through several rounds of negotiations. Other contributors included computers, intercontinental jet travel, improved communications, the Internet, and the opening of China and the fall of the Iron Curtain. Containerization's role in the process was to provide an efficient freight transportation system that contributed to the development of global markets. It succeeded to a degree far beyond what anyone anticipated a half-century ago.

How much containerization contributed to the development of today's global economy is impossible to quantify. Apparently

Opposite: A ship is unloaded at New York Container Terminal on Staten Island.

A container crane operator at Hamburg has a bird's eye view.

no economic data exist that accurately estimate the portion of globalization that is attributable to containerization. There are statistics, however, that suggest containerization has a greater role than is widely recognized. Between 1982 and 2005, international trade volume increased more than twice as fast as gross domestic product of the world's nations. Containerized cargo volume, meanwhile, increased three-and-a-half times as fast as the world GDP. Some of the increase in containerized volume undoubtedly resulted from the shipment in containers of commodities that previously moved by other means. But although the impact of containerization on the world economy cannot be precisely quantified, there is ample anecdotal evidence to support the argument that containerization has expanded world trade by creating new markets.

The different global economies that existed before containerization focused on trade in specific goods that were scarce and expensive, such as silk and gold; or on goods that could only be produced in certain regions, such as sugar, tobacco and tropical spices; or on goods that met specific needs that could not be sat-

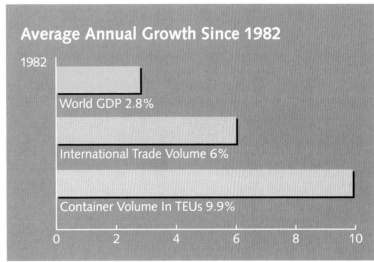

Average Annual Growth Since 1982

1982

World GDP 2.8%

International Trade Volume 6%

Container Volume In TEUs 9.9%

0 2 4 6 8 10

Sources: International Monetary Fund, Drewry Shipping Consultants Ltd.

isfied locally, such as grain, fish or petroleum. Globalization, and containerization, changed that formula by allowing manufacturers to seek the lowest labor and production costs and the most favorable regulations anywhere in the world.

Transportation efficiency has a direct effect on international trade. Faster, more reliable transportation makes a nation's goods more attractive to buyers from other nations. Economist David Hummels has written about the importance of time as a trade barrier. Hummels says each additional day of transportation time is estimated to reduce by 1 percent to 1.5 percent the likelihood that those goods will be purchased by U.S. companies.

Faster transit time is only one aspect of containerization's role as a building block of the global economy. Reduced damage, improved reliability and flexible sourcing also have helped reduce the "cost of distance." Changes in domestic demand now quickly stimulate global responses, making local and world markets one. Today, because of containerized shipping, consumers in developed nations are immediately and thoroughly involved in the global economy. Producers of goods, meanwhile, have a global market for their products. The global economy is no longer a second or alternative market; it is *the* market for all but the most local or specialized products.

The low-cost transportation provided by containerized shipping has helped to blur the traditional distinction between domestic and global economies. The result: Marshall McLuhan's global village of information is paralleled by containerization's global village of goods.

*   *   *

Creating this new kind of global market was not something the founders of containerization anticipated, and this consequence of containerization is still not widely appreciated by the average person. But containerization has redrawn the world's economic map.

In early 2006, China became the world's fourth-largest national economy, behind the United States, Japan and Germany. All

211

A Hapag-Lloyd ship at Hamburg. Imports from Asia dominate trade at North European ports.

these nations, and all those in the next tier, are deeply committed to participating in today's global economy. Technological innovation and industrial production are no longer concentrated in one or two nations or coastal regions.

Protesters at international trade meetings regularly command media attention, but more thoughtful observers have published powerful arguments for the increased integration of the global economy. Many economists have made the case for seeking global progress though the development of market economies. Books such as Jagdish Bhagwati's *In Defense of Globalization* (2004), Amartya Sen's *Development as Freedom* (1999) and Martin Wolf's *Why Globalization Works* (2004) present economic arguments that increased trade promotes human progress. Wolf states that his defense of contemporary globalization "starts from the proposition that a world integrated through the market should be highly beneficial to the vast majority of the world's inhabitants....The market is the most powerful institution for raising living standards ever invented: Indeed there are no rivals." But Wolf acknowledges that markets alone are not enough.

"Markets need states, just as states need markets," he says. "In a proper marriage between the two, one has contemporary liberal democracy, incomparably the best way to manage a society....The problem today is not that there is too much globalization, but that there is far too little."

These authors are well aware of their debt to Adam Smith's classic *The Wealth of Nations*. Writing in 1776, Smith was astonished by what he called the "opulence" of his age. Great Britain was then the world's foremost colonial power and a singularly wealthy kingdom. Smith explained the source of this wealth by focusing on the connections between specialized manufacturing, the cost of transportation and the extent of markets. Writing well before the development of compact steam engines, railroads or other products of the Industrial Revolution, Smith described how the division of labor promotes productivity and how productivity creates wealth.

In his famous example of the pin factory, Smith tells us that an individual working alone might produce 10 pins in a single day but that when 10 workers produce pins together, with each worker concentrating on just one step in the process, they can produce 48,000 pins a day. Smith understood, however, that faster production and lower costs alone do not guarantee wealth. If all of those pins were put on sale in a single local market, there would be too few buyers for the factory to succeed.

The solution is a larger market, Smith wrote. If the market is insufficient, the pin factory could not achieve the scale of operations that would permit the division of labor needed to achieve high productivity. According to Smith, the market is the "mechanism" that encourages the division of labor and provides all the gains that flow from it. A student of human nature, Smith theorized that most people have "a certain propensity to truck, barter and exchange one thing for another." He also recognized that entrepreneurs did not innovate merely for innovation's sake and that workers would not accept the monotony and repetition of specialized work merely for the good of society as a whole. They will do so

Containers have been designed to carry cargoes that don't fit in a regular box. The tank container at top is filled with chlorine gas. A flat-rack frame allows a bus to be carried on a container ship.

An Amsterdam terminal uses cranes that load and unload a ship from both sides at once.

only when they share in the benefits that markets make available. When one person trades with another, Smith wrote, "he intends only his own gain, [but] in this, as in many other cases, [he is] led by an invisible hand to promote an end which was no part of his intention."

Smith also discussed the influence of the size and breadth of markets: "As it is the power of exchanging that gives occasion to the division of labour, so the extent of this division must always be limited by the extent of that power, or, in other words, by the extent of the market." This is where the cost of transportation becomes crucial. Smith carefully compared the costs of carrying goods overland in horse-drawn wagons and of carrying them between seaports in ships. Like Malcom McLean two centuries later, he reached the unsurprising conclusion that distant markets near ports can be most economically served by using ships. This demonstration then enabled him to explain why in the 18th century Great Britain was able to generate such great wealth by engaging in oceanic commerce. "As by means of water-carriage a more extensive market is opened to every sort of industry than what land-carriage alone can afford, so it is upon the seacoast, and along the banks of navigable rivers, that industry of every kind naturally begins to subdivide and improve itself."

Smith never saw a container or a steamship. His writing predated both. But the title of Chapter 3 of *The Wealth of Nations*, "That the Division of Labour is limited by the Extent of the Market," explains why containerization has been such a notable source of wealth for both recently industrialized and long-established nations. The costs of producing goods and of taking them to market are the two largest costs of trade, and containerization has dramatically reduced transportation costs. This reduction has greatly extended global markets, especially for goods of lower value. This in turn has encouraged further specialization through the "division of labour" that Smith discussed.

Examples abound. Toyota automobile parts are packed in containers in Japan for assembly in Georgetown, Kentucky. Textiles from various countries are shipped to the Philippines for the production of men's suits sold at J.C. Penney. Slabs of Brazilian granite are shipped in containers to the United States to be cut and finished into kitchen countertops marketed by Home Depot. Hay bales from the Pacific Northwest are shipped to Japan to feed racehorses.

Containerization has given rise to incredibly complex patterns of exchange among a wide variety of suppliers and customers. But fundamentally, international trade still responds to the circumstances and concerns that Adam Smith described over two centuries ago. What has changed is the transportation technology, and that change has in turn changed everything. Containerization is not a high-tech innovation, but it has altered the contemporary world far more profoundly than have many more dazzling high-tech innovations. Adam Smith would have understood.

CHAPTER NINE

The Revolution Continues

"The system that underpins the incredibly efficient, reliable and affordable movement of global freight has one glaring shortcoming in the post-9/11 world – it was built without credible safeguards to prevent it from being exploited or targeted by terrorists and criminals."

—Steven E. Flynn, Council on Foreign Relations

During its first half-century, containerization grew from a novel idea pursued by an innovative trucker into a mature global transportation industry. Such rapid development seems astonishing, but there are many other new industries that have matured even more quickly. It took only 41 years from 1882, when Thomas Edison built the first central power station in lower Manhattan, for his former secretary, Samuel Insull, to develop the electrical holding company as a new form of industrial organization. Aviation progressed rapidly from the Wright brothers' first powered flight in 1903 to the crucial role it played in World War II only 40 years later. Mass production required even less time to transform manufacturing after Henry Ford's 1913 installation of a moving assembly line at his Model T factory in Detroit.

Today containers are ubiquitous on highways and railroads and in seaports. In 2005, container shipping lines' annual revenue was estimated at $181 billion. Like electric power, airplanes and mass production, containerization has become so firmly established that 50 years after its introduction it is considered a standardized utility that is routinely taken for granted.

In our industrial age we have become so used to assimilating innovations that we seldom notice how frequently and rapidly they transform our world. But unanticipated anxiety often arises when it is realized that the benefits of new technologies are unavoidably accompanied by new problems and vulnerabilities. These collateral problems and vulnerabilities are receiving increased attention as containerization enters its second half-century.

*   *   *

Opposite: South Korea's Hyundai Merchant Marine is among the world's top 15 container ship lines.

After terrorists destroyed New York City's World Trade Center on September 11, 2001, containerized shipping suddenly attracted an unprecedented level of attention from the press and broadcast media. Before then, few had given more than a passing thought to the possibility that a terrorist might try to smuggle weapons across borders inside a shipping container. But the heightened public concern about the possibility of other terrorist attacks quickly focused attention on the tens of millions of containers that circle the globe every year. Many of these boxes come ashore in American ports without being inspected. Suddenly these seemingly harmless cargo boxes were potential "Trojan boxes," disguised delivery systems that could slip ashore and carry nuclear, chemical or biological weapons to American targets.

U.S. policymakers quickly realized that the container system represented a gaping hole in the nation's defenses against terrorism and that a suitable response was needed. Only a month after 9/11, headlines trumpeted that in the Italian container port of Gioia Tauro, a container had been discovered that was equipped as a traveling compartment for a stowaway. The container had been fitted out with a bed, a laptop computer, and mobile phones, and its occupant was carrying a Canadian passport, an airport security pass, and a certificate stating that he was an aircraft mechanic. The container had been place aboard the ship in Egypt, and its discovery was cited innumerable times in subsequent years to justify stronger measures to secure the ocean container system.

There were also strong economic reasons to be concerned about possible terrorist attacks on seaports. In 2002 the consulting firm Booz Allen Hamilton conducted a simulation of the effects of discovering two "dirty" radioactive bombs inside containers. The firm found that the probable response would be an order to close all U.S. ports for more than nine days – an action that would generate a loss of $58 billion from backlogs, lost sales, spoilage and disrupted manufacturing.

The "Trojan box" threat is real, just as the possibility that nuclear power plants may be sabotaged is real, but it also became clear following 9/11 that clumsily applied security measures can easily disrupt legitimate trade. This was illustrated by the case of the *Palermo Senator*, a container ship that was ordered to leave the Port of New York/New Jersey to an offshore anchorage in September 2002 after agents detected low-level radioactivity. The source of the radioactivity turned out to be the normal level

The 6,000-TEU Regina Maersk called at New York in 1996 to dramatize the need to deepen the port's harbor to handle large ships.

of emission from clay tiles that the ship was carrying, but the incident resulted in the ship and its containers being delayed for three days.

Since 9/11, the effort to secure containers against terrorism has taken several forms. U.S. officials have developed technology to screen each incoming container for signs of significant radiation that might indicate the presence of a nuclear device. U.S. Customs and Border Protection has provided incentives for private-sector cooperation through the Customs-Trade Partnership Against Terrorism. C-TPAT participants agree to adopt tighter security standards in exchange for promises that their containers will be subject to fewer inspections by Customs. In 2003 Customs implemented the "24-hour rule" requiring ship lines to electronically transmit their vessel manifests to the agency a day before the cargo is stowed on a U.S.-bound ship. The information helps Customs agents target suspicious shipments for inspection, but there is widespread concern that the information is not reliable enough to allow Customs to effectively assess the risks of each container. In the years to come, cargo shippers are likely to be required to furnish additional data in advance of shipments.

The future of container security lies in technology. C-TPAT

members are being encouraged to attach high-security seals on all containers. This requirement could lead to widespread implementation of electronic seals that would enable a radio-frequency identification scanner to detect tampering while confirming information about the container's contents. Other ideas being discussed include sensors that would track containers and warn of tampering. Each of these technologies offers opportunities for commercial benefit as well as imposing new costs on operators, and their possible uses will be much discussed in the years ahead.

*　　*　　*

Another issue of growing concern as containerized shipping neared its half-century mark was the need to expand the industry's capacity to keep up with the rapid growth in international cargo volume. Between 1994 and 2004, container shipping volume increased at an average annual volume of 8.3 percent. Ports, highways, railroads and the companies that serve the industry have struggled to deal with the growth. Delays at ports and on inland transportation networks have become frequent in North America and Europe. The problem is complicated by the shift in global production to the Asia-Pacific region, primarily China. This shift has led to a largely one-way cargo flow that has added to container ship lines' difficulties in repositioning containers. Today the highest-volume containerized commodity carried by ocean shippers is air – it is estimated that more than 20 percent of containers moving by sea are empty.

Larger ships provide economies of scale at sea, but they also create problems at ports and on roads and rail systems. An 8,000-TEU container ship can disgorge enough containers to fill 20 miles of railcars. In the future, ports will have to stack containers higher and keep truck gates open longer to squeeze more capacity from limited acreage. In 2005, Southern California terminal operators introduced PierPass, a program that imposes a fee on weekday shipments to help offset the cost of operating terminal truck gates on weeknights and Saturdays. As with security, technology will be key to expanding the system's capacity to handle containerized trade. Shipping lines, freight forwarders and other intermediaries and users of container shipping services are investing heavily in technology to track containers and speed their flow. A sizable and growing industry has sprung up to meet this demand – one more example of how a new technology creates new markets.

The MSC Texas can barely fit under the Desmond Bridge at Long Beach. As container ships become larger, bridge clearance has become an issue at some ports.

Other questions surrounding container shipping's future are related to the environment and the economy. Larger ships create a demand for deeper port channels, which sometimes requires controversial dredging. In some ports, the latest generation of big ships can barely squeeze under highway bridges that were built long before anyone considered the possibility of a 10,000-TEU ship. Air pollution at ports has become an issue. The ports of Los Angeles and Long Beach have begun to require some ships to

Many container ships are too large for the Panama Canal's locks. Proposals to build larger locks could alter shipping patterns in the 21st century.

operate from shore-side electrical power instead of running their engines while docked. Expansion of ports and intermodal networks frequently generates a backlash from local communities that object to the traffic and pollution that accompanies the economic bene- fits of containerization. The result- ing controversies will be hashed out locally and nationally, and in some cases on the international level.

Another question is the future of global trade. Like any other fundamental industrial change, globalization is subject to resist- ance from those who oppose change or are dissatisfied with its consequences. Containerized shipping is an industry whose for- tunes are inseparable from those of international trade.

It's safe to say that few, if any, of these issues were topics of conversation on the dock at Port Newark on the morning of April 26, 1956. Containerization grew up quickly, but to say that the container industry had reached maturity by the 21st century is not to say that it has become static. Competition among liner service companies remains intense, technological change con- tinues, trade patterns continue to shift, the size of container ships and the volume of container movements continue to grow, security remains a thorny issue, and a whole host of problems, from piracy to exploitive employment practices, remain unsolved. But while the industry itself faces many problems, containeriza- tion is also undeniably one of the great industrial achievements of the 20th century. It has enlarged and integrated the global economy in ways that were simply unimaginable 50 years ago, and it seems certain that in its next half-century containerization will continue to generate wealth and trade through increased global commerce.

Authors' Acknowledgments

ARTHUR DONOVAN wishes to acknowledge with gratitude the late Andrew Gibson, who urged him to concentrate on maritime history and got him started on the history of containerization; the dozen Founding Fathers of containerization who agreed to be interviewed in the Donovan-Gibson oral history project sponsored by the Smithsonian Institution; the talented team at *The Journal of Commerce*; the staff of the Kings Point Library, and especially Donald Gill, for research assistance; his faculty colleagues in the Kings Point Department of Marine Transportation, Gerhardt Muller and Jon Helmick; and his wife, Carolyn, who once again patiently listened to more than she ever wanted to know about a subject that never really did become the primary focus of her attention.

JOSEPH BONNEY acknowledges and thanks the many people who generously took time to share stories and photographs, answer questions and track down details related to the history of containerization. At the top of the list is Captain James McNamara, president of the National Cargo Bureau, who shared his wonderful photo collection, encyclopedic industry knowledge, and friendship and good cheer. Special thanks also to Keith W. Tantlinger, the mechanical genius who helped Malcom McLean's vision become reality; John Griffith and Lewis Welter, who journeyed to Newark to share photo albums and recollections; James LaRose and Terry Jaquess of Gottlieb, Barnett and Bridges, successor firm to Ewin, Campbell and Gottlieb; Ron Katims; Paul Richardson; Irena McLean; Jeff Hull of Matson Navigation Co.; and Constantia Constantinou and her staff at the New York State Maritime Academy Library at Fort Schuyler. Many others also helped with this project, including Charles R. Cushing, Gerard Ekedal, Jake Coakley, John Heeren of Maersk Line, Arthur Novacek, Sol Katz, John McCown, Doug Cole of NYK, Anastasia Kontos, Charles "Chuck" Hotchkiss of the North Carolina Transportation Museum, B Carroll Miazza, Mark Miller of Crowley Maritime Corporation, Jeff Parker, Sara Diamond of the San Francisco Maritime National Historical Park, Molly Rawls of the Forsyth County Public Library in Winston-Salem, North Carolina, Margaret Stocker of India House, Mike Zampa of APL Limited, Mike Moriarty, Bill Hensel Jr., Donald Brush, Howard Finkel, Joseph Alagna, Allen Clifford, Elizabeth Bonney, Gordon Forsyth IV and Barbara Yeninas. The unsung heroes of *The Journal of Commerce* editorial staff – Larry Treat, Marsha Salisbury, Barbara Wyker, Sue Boehning, Danielle Corso, Chris Brooks, Bob Edmonson, Alan Field, Peter Leach and Bill Mongelluzzo – contributed in ways large and small, as did Peter Tirschwell, JoC vice president and editorial director, Doreen Savolskis and Rosemary Ferrara. Graphic designer Nancy Graham worked on deadline to combine words and photos into an attractive design. Finally, it's said that a skilled copy editor and proofreader is a writer's best friend. In this case, she truly is. Thanks to my wife, Donna, for applying her editing expertise and proofreading skills and to my family for their patience and support.

GENERAL WORKS

Broeze, Frank. *The Globalization of the Oceans: Container-ization from the 1950s to the Present*, Research in Maritime History No. 23, St. John's, Newfoundland: International Maritime Economic History Association, 2002.

Chang Yung-fa. *Tides of Fortune*. Singapore: Times Books International, 1999.

Childs, William R. *Trucking and the Public Interest*. Knoxville: University of Tennessee Press, 1985.

Containerisation International Yearbooks. London: Containerisation International, 1970-2004.

Containerization Oral History Collection, 1995-1998. Interviews with 12 container-industry executives who were "present at the creation." Smithsonian Institution Research Information System, www.siris.si.edu, "Archival, Manuscript, and Photographic Collections."

Containerization: The First 25 Years, Containerization & Intermodal Institute, 1981.

Cudahy, Brian J. *Box Boats: How Container Ships Changed the World*. New York: Fordham University Press, 2006.

DeBoer, David. *Piggyback and Containers*. San Marino, Calif.: Golden West Books, 1992.

De La Pedraja, Rene. *The Rise & Decline of U.S. Merchant Shipping in the Twentieth Century*. New York: Twayne Publishers, 1992.

De La Pedraja, Rene. *A Historical Dictionary of the U.S. Merchant Marine and Shipping Industry Since the Introduction of Steam*. Westport, Conn.: Greenwood Press, 1994.

Federal Maritime Commission. *Seminars On The Container Revolution*, prepared for the Senate Commerce Committee, Washington, D.C.: U.S. Government Printing Office, 1968.

Felice, Mark. Unpublished manuscript. Matson Navigation Company collection, San Francisco Maritime National Historical Park, SAFR Accession 1849.

Fuson, Jack. *Transportation and Logistics*. Washington: Center of Military History. U.S. Army, 1994.

Gibson, Andrew, and Donovan, Arthur, *The Abandoned Ocean, A History of United States Maritime Policy*, Columbia, S.C.: University of South Carolina Press, 2000.

Goddard, Stephen B. *Getting There*. Chicago: University of Chicago Press, 1994.

Greh, Thomas. *The Container Story*. Bremen: film by trifilm GmbH, 2004

Heiser, Joseph M. Jr. *Logistic Support*. Washington: Vietnam Studies Series. U.S. Army, 1974.

Hornby, Ove. *'With Constant Care...' A.P. Moller: Shipowner 1876-1965*. Copenhagen: H. Schultz Information, 1988.

Lane, Frederic C., et al. *Ships for Victory: A History of Shipbuilding Under the U.S. Maritime Commission in World War II*. Baltimore: Johns Hopkins University Press, 1951, reprinted 2001.

Larrowe, Charles P. *Harry Bridges: The Rise and Fall of Radical Labor in the U.S.* Lawrence Hill & Co., 1972.

Lawrence, Samuel A. *United States Merchant Shipping Policies and Politics*. Washington: Brookings Institution, 1966.

Mahoney, John H. *Intermodal Freight Transportation*, 1st ed., Westport, Conn.: Eno Foundation for Transportation, Inc., 1985.

Mitchell, C. Bradford. *Have Served, The National Cargo Bureau's First Quarter-Century*. New York: National Cargo Bureau Inc., 1977.

Mueller, Edward A. *Steamships of the Two Henrys*. Jacksonville, Fla.: privately published, 1996.

Muller, Gerhardt. *Intermodal Freight Transportation*, 3rd ed., Landsdowne, Va.: Eno Transportation Foundation Inc. and Intermodal Association of North America, 1995.

Niven, John. *The American President Lines and its Forebears 1848-1984*. Newark, Delaware: University of Delaware Press, 1987.

Richter, William L. *Transportation in America*. Santa Barbara, Calif.: ABC-CLIO, 1995.

Shields, Jerry. *The Invisible Billionaire – Daniel Ludwig*. Houghton Mifflin, 1986.

The Box, An Anthology Celebrating 25 Years of Containerization and the TT Club. London: EMAP Business Communications on Behalf of the TT Club, 1991.

Van Den Burg, G. *Containerization and Other Unit Transport*. Hutchinson Benham,1982.

Worden, William L. *Cargoes: Matson's First Century in the Pacific*. University of Hawaii Press, 1981.

Zweig, Phillip L. *Walter Wriston, Citibank and the Rise and Fall of American Financial Supremacy*. Crown Publishers, 1995.

CHAPTER 1

Much of the information on Malcom McLean's background and early years is from his first-person account in "Opportunity Begins At Home," *American Magazine,* May 1950; from the Maxton Historical Society; and from Oliver E. Allen, "The Man Who Put Boxes on Ships," *Audacity*, Spring 1994.

Details on McLean Trucking's development come from McLean in *American Magazine* and from *Fortune*, March 22, 1982; and Paul Richardson oral history. The McLean quotation at the start of the chapter is from *Fortune*, March 22, 1982.

Information on Seatrain's railcar-on-ship operation is from several sources, including David Hendrickson, "From Boxcars to Boxships: The Ships of Seatrain Lines", *Steamboat Bill* (Journal of the Steamship Historical Society of America), Summer 2005; "Rails Extend Overseas – Seatrain Service is Here!" *Port of New York*, September 1932; *Marine Engineering and Shipping Age*, October 1932; De La Pedraja's *Historical Dictionary*; and Flagg.

Brian Cudahy shared details on port calls of the *Examelia* and *Seatrain Havana*, and on the Havana dockworkers' protest.

CHAPTER 2

The chapter-opening quotation is from Allen in *Audacity*. The ICC's piggyback rulings are discussed by DeBoer in *Piggyback and Containers* and Mahoney's *Intermodal Freight Transportation*.

Information on the development of McLean's "sea-land" plans comes from numerous magazine and newspaper articles, including *Business Week*, April 9, 1956; *New York Times*, Feb. 17, May 6, and Oct. 8, 1954, and Sept. 24, 1955; *Baltimore Sun*, Jan. 22, 1955; *Time*, March 1, 1954; *Marine Engineering*, April 1954; and Richardson oral history.

Details on McLean's Pan-Atlantic and Waterman acquisitions are primarily from Zweig; *New York Times* of April 2, and Sept. 15, 1955; *Business Week*, April 16, 1979; and *Mobile Press*, Jan. 21, 1955, quoted in an unpublished history of Waterman Steamship Corporation, c. 1959.

Information on "The Higgins Box" is from *Journal of Commerce*, Sept. 25, 2000, based on Higgins sales brochure provided by Jerry E. Strahan, author of *Andrew Jackson Higgins and the Boats That Won World War II* (LSU Press, 1994).

Details on Alaska Steamship are from S.G. Hayman, *Ships and the Sea;* and *Seattle Post-Intelligencer*, April 19, 1972.

Information on McLean's relationship with Ludwig is from De La Pedraja; Shields; and *Business Week*, April 15, 1961.

CHAPTER 3

The quotation by Mark Rosenstein is from his master's thesis, *The Rise of Maritime Containerization in the Port of Oakland,* New York University, 2000.

Sources on McLean's plans to build trailer ships include *Baltimore Sun*, Nov. 16, 1956; and *U.S. Shipping*, January 1956.

Keith W. Tantlinger was a primary source of information on the technical aspects of McLean's entry into containerization. He provided a vivid account in "U.S.

Containerization: From the Beginning Through Standardization," a paper presented to the Trailer Manufacturers Association, 1981, and shared other information in a letter and in telephone conversations.

Two excellent magazine articles on the subject are by James LaRose, "Twist in the tale of containerization," *CargoSystems*, June 2004; and Matt Baratz, "Fantastic Voyage," *Via Port of New York and New Jersey*, March/April 1996.

Also see James J. Henry and Henry J. Karsch, "Container Ships," presentation to Society of Naval Architects and Marine Engineers, Nov. 10-11, 1966, and Doros A. Argyriadis, "Cargo Container Ships," presentation to Institution of Naval Architects, March 25, 1959.

All Richardson quotations are from his oral history. R.K. Johns' quotations on sales are from *American Shipper*, May 1996. Pan-Atlantic's launch of containerization also is drawn from *New York Times*, April 20, 1956; Nov. 19, and 23, 1958.

The railroads' counterattack on coastwise container service is described in *Decline of Coastwise and Intercoastal Shipping Industry*, Hearings of the Merchant Marine and Fisheries Subcommittee of the Committee on Interstate and Foreign Commerce Committee, U.S. Senate, 86th Congress, 2nd session, Government Printing Office, Washington, 1960.

Information on Matson's containerization comes from several sources, including Worden; Felice; Foster Weldon, "Cargo Containerization in the West Coast-Hawaiian Trade," *Operations Research*, September-October 1958; L.A. Harlander, "Engineering Development of a Container System for the West Coast-Hawaii Trade," presented at June 1959 meeting of Northern California Section of the Society of Naval Architects and Marine Engineers; Charles Regal, "20 Years of Containerization in the Pacific," *Ampersand*, Spring 1978; and the oral histories of Stanley Powell and Robert Pfeiffer.

Primary sources on the ILWU's M&M Agreement are Felice; Larrowe; and *Seminars On the Container Revolution*. *Wall Street Journal* editorial was published Oct. 21, 1960.

Except as otherwise noted, Charles Cushing and Ron Katims quotations are from their oral histories.

Information on McLean's acquisition and conversion of war-built ships is from *The Shipping World and World Shipbuilding*, April 16, 1968; and *Marine Engineering/Log*, May 31, 1958.

Information on Grace Line's experience in Venezuela comes from *Marine Engineering/Log*, February 1960; Gibson and Donovan; and Cudahy.

CHAPTER 4

The quotation by Wayne Franklin is from his speech to the Containerization and Intermodal Institute, New York, Feb. 7, 1972.

John Griffith kindly provided a copy of his Aug. 27, 1965, report to U.S. Lines management on the economics of containerization in the North Atlantic and shared photographs and details of the company's launching of container service in the Atlantic and Pacific markets.

Scott Morrison's quotations are from his oral history. Sea-Land's launching of North Atlantic service also draws from *New York Times*, April 24, 1966; Allen; and *Marine Reporter/Engineering News*, June 1, 1969.

Many details of the North Atlantic consortia and services are from Broeze; *Journal of Commerce*, May 1, 1967; *New York Times*, Nov. 7, 1967; and *Distribution Age*, October 1966.

The quotation by ACL's Otto Portman comes from *Seminars on the Container Revolution,* prepared by the Federal Maritime Commission for the Committee on Commerce, U.S. Senate, 90th Congress, 2d session, Senate Commerce Committee. Washington: Government Printing Office, June 1968.

The discussion of containerization in Vietnam draws on Katims; Fuson; Heiser; Helen Delich Bentley, "Containerships and the U.S. Navy," *Our Navy*, June 1968; and *Wall Street Journal*, March 30, 1967.

Details on the dispute over container sizes are from Bentley in *Our Navy*, and *Baltimore Sun*, May 29, 1967.

Information on Japanese lines' development of containerization is from sources including Broeze; Rosenstein; *Containerisation International,* March 1984, March 1986; *Intermodal World,* September 1975; and *New York Times,* Aug. 27, 1968, and Aug. 10, 1969.

Boylston's account of SL-7s is from his oral history.

Much of the information on McLean's sale of Sea-Land is from "Malcom McLean's $750 Million Gamble, *Business Week,* Aug. 6, 1979.

The Katims quotation on "McLean Tech" is from *American Shipper,* July 2001. The George Marshall quotation is from *Journal of Commerce,* July 23, 1999.

Field lawsuit against Battery City Park is from *New York Times,* April 16, 1969.

CHAPTER 5

The quotation by Karl Heinz-Sager comes from *Fairplay,* 1981, quoted in *The Box* (TT Club, 1991).

Details of Chang Yung-fa's early years and all his quotations are from his memoirs, *Tides of Fortune,* and from *Journal of Commerce,* April 6, 1999.

Trio Group details are from Broeze and *Lloyd's List,* Aug. 20, 1982, and *Containerisation International* yearbooks.

McLean's "I am a builder" quotation is from *Business Week,* April 16, 1979.

The description of U.S. Lines before McLean's acquisition, the account of McLean's talk at Kings Point and the quotation by William Hubbard come from *American Shipper,* January 1983.

Gilbertson quotation comes from *Wall Street Journal,* Sept. 26, 1986.

Details on Maersk and Evergreen in the 1980s come from *Containerisation International,* March 1983, May 1984 and May 1986.

Much of the detail on U.S. Lines' losses and bankruptcy comes from R.F. Gibney, *Container Briefing,* February

1987; *Journal of Commerce,* incl. June 11, July 28, Nov. 26, 1986; *Business Week,* Dec. 8, 1986; *Wall Street Journal,* Sept. 28, 1986.

McLean's "I've made…" quotation is from *Journal of Commerce,* Sept. 4, 1996.

CHAPTER 6

Details on APL's history and experiences in containerization come primarily from Niven; W. Bruce Seaton's oral history; and *Journal of Commerce* coverage. All quotations by Seaton are from his oral history.

Information on Seatrain's introduction of mini-bridge is from *Containerisation International,* June 1972.

Details on the growth of large container ships come from *Journal of Commerce,* various issues, 1986-2006; and *American Shipper,* July 1996.

CHAPTER 7

Information in this chapter is taken from coverage in *Journal of Commerce,* various issues, 1990-2006, unless otherwise noted.

The quotations by Aponte come from *Fairplay,* April 10, 2003.

CHAPTER 8

The quotation by Peter F. Drucker is from *Innovation and Entrepreneurship,* New York: HarperCollins, 2005.

CHAPTER 9

The quotation by Steven Flynn is from "Cargo Containers: The Next Terrorist Target?", his testimony to the Senate Committee on Governmental Affairs, March 20, 2003.

PHOTO CREDITS

The Containerization & Intermodal Institute would like to thank all of the companies and organizations whose generosity and understanding helped make this book possible, allowing CII to continue its mission since 1960 of education and outreach in the international transportation industry.

DEDICATION

Evergreen Group
Horizon Lines LLC
Maersk Inc.
New York Shipping Association
Port of Houston Authority

ACKNOWLEDGEMENT

APL Limited
American Trucking Associations
BNSF Railway Company
Calhoon MEBA Engineering School
China Shipping (North America) Holding Co., Ltd.
CMA CGM (America) Inc.
Columbia Coastal Transport
COSCO Group
CSX Intermodal
Georgia Ports Authority
Global Terminal & Container Services, Inc.
Hapag-Lloyd (America) Inc.
Hatsu Marine Ltd.
Italia Marittima SpA
Maher Terminals, Inc.
Marine Terminals Corporation
Matson Navigation Company
Mediterranean Shipping Company (USA) Inc.
New York Container Terminal
Port Authority of New York and New Jersey
Port of Los Angeles
Port of Tacoma
Trailer Bridge, Inc.
United States Maritime Alliance, Ltd.
United Arab Agencies, Inc.

CONTAINERIZATION & INTERMODAL INSTITUTE

Part of the ≋NOL Group

April 26, 2006

On this 50th anniversary of containerization,

Congratulations to the Containerization & Intermodal Institute and the Journal of Commerce for producing this fine tribute to the first 50 years of container shipping. Thank you for providing us an opportunity to pause and reflect on what our industry has accomplished.

At APL we've been honored to help shape the course of shipping for 158 years. More than a century ago we were the first steamship company to provide regular transpacific service. In the 20th century we pioneered intermodal transport by developing Stacktrain technology and introducing Linertrain service from coast-to-coast. And in the 21st century we've been a leader in guiding customers to the Internet to conduct business.

Commerce on the high seas is an ancient and noble profession. But it's not a staid or mature business despite roughly 6,000 years of history. As this milestone reminds us, the shipping industry must continually evolve. Our customers demand it. The global economy depends on it.

So now that we've stopped to congratulate ourselves on 50 years of containerization, it's time to get back to work. We need new innovations that – like the container a half century ago – foster world trade, control costs for consumers and strengthen the transportation network that links nations.

It took collaboration among carriers, shippers, labor and others to develop the containerized shipping industry that underpins global trade today. That's what it will take to develop the next big breakthrough. We look forward to playing a leading role in the effort.

Sincerely,

Ronald D. Widdows
Chief Executive Officer
APL

APL is a global container transportation company offering more than 60 weekly services and nearly 300 calls at more than 90 ports in Asia, Europe, the Middle East and the Americas. It combines world-class intermodal operations with leading edge IT and e-commerce. APL is a unit of Singapore-based Neptune Orient Lines (NOL), a global logistics and transportation company.

April 26, 2006

On this 50th anniversary of containerization,

American Trucking Associations and its Intermodal Motor Carriers Conference are pleased to mark this major transportation milestone with our congratulations and admiration for a half-century of service that has revolutionized the freight transportation system worldwide. That this transportation innovation was developed by a motor carrier owner makes this occasion particularly auspicious to the trucking industry.

The vision of Malcom McLean has led to the creation of a modern marine transportation-freight containerization system that is integral to the transport sector of every nation of the world and indispensable to every country that seeks to reach its fullest economic potential.

Simply put, the "box that changed the world" was created by an "outside of the box" thinker. McLean brought to life a revolutionary concept of packaging freight in containers. These boxes could be efficiently moved and transloaded at ports and terminals and across America's highways by trucks that generally make the first and last intermodal move.

Containers have extended the reach of global trade to our domestic markets. A bedrock of budding to fully developed state-of-the-art transportation systems, the container has become a major player in the operations of every mode within the freight transportation sector.

The entire freight transportation sector can celebrate with pride Malcom McLean's vision. Our collective participation in a dream-turned-into-reality continues to advance progress and prosperity around the globe.

Sincerely,

Bill Graves
President & Chief Executive Officer
American Trucking Associations

The American Trucking Associations is the largest national trade and safety advocacy association for the trucking industry. Through a federation of trucking groups, industry-related conferences, and its 50 affiliated state trucking associations, ATA represents more than 37,000 members covering every type of motor carrier in the United States.

April 26, 2006

On this 50th anniversary of containerization,

BNSF Railway Company is proud to have been not only a beneficiary, but also a benefactor of containerization.

BNSF and its predecessor railroads were rail industry pioneers in the movement of trailers on flatcars referred to as piggyback. The movement of containers by rail developed in conjunction with the movement of ocean-going containers and the growth of international trade.

The success of intermodal movement of international containers made it clear that containerization also offered efficiencies for domestic movements.

One of the biggest successes was a historic agreement between Santa Fe Railway and J.B. Hunt. This not only validated intermodal as an efficient means of ground transportation, but also popularized the use of domestic containers in the traditional full truckload market.

And today, intermodal transportation is even more important to BNSF. As the world's largest rail intermodal carrier, BNSF moves more than 5 million containers and trailers annually, accounting for more than 50 percent of BNSF's total volume. We believe intermodal will continue to grow.

Containerization has played a significant role in rail transportaton for the last 50 years. Its role in the next 50 years will be even more important as the need to facilitate the efficient and effective movement of goods within our country also continues to grow.

Sincerely,

Steve Branscum
Group Vice President - Consumer Products
BNSF Railway

A subsidiary of Burlington Northern Santa Fe Corporation (NYSE: BNI), BNSF Railway operates one of the largest railroad networks in North America, with about 32,000 route miles in 28 states and two Canadian provinces. The railway is among the world's top transporters of intermodal traffic.

April 26, 2006

On this 50th Anniversary of containerization,

I was asked by Ron Davis, the President of the Marine Engineers'
Beneficial Association and the Chairman of the MEBA Training Plan
Board of Trustees, to write a brief reflection on this, the 50th anniversary
of containerization. It is hard to believe that it has only been 50 years since
the first containers were loaded aboard a vessel and shipped worldwide.
Containerization has become so fundamental to what we do in maritime
that it is difficult to believe that cargo was ever shipped another way.

As the school that provides ongoing training for licensed deck officers and
engineers onboard the U.S.-flag ships of the American merchant marine,
the Calhoon MEBA Engineering School continues to train the members
of MEBA. Today, containerization seems obvious and clear – like so many
ground-breaking ideas. The container has been to maritime in the 20th
century what steam power was to maritime in the 19th.

The maritime industry – in fact, all of industry – will forever be indebted
to Malcom McLean and the revolution that was touched off by containerization. Like many American pioneers, Mr. McLean proved yet again that
the world can be changed by one man with one idea.

As we look back on the last fifty years and look forward to the decades to
come, we should be as willing as Malcom McLean was to embrace change.
There are more revolutions like containerization that are waiting to happen
– all they need is one individual willing to challenge the way things have
always been done.

Sincerely,

Joyce H. Matthews

Joyce H. Matthews
Director
Calhoon MEBA Engineering School

*Calhoon MEBA Engineering School is celebrating its 40th year of excellence in maritime training for MEBA
Members, as the Marine Engineers' Beneficial Association celebrates its 131st year of representing the best of
maritime officers. We train for tomorrow ... today.*

April 26, 2006

On this 50th anniversary of containerization,

China Shipping is a relatively new company in the world of containerization. When the dawn of containerization occurred fifty years ago, the world was a very different place. World trade was a fraction of today's volume and was clogged with high inefficiencies.

As in all entrepreneurial enterprises, Mr. Malcom McLean decided on a revolutionary way to change the way business in world trade was done for general cargo. His decision was driven by the opportunity to enrich himself and his investors by bringing forth efficiencies that would be redeemed by new profits derived from a better way of carrying and delivering freight on a worldwide basis. This also resulted in a complete change in the way all maritime companies did business. In order to compete, the maritime companies' focus became adapt or die. Many companies with long histories in world trade did not survive and many were absorbed or merged into new corporate entities. New companies with new visions sprung up to take on these new opportunities that were provided by the amazing expansion of world trade.

China Shipping is a new company, a young company, from a very old civilization. We see our place as continuing the growth of world trade from which all countries have derived wealth and prosperity. China Shipping wants to continue in the tradition of Mr. McLean, by expanding opportunities for all by efficient world trade.

Sincerely,

Zhang Bing
President
China Shipping (North America) Holding Co., Ltd.

At China Shipping, solid connections in China and around the globe are surpassed only by our reputation as the fastest growing container carrier in the world. Operating the youngest fleet of container vessels with over 350,000 TEU space, China Shipping is constantly refining its service network and expanding its international routes to serve customers on six continents.

April 26, 2006

On this 50th anniversary of containerization,

In April 1956, the *Ideal X* with 58 containers aboard sailed from Newark, N.J., to Houston, Texas. Fifty years later, CMA CGM is taking delivery of four 9,400 TEU ships that will be deployed on the Europe / Arabian Gulf / Asia / Europe service.

The concept of containerization clearly revolutionized the transportation industry. It also opened new vistas for import and export trade and directly contributed to the international supply chain logistics concepts we enjoy today. This seemingly simple concept enabled the small entrepreneurial family-owned business to compete in global trade and became a cornerstone in building international corporations that source from all over the world.

Containerization brought the world closer by providing transportation directly from the manufacturing site using a combination of truck, rail, and container ships to the final destination. Now you can ship from the manufacturing site 1,000 miles inland in China over 6,500 miles of ocean in 12 days and have cargo arrive secure and damage free to the distribution center 1,300 miles away in Omaha, Neb.

Could Malcom McLean have known that his frustration over having to wait for a load of cotton to be re-handled by tired stevedores would generate countless employment opportunities ranging from the manufacturing and repair of containers to a revitalization of the railroads with stack train operations?

CMA CGM salutes the vision of Malcom McLean for recognizing that there had to be a better, faster more secure way to move cargo from the docks and for developing the solution upon which the CMA CGM group has demonstrated phenomenal growth and success.

Sincerely,

Frank J. Baragona
President
CMA CGM (America) Inc.

CMA CGM led by its founder, Jacques R. Saade, is the 3rd largest worldwide container shipping line. The group operates a modern fleet of 245 vessels serving over 86 major routes, of which 22 are to and from the USA. CMA CGM has a strong worldwide network offering one of the largest scopes of origins and destinations to its customers.

April 26, 2006

On this 50th anniversary of containerization,

History shows us that the true value of a new idea is not fully appreciated until years later, after it has withstood the test of time. Today, anyone working in a business connected to cargo shipping views containerization as the norm. Understandably so, when you consider the volume of containers moving over U.S. ports each year to and from destinations around the globe.

The sheer magnitude of this business pays tribute to Malcom McLean's vision and persistence – his vision of a metal box carrying freight by sea or by land, and the persistence to push through the changes needed to make it a viable mode of transport.

The launching of Columbia Coastal Transport in 1990 marked another milestone in the evolution of containerization. For the first time, containers could move between U.S. ports using an all-water mode of transport. Container barge service let steamship lines access alternate U.S. ports without the expense of direct ship calls; multiple containers could be moved at one time; and transit times were often improved. None of this would be possible if cargo wasn't moving in containers – and so our company is yet another expression of containerization at work.

Today, there is much talk in the U.S. about Short Sea Shipping, using inland waterways and alternate inland ports to receive and deliver containerized freight. This is the "new trend" for discussion and debate at trade conferences. However, without sufficient funding to establish – and maintain – short sea shipping networks, it is an idea whose time has not yet come.

But that box idea of Malcom's? It's a keeper.

Sincerely,

Bruce Fenimore

Bruce Fenimore
President
Columbia Coastal Transport

Columbia Coastal Transport is the premier container barge operator serving the U.S. Atlantic and Gulf Coasts plus Freeport, Bahamas, and Cuba. The company deploys U.S.-flag container barges in regularly scheduled feeder service linking 11 different U.S. ports, and offers expert project cargo services as well. It is one of the Columbia Group of Companies.

April 26, 2006

On this 50th anniversary of containerization,

I would like to thank the pioneers before me, who helped create a dynamic, fast growing and exciting industry that my company and I are proud to be integral members of.

Containerized shipping made the world a lot smaller. In 1956 containerization began here in the U.S. Just five short years thereafter, on April 27, 1961, COSCO was established in China. It has truly been my pleasure to witness so many great milestones in our industry. Among which are the sailings of COSCO's m.v. Liu Lin Hai from Shanghai to Seattle in 1979 soon after the diplomatic relations were normalized between China and the United States. Today, the trade between our two countries has grown to the largest container volume in the world. COSCO began container service with 200 TEU ships in 1978. Today, 8,000 TEU ships are deployed into the Trans-Pacific services and we are looking forward to welcome the first 10,000 TEU ships into our fleet in 2007.

Being the CEO and President of one of the largest carriers worldwide, I often run into people who are willing to understand more about our businesses. This book serves that purpose. I am sure readers will take another look at this great innovation and join all industry leaders and myself to seek more efficient, cost-effective, safer and more secure services in marine transportation and the supply chain globally.

Sincerely,

Capt. Wei Jiafu
President and CEO
COSCO Group

COSCO is a diversified transportation services company with one of the most recognized and admired brand names in the world focusing mainly on shipping and modern logistics businesses. The group also serves as an independent ship agency and provides services in freight forwarding, newbuilding, shiprepairing, terminal operation, container manufacturing, trade, financing, real estate, IT and contract employment.

April 26, 2006

On this 50th anniversary of containerization,

We at CSX Intermodal are proud to be a part of this important occasion. As we reflect on 50 years of containerization we recall the genesis of our own company and a direct link to Malcom McLean. In 1986 CSX/Sea-Land Intermodal was created to link CSX's desire to develop inland intermodal service with Sea-Land's proven success on the ocean. The acquisition turned CSX's small intermodal franchise into the first transcontinental intermodal network.

The CSX/Sea-Land combination created value well beyond the visionary success Sea-Land developed in the ocean trade. The value was further refined with dedicated, double-stack trains allowing for efficient service for both domestic and international cargoes. This service today remains as a backbone of CSX Intermodal's service product where over 2 million container shipments are handled each year.

The future of containerization specifically, and intermodal in general, is very bright. The inspiration from Malcom McLean drives us today to constantly improve and innovate new products and services. Growth from China, congested highways and the growing needs placed on logistics in today's business mean high-speed, reliable intermodal networks are key to our economy and will continue to drive the demand for intermodal services even farther.

CSX Intermodal is committed to fully developing the concept of the container and the intermodal industry. From humble roots we have come a long way and we continue to strive to greater heights using Malcom McLean's vision as inspiration.

Sincerely,

James R. Hertwig
President
CSX Intermodal

CSX Intermodal is one of the nation's largest coast-to-coast intermodal transportation providers handling over 2 million loads each year. We offer customers the value of rail combined with the advantages of trucking in this increasingly competitive alternative to long- and medium-haul trucking.

April 26, 2006

On this 50th anniversary of containerization,

Fifty years of containerization presents truly a golden opportunity for those of us involved to take a broad view of how far we have come…and where we still have to go. There is no question that the advances in technology have moved trade beyond any vision we may have had in the early years. The people of Evergreen are pleased to have played a role in this venture.

We must also acknowledge the others that have moved us forward. In this regard, we also salute the ports, inland transportation providers, equipment builders and the various industries that make up this interdependent business in which we all work. Without the cooperation of everyone, we could not celebrate the success of anyone.

Indeed, the success of the entire world economy and the well-being of all of the world's people depends on our ability to meet all the challenges at this critical juncture in our industry's history. During this defined moment in our history – a half-century of progress and unfathomable development – we must reflect on what is ahead.

While we celebrate our accomplishments, we at Evergreen look forward to what is ahead and anticipate that over the next years we can celebrate a world marked by peace, prosperity for all people and other milestones of which we can be proud.

Sincerely,

Kuo-Cheng Chang
Chairman
Evergreen Marine Corp.

Since its establishment by Evergreen Group Chairman Dr. Yung-fa Chang in 1968, Evergreen Marine Corp. (EMC) has secured its place in shipping history. Both in terms of the magnitude of its fleet and its cargo loading capacity, EMC ranks among the world's leading international shipping companies serving more than 240 locations in 80 countries touching six continents of the globe.

Georgia Ports Authority

April 26, 2006

On this 50th anniversary of containerization,

"Wouldn't it be great if a trailer could simply be lifted up and placed on a ship without its contents being touched?" That was the question posed by Malcom McLean in 1937. Nineteen years later Mr. McLean's controversial idea, considered by many to be utterly impractical, set sail from New York to Houston aboard the *Ideal X*. Over the next decade in a turn of events that would forever change the face of global transportation, containerization was not only born, it was the future.

But what if containerization had never existed? Would America's interstate system have evolved to be the greatest in the world? Would the fortune of the world's largest ports have been reversed? Would the U.S. economy have grown to be the single largest consumer market? Would we have seen the emergence of America's largest retail giants? Those are some fairly big "what ifs". Fortunately for global trade and transportation, industry pioneers like Malcom McLean had the strength of character to move forth with the necessary vision, innovative thinking and financial support to make "an impractical idea" a proven reality.

In an era that has seen man's first steps on the moon, as well as the development of the mechanical heart, history will note that, among mankind's greatest accomplishments, the modern era of containerization is only second to the development of the internet as innovations that sent global trade surging, while profoundly enhancing the quality of living for the next great generation.

Sincerely,

Doug J. Marchand
Executive Director
Georgia Ports Authority

Georgia Ports Authority owns and operates the Port of Savannah, which has become the fifth largest U.S. container port in the United States and the largest single terminal container facility on the U.S. East and Gulf Coasts. Fiscal Year 2005 throughput was 1.7 million TEU.

April 26, 2006

On this 50th anniversary of containerization,

On behalf of all employees of Global Terminal & Container Services, Inc., I wish to thank co-authors Arthur Donovan and Joseph Bonney and the Containerization & Intermodal Institute for undertaking the task of compiling and publishing "The Box That Changed The World" forever preserving the historic development and impact of containerization.

During 34 years of operations at Global Terminal, container handling methods have evolved from wheeled to semi-wheeled to fully-grounded utilizing equipment to maximize terminal capacity to meet the demands of continued container cargo growth. Dramatic changes have occurred not only in the physical handling of containers. Information management and processing through ever changing technologies has far exceeded the possibilities envisioned in what seems just a few years ago.

This book chronicles that evolution during the past 50 years and for those of us who have witnessed and experienced a majority of those years we can only imagine the changes yet to come.

Sincerely,

Maurice C. Byan
President & CEO
Global Terminal

Construction of Global Terminal in the Port of New York/New Jersey was completed in 1972. Designed as a marine container handling facility, it was engineered to incorporate the latest technology of the time. The philosophy of providing the highest level of service to its customers has continued through the years with capital investment to keep ahead of the many changes our industry has and continues to undergo.

Hapag-Lloyd
Container Linie

April 26, 2006

On this 50th anniversary of containerization,

On behalf of Hapag-Lloyd I extend my congratulations to the Containerization and Intermodal Institute on the successful completion of this book to commemorate the 50th Anniversary of containerization.

Who would have thought, 50 years ago, that the concept to move cargo in containers, could have had such a far-reaching impact on not only freight transportation itself, but would also have a profoundly positive effect on the global economy, truly making the world both smaller and better, benefiting us all in our daily lives.

It is now incumbent upon us all to ensure that we continue to improve on this idea.

Forecasts predict that the global container market will double during the next 20 years, as more and more companies continue the global outsourcing to an even greater extent. This will result in the need for larger and more expensive vessels, which are already being planned. In this context our customers must appreciate that carrier profitability is an essential tool to continue to offer, and improve upon, a longer term service, with the required hard-ware investments, which is expected and to which they have become accustomed.

It is, however, equally important that continuous infrastructure improvements are made on other legs of the supply chain, including port, terminal, canal and rail capacity expansion. Adequate labor must be available, and IT systems integration and enhancement solutions must be found in order for us to continue to handle the increased volumes timely and effectively. All these tasks can only be resolved jointly.

My best wishes to all for the successful next 50 years of containerization.

Sincerely,

R. Mack
President,
Hapag-Lloyd (America) Inc.

Hapag-Lloyd group focuses on global container liner shipping. More than 260 sales offices are located in over 90 countries. With its recent acquisition of CP Ships, Hapag-Lloyd has joined the Top 5 in global container shipping with a combined fleet of more than 130 vessels and a total capacity of 980,000 TEU. The company is owned by TUI AG, based in Hannover, Germany.

April 26, 2006

On this 50th anniversary of containerization,

At this time in history, as containerization marks its 50th anniversary, I would like to introduce what is perhaps the world's newest container carrier, Hatsu Marine Ltd. Hatsu Marine was established in January 2002, launching a fleet of UK-flag post-Panamax ships into the transpacific trades as cargo volumes from China to North America were experiencing double-digit growth.

The primary reason for commencing a new ocean carrier was to provide the world's shippers with a strong Evergreen Group presence in Northern Europe. We are working to develop markets throughout Europe, establish greater relationships with other carriers and to build a feeder network that would provide customers with an enhanced range of European port calls.

While pursuing these goals, we have relied on the experiences of those who came before us and, in this regard, can identify with the pioneers a half-century ago whose vision established this dynamic industry in which we all thrive. Those pioneers had to meet and overcome many challenges and convince the non-believers that there was a newer and better way to move cargo around the world.

We salute them for their steadfast commitment to containerization. Importers and exporters have greatly benefited from that mission and the world at-large has enjoyed the incredible growth this simple idea provided. They facilitated the dream of global trade and Hatsu Marine and others will continue to build on the foundations they provided.

Sincerely,

Slin Yeh
Chairman
Hatsu Marine Ltd

Hatsu Marine Ltd was established in London in January 2002. By mid 2006, its owned fleet will stand at eleven vessels, nine of which are post-Panamax, and be complemented by a further two 8,000 TEU ships on long-term charter. Through slot-sharing and joint service agreements, Hatsu offers a network of services embracing Asia, North America and Europe.

April 26, 2006

On this 50th anniversary of containerization,

This is a milestone year for our industry and for Horizon Lines, a direct descendant of the pioneering Sea-Land. Today we continue to ply the domestic trade routes that marked the inaugural containerized sailings as the nation's largest Jones Act carrier, serving the burgeoning and vital offshore American marketplaces.

Looking proudly at the past, however, underscores the importance of continuing to look at the future – which we have done for a half-century. Information technology moves us forward, as does the importance of the country's cabotage laws, the vast security initiatives to keep our nation safe and the ongoing role of innovation to keep us cutting edge.

We must explore short sea shipping and other alternative methods for moving cargo to keep our highways open for their most necessary needs. We must look at new initiatives to partner with labor on issues of mutual concern that will keep us all competitive. We must begin to take action to keep ours a sustainable business.

The people of Horizon Lines who are always there and always delivering are our greatest asset and each and every one carries the legacy of Sea-Land and the heritage of service. We salute the genius of American innovation and congratulate the rest of the world for their commitment to containerized shipping, which has allowed trade to expand beyond our imagination.

Sincerely,

Chuck G. Raymond
CEO
Horizon Lines

Horizon Lines is the leading ocean container shipping and logistics company serving the U.S. domestic markets of Alaska, Hawaii, Guam and Puerto Rico. The company is headquartered in Charlotte, N.C., and traded on the New York Stock Exchange under the stock symbol HRZ.

ITALIA MARITTIMA S.p.A.

April 26, 2006

On this 50th anniversary of containerization,

In the very year we celebrate 50 years of containersation, it is fitting that the company I represent, known for many years to you all as Lloyd Triestino, is celebrating its 170th birthday and a brand new identity. We now provide global container services to our customers under the banner of Italia Marittima.

Our decision to rebrand a company that has been around for so many years and to replace a name recognized as a pioneer in the development of Europe's containerized shipping business back in the 1970s, is based on commitment to the market. We would like to ensure a brighter future for our customers and ourselves in this industry while strengthening our Italian national identity worldwide.

We are also bound to the wonderful city of Trieste – to its people, its port and its potential. With a modern fleet, including some of the largest containerships plying the oceans today, Italia Marittima will continue to connect its home city and indeed its homeland with almost every major port around the world.

On a broader scale, my vision for the future, for the next 50 years of containerization, is for a more socially and environmentally responsible industry. We are making a promising start, but there is still some way to go. Sensible rate structures, investment in people and stable relations are crucial to further progress.

At Italia Marittima, we look forward to playing our part in working with you, our industry peers, for a brighter future for all.

Sincerely,

Pier Luigi Maneschi
Chairman
Italia Marittima SpA

Italia Marittima was incorporated on Aug. 2, 1836, in Trieste as Oesterreicher Lloyd, later named Lloyd Triestino. In the 1970s, it became a pioneer in Europe's containerized shipping business when it introduced a fleet of purpose-built vessels. Today the company, with its brand new identity as Italia Marittima SpA, is a truly global carrier, with east-west and north-south routes serving almost every major port in the world.

April 26, 2006

On this 50th anniversary of containerization,

It is appropriate to acknowledge its founder, Mr. Malcom McLean, a consummate entrepreneur, together with many other industry pioneers, whose collective determination to find a more efficient method of transporting goods led to the development of the marine container and containerization. This innovation revolutionized the maritime industry and continues to have a profound impact on the globalization of commerce. The efficiency that containerization has brought to global trade has contributed significantly to facilitating the historic growth of international goods movement. Today, containerization handles the overwhelming majority of world trade and continues to grow at a remarkable pace.

By 1956, when the *Ideal X* sailed out of Port Newark, N.J., Maher Terminals was well on its way to establishing itself as an important operator at the port. For the container to initially succeed, ships as well as port and marine terminals and inland transportation systems required extensive modification.

Some 50 years since that first container shipment, the scope of containerization continues to expand aggressively. Ever larger vessels are being deployed by the world's ocean carriers, while many port and marine terminals have undertaken capital-intensive expansion and modernization initiatives in order to handle the unprecedented growth of container volumes.

The maritime industry continues to face some significant challenges in accommodating the dramatic growth of trade particularly between the Far East and North America. A renewed emphasis on increasing container throughput capacity and challenging of the status quo by embracing the innovative spirit of Mr. McLean and that of the many early pioneers will be essential to ensure the efficient handling of containerization's long-term growth.

Sincerely,

Mr. M. Brian Maher
Chairman & Chief Executive Officer
Maher Terminals, Inc.

Maher Terminals, Inc., is a major multi-user marine terminal operator that has operated in the Port of New York/New Jersey for nearly 60 years. At North America's third largest port, Maher Terminals handles approximately 50% of the port's total container traffic. Maher Terminals was founded in 1947 by Michael E. Maher and remains privately held.

April 26, 2006

On this 50th anniversary of containerization,

I very vividly remember my first exposure to containerization. I had gone to work for U.S. Lines in the waning days of their Far East break bulk service. I was stationed as a company clerk at Pier 76 North River in Manhattan handling the "Challenger" class vessels, some of the most beautiful general cargo vessels ever built.

Shortly after starting work, I was sent for an orientation to Port Elizabeth where the U.S. Lines' vessels worked at the former ITO terminal. I was deposited at the office trailer alongside the string piece and was awestruck by the sheer enormity of size of everything about the operation. The straddle carriers, the gantry cranes and the "Lancer" class vessels themselves. Everything seemed to dwarf me and that image is forever seared in my memory.

Of course, by today's standards the Lancer vessels would be feeder-sized and the cranes mere toys compared to the ZPMC behemoths that populate so many of the world's ports. In the 37 years following that first exposure I am still struck by the enormity of container operations. The box has facilitated world trade growth, and advanced the global economy in ways that were unimaginable in 1969. The container industry has responded with ever increasing adaptations in scale. Standing on the dock of a 400-acre facility watching an 8,500 TEU vessel work still has the same feeling for me as that day in 1969 had.

Sincerely,

Douglas A. Tilden
President and CEO
Marine Terminals Corporation

Marine Terminals Corporation is a privately owned stevedore and terminal operator with operations throughout the United States. The company handles a broad range of commodities and has large scale container operations. In 2005 the company handled 7 million TEU. MTC has a major commitment to and investment in container terminal technology including web enabled customer applications.

Matson.

April 26, 2006

On this 50th anniversary of containerization,

Containerization is clearly the most significant innovation in 20th century maritime history. The container revolution that was led by Malcom McLean's Sea-Land in the Atlantic in 1956 and Matson in the Pacific in 1958 made waves that reverberated in the transportation industry worldwide. Matson's research department, which was formed in 1954, developed a system of handling, gathering and distributing cargo – a process that had changed very little since the time of the Phoenicians. In order to design an optimum system, transportation and distribution had to be studied as a whole, starting with the origin of goods in the factory all the way to the point where they were consumed. This involved developing a container freight system that encompassed ships, rail and trucks. With this system came the advent of A-frame gantry cranes, cellular ships, intermodal operations and container handling equipment. While the high costs of capital investments did not deliver immediate financial benefits, by 1967 the system proved a boon to all parties involved. Customers' costs were reduced. Distribution savings were realized. And Matson's operation was profitable.

It's hard to imagine modern supply chain management systems operating efficiently without the seamless interchange the industry has today, moving goods from the manufacturing plant to virtually any point in the world, using multiple modes of transportation. Matson is proud and gratified by the success of the containerization system it pioneered in the Pacific. Today, we continue to build on that platform, delivering to our customers modern and efficient ocean transportation, intermodal and logistics services in the Pacific and throughout North America.

Sincerely,

James S. Andrasick
President and Chief Executive Officer
Matson Navigation Company

Matson Navigation Company is one of the leading U.S.-flag carriers operating in the Pacific. Founded in 1882 and incorporated in 1901, Matson is the principal carrier of containerized freight and automobiles between the West Coast and Hawaii, Guam, China and the Mid-Pacific, and is the largest subsidiary of Honolulu-based Alexander & Baldwin, Inc. Matson's two subsidiaries are Matson Integrated Logistics (MIL) and Matson Terminals, Inc. MIL is a leading provider of multimodal transportation services to the North American market.

April 26, 2006

On this 50th anniversary of containerization,

When Malcom McLean first pondered how cargo might be loaded faster onboard and better secured while transported at sea, his vision of a metal box to be lifted on and off of ships would change the way our industry did business forever. The impact of that vision could not have been foreseen, nor fully appreciated, until years later. No one cheered this creation at its onset; no labor union, no ports, no terminals, no ship owners were pre- pared to handle containers. But that did not deter Mr. McLean.

Mediterranean Shipping Company attests to how far containerization has come since that first ship, the *Ideal X*, sailed 50 years ago from Newark to Houston. Fourteen years after that event, in 1970, a young Italian man, Gianluigi Aponte, would launch his company's first ship, a 3,000-ton freighter, with a vision to create a global shipping company. I was fortunate to work with Mr. Aponte when in 1985 MSC converted to containerships, a decision that would lay the groundwork for MSC's meteoric growth.

Today, MSC is a premier ocean container carrier serving world commerce, and another example of how one man's vision can make a dream reality. Never once in my 45 years working in this industry have I found it any- thing less than challenging, stimulating and, in the end, satisfying. Satisfying to be part of such a dynamic industry; to work with a company like MSC that provides jobs for thousands of employees worldwide so that they can raise families and earn a living; and to know that, at the end of the day, we have served our customers well.

Sincerely,

Nicola Arena
Chairman & CEO
MSC (USA) Inc.

Mediterranean Shipping Company is the second largest containership operator in the world. Its fleet of 275 containerships is one of the most modern, and it includes some of the largest ships serving global commerce today. Founded in 1970 and still privately held, the company is headquartered in Geneva, Switzerland.

April 26, 2006

On this 50th anniversary of containerization,

They were wrong, at least partially. With the first vessels to sail
carrying modular intermodal boxes, the wisdom at the time by all
the established steamship people was that this concept will not
last. History has now shown that while neither the first 33-foot
aluminum container nor the founding company Sea-Land Service
has survived, clearly the concept has endured and truly has
changed the world.

What has also survived is the competitive nature of international
shipping. The landscape is literally changing every day with further
consolidation and in some cases liquidation. What has also survived
is the relatively close knit shipping community. Sea-Land was blessed
with having a truly family-oriented culture in the beginning which
allowed those who had the opportunity to work for it to grow, learn,
make mistakes and move on in an extremely challenging and
rewarding environment. As someone who has had the pleasure of
working in the industry for the last 33 years, I am pleased that we
are taking time to celebrate the creation of an industry which is
helping to bring the world closer together and hopefully closer to
world peace as nations become interdependent thanks to "the box
that changed the world".

Sincerely,

James J. Devine
President and CEO
New York Container Terminal

*New York Container Terminal, currently a moderate sized marine terminal located in Staten Island, New
York, has the pleasure of carrying on the great tradition of marine commerce in a working waterfront which
started back in the early 1600's. The facility has 3,000 feet of berth, 9 cranes, state-of-the-art gate system
and is currently capable of handling 751,000 TEUs.*

New York Shipping Association, Inc.

April 26, 2006

On this 50th anniversary of containerization,

We are proud to say this is where it all started, right here in the Port of New York and New Jersey. As we join with all members of our industry to recognize and celebrate the genius of Malcom McLean, we also acknowledge the vision of the men and women of the New York Shipping Association and the International Longshoremen's Association who collaborated in the successful completion of the *Ideal X* voyage, and then carried that heritage forward to this auspicious date.

Our industry has evolved tremendously in only 50 years with the development of new operational and safety standards, extremely efficient operations, highly specialized equipment, advanced management techniques, intensive training, and, of course, a highly skilled workforce that now moves 90 percent of all the cargo in the world...in containers. From a single vessel with 58, 33-foot trailers in 1956, some 75 container-carrying steamship lines now deliver more than 2.8 million containers annually to the Port of New York and New Jersey carrying more than $115 billion in cargo to the customers in this region. That activity is the primary source of more than 229,000 jobs and $20 billion in regional gross domestic product.

Not bad for one man from North Carolina.

On behalf of the members of New York Shipping Association, I offer our sincere respect, appreciation and admiration for Mr. McLean, the visionaries that followed, and the men and women of today who carry on the tradition. Now let's move that cargo!

Sincerely,

Frank M. McDonough, Esq.
President
New York Shipping Association, Inc.

New York Shipping Association is an organization of ocean cargo carriers, terminal operators, stevedores and marine related businesses which negotiates the labor and security officer contracts, hires, trains and dispatches the workers that maintain the equipment and move the cargo in the Port of New York and New Jersey.

THE PORT AUTHORITY OF NY & NJ

April 26, 2006

On this 50th anniversary of containerization,

The Port Authority of New York and New Jersey is especially pleased to participate in celebrating the 50th Anniversary of Containerization. The very first vessel to carry containers, the *Ideal X*, left from our facility in Port Newark, New Jersey.

Containerization revolutionized the shipping industry, and the Port Authority of New York and New Jersey responded to that innovation by building the first container terminal in the country at the Elizabeth Port Authority Marine Terminal. Today we move millions of containers annually at container terminals located in both New York and New Jersey. These facilities can now accommodate all the new classes of container ships that have been built since that "first generation" vessel left our berth.

We are prepared to meet the needs of the future, and are investing almost $2 billion in infrastructure, expansion projects and channel deepening, while preserving and protecting the environment that surrounds us.

We join the many other industry leaders in acknowledging this momentous occasion!

Sincerely,

R.M. Larrabee
Director
Port Commerce Department

The Port Authority of New York and New Jersey operates many of the busiest and most important transportation links in the region. They include John F. Kennedy International, Newark Liberty International, LaGuardia and Teterboro airports; AirTrain JFK and AirTrain Newark; Port Newark; the Elizabeth-Port Authority Marine Terminal; the New York Container Terminal on Staten Island; and the Brooklyn Piers/Red Hook Container Terminal.

April 26, 2006

On this 50th anniversary of containerization,

It is truly gratifying to reflect on the Port of Houston Authority's past, present and future as a pioneering leader in containerized cargo shipping.

Since the world's first container ship, the *Ideal X*, arrived in Houston from New York in 1956 carrying 58 "containers," the world has embraced this innovative shipping concept. By 1970, more than half of the non-bulk freight on the North Atlantic was moving in containers – many of them destined for the Port of Houston Authority.

This led the PHA to take a risky gamble in 1970 with the decision to build the Barbours Cut Container Terminal. I was the planner/design engineer for the multi-million dollar facility, which opened in 1977 and quickly became the crown jewel of containerized shipping on the U.S. Gulf Coast. Over the past few years, this facility has been operating beyond capacity. Yet, it has continued to achieve record double-digit increases in annual tonnages, TEUs, and revenues.

To help alleviate the capacity crunch, the PHA is building the $1.2 billion Bayport terminal. The first phase – including 1,660 feet of the ultimate 7,000 ft. wharf and approximately 65 acres of the ultimate 1,043 acre facility – is scheduled for completion this summer. In the coming years, Bayport will have enough space for seven ships and a 378-acre container storage yard with a maximum capacity of about 2.3 million TEUs – a 200 percent increase over PHA's current capacity.

Clearly, Bayport heralds the next era of containerization and solidifies Houston's leadership in global logistics.

Sincerely,

H. Thomas Kornegay, P.E., P.P.M.
Executive Director
Port of Houston Authority

The Port of Houston Authority owns and operates or leases the public facilities located along the Port of Houston, the 25-mile long complex of diversified public and private facilities designed for handling general cargo, containers, grain and other dry bulk materials, project and heavy lift cargo, and other types of cargo. Each year, more than 6,600 vessels call at the port.

April 26, 2006

On this 50th anniversary of containerization,

The Port of Los Angeles is pleased to join the maritime industry in commemorating the 50th Anniversary of Containerization. As with ports around the world, the invention and introduction of the "box" revolutionized the operations of our harbor, efficiently and safely bringing nearly every conceivable type of product to millions of homes and businesses across the nation.

Today, as America's leading containerport, the Port of Los Angeles proudly acknowledges our container operations as the key to financial stability, diversification of our facilities, and efficiencies in a Pacific Rim gateway that manages more than 20 percent of the containerized goods entering the U.S. each year. We are looking forward to the future challenges of containerization, which we believe will combine operational efficiencies with technological innovations, bringing new and higher environmental standards to our industry. Looking back on decades of innovation, it is our firm belief that the shipping industry has the expertise, creativity and operational savvy to bring about broad-ranging and sustainable programs that will pave the way for a cleaner, greener business environment.

On the horizon, we foresee further growth in intermodal and terminal velocity, helping to expedite the flow of goods through our ports and on to their final destinations. Innovation is an industry-wide effort requiring the same type of foresight that brought the container to the forefront of our cargo handling capabilities.

The Port of Los Angeles will serve as America's premier port as we continue on this road started 50 years ago.

Sincerely,

Geraldine Knatz, Ph.D.
Executive Director
Port of Los Angeles

As the leading containerport in the nation and a critical hub in the international supply chain, the Port of Los Angeles handles more than seven million TEUs annually, with a total cargo value in excess of $122 billion. The Port also places a high priority on clean growth initiatives combined with high security, environmental stewardship and community outreach. The Port of Los Angeles — A cleaner port. A brighter future.

April 26, 2006

On this 50th anniversary of containerization,

We reflect on history and look forward to future challenges.

The containerization revolution led to the evolution of ports and supply chain infrastructure, new concepts in supply chain logistics for manufacturers and retailers, and a more peaceful and prosperous world. Indeed, well known companies like Wal-Mart and Dell would not exist without containerization. The historic downward movement of global transportation costs has allowed new entrants into international trade from all parts of the globe, spreading wealth and better living conditions the world over.

The Port of Tacoma is proud to be the global leader in pioneering on-dock rail, building upon Malcom McLean's revolutionary vision of intermodalism. We built the first on-dock intermodal yard 25 years ago, and our Port has seen steady growth ever since, today comprising five container terminals, each with on-dock rail service. Now handling more than 2 million TEU annually, the Port of Tacoma continues to invest in new terminals and transportation improvements to facilitate the growth of transpacific trade. Our goal is to be the most efficient and reliable intermodal gateway in North America, and we strive every day to make that goal a reality.

The Port of Tacoma salutes Malcom McLean on this 50th anniversary of containerization, along with all of those who have made his vision a world-changing reality.

It is truly The Box that Changed the World.

Sincerely,

Timothy J. Farrell
Executive Director
Port of Tacoma

The Port of Tacoma is one of the leading international ports on the West Coast, handling more than $35 billion in global trade and more than $3 billion in Alaskan trade each year. Its imports include everything from automobiles and electronics to footwear, while its exports include plastics, grain, and more. A five-member Commission, elected by Pierce County citizens, serves as the board of the directors of the port.

Trailer Bridge, Inc.

April 26, 2006

On this 50th anniversary of containerization,

Long before it was a popular business mandate to "think outside the box" Malcom McLean did just that by directing shippers to "think inside the box". His idea to move goods in containers came alive with the sailing of the *Ideal X*. In 1956, the *Ideal X* embarked on a voyage that would forever change freight transportation and the world.

Containerization was a big idea that helped make the world smaller. Its logic and efficiency was embraced worldwide, turning strangers into trading partners. Today, the transportation system created by containerization is the largest hard asset network in the world. Malcom's idea to transport freight in containers is directly tied to the current mega growth in trade. Millions of containers filled with trillions of dollars worth of goods cross the globe yearly, increasing living standards for billions of people. Because containerization empowers world trade, it promotes world peace. What a legacy!

Fifty years after the *Ideal X* set sail, Malcom McLean's innovative thinking lives on in Trailer Bridge. Here, he created a business model that increased box size and decreased operating costs. Every day, Trailer Bridge proves the efficacy of this model by moving more freight for less cost in the Puerto Rico trade lane.

All of us at Trailer Bridge celebrate the golden anniversary of containerization and take pride in being part of Malcom McLean's enduring vision. Our founder taught us well. When it comes to freight, we will never stop thinking "outside the box".

Sincerely,

John D. McCown
Chairman & CEO
Trailer Bridge, Inc.

Founded by Malcom McLean in 1991, Trailer Bridge is a U.S.-flag carrier with an integrated freight system built around 53-foot containers, cost-efficient tug/barges and tractors that move freight between the mainland and Puerto Rico.

260

April 26, 2006

On this 50th anniversary of containerization,

It took a West Coast ports work stoppage a few years ago to draw public attention to the containerized liner shipping business. Currently the "box" is gaining the attention of lawmakers for the wrong reasons – they see a Pandora's box that may contain within it a WMD. The negativity notwithstanding, the benefits of the container revolution in the past 50 years is too numerous to mention.

What about the next 50 years? We should bring nanotechnology into play to determine if a general purpose container could be manufactured using lighter yet strong material – a box that is fully collapsible. Imagine the savings in supply chain costs to shippers and carriers, if a light and collapsible general purpose container could be developed that is fully stackable.

What if the current lo/lo method of container handling is replaced by a ro/ro method, whereby a conveyor belt type mechanism on and off the vessel could roll off the boxes almost like driving a stack train on and off the ship? Mega ships would spend less time in port and more at sea, thereby reducing the number of ships deployed.

We have made great strides in expansion in size from ships, cranes, terminal size, etc. but no dramatic change in the concept of container handling. The greatest tribute we could pay Malcom McLean is to improve upon the historical concept that he pioneered 50 years ago.

Sincerely,

Dr. Anil J. Vitarana
President
United Arab Agencies, Inc.

UASC has a milestone year, celebrating its 30th anniversary. The company owned by six Arab Gulf countries is a top 20 container carrier that expects to double its liftings of a little over a million TEUs in the next three years. UASC has a proud track record of 12 straight profitable years. United Arab Agencies, Inc. is the North American General Agent for United Arab Shipping Company (UASC).

April 26, 2006

On this 50th anniversary of containerization,

The United States Maritime Alliance, Ltd. is proud to have played a small part in the revolution that has defined international transportation. Since we have only been a part of this industry for the past decade, we look forward to contributing to the continuing evolution of containerization.

Labor and management have helped shape the destiny of the industry since its inception. We have all strived to do what is necessary to ensure that the transition from the old break-bulk days to modern containerization was done in such a way as to not only allow for the technological break-throughs, but also continue to provide a good livelihood to the men and women who have been the backbone of the industry.

With that transition almost complete, we must look forward together to address the challenges we now face. A great first step is to continue to maintain labor peace on the waterfront. Our current landmark six-year collective bargaining agreement is testimony to the will and desire on both sides to move forward together. We must now address the problems that could prevent this great industry from having the tremendous impact that the first 50 years of containerization have had.

We are sure that the innovation that Malcom McLean gave us is alive and it will continue to flourish as we create history for the second half of our first century.

Sincerely,

James A. Capo
Chairman/CEO
United States Maritime Alliance, Ltd.

Founded in 1997, USMX is an alliance of container carriers, direct employers, and port associations serving the East and Gulf Coasts of the United States. While serving as the representative of the Management groups in Master Contract bargaining, the Alliance also articulates industry positions on regulatory and safety issues; oversees coastwide training, retraining, certification, and recertification programs; and is responsible for administering coastwide fringe benefit funds and programs.

Southampton
SOLENT
iv